WITHDRAWN

W9-AQW-312

A12900 306975

ILLINOIS CENTRAL COLLEGE
PN6231.P6F82
STACKS
The Fun and laughter of politics /

A12900 306975

PN
6231
.P6
F82   The Fun
         of politics

DATE			

I.C.C. LIBRARY

© THE BAKER & TAYLOR CO.

The Fun and Laughter of Politics

The Fun and Laughter of Politics

Senator John F. Parker

MINORITY LEADER
MASSACHUSETTS STATE SENATE

DOUBLEDAY & COMPANY, INC.
GARDEN CITY, NEW YORK
1978

66288

I.C.C. LIBRARY

PN
6231
.P6
.F82

ISBN 0-385-12354-X
Library of Congress Catalog Card Number 76–56325

Copyright © 1978 by John F. Parker
ALL RIGHTS RESERVED
PRINTED IN THE UNITED STATES OF AMERICA
FIRST EDITION

This book is dedicated to Dear Mae, my wife—by my side through all the storms of politics and who, no matter how many times she has heard my political jokes, is always the first one to laugh.

ACKNOWLEDGMENTS

I am grateful to a host of politicians, in and out of office, who have contributed personal experiences and reminiscences to the fun-filled pages of this book. It has been enjoyable talking to (and snatching jokes from) the great, the near great, and those who tried and missed.

This book never would have been possible had not the politicians of the world embellished the serious business of politics and government with plenty of wit and humor, fun and laughter.

I am indebted to the staffs of the Massachusetts State House Library, the Boston Public Library, and the New York Public Library for their help in providing material. Also a special "thanks" to George Gloss, of Boston's historic Brattle Book Store, for his encouragement and excellent political material.

—Senator John F. Parker

Contents

Introduction

"A little nonsense now and then
Is relished by the best of men."
—Anonymous

This book is not intended to change the course of history. It is simply a compilation of the humorous things that have taken place in the political lives of men and women who, in their time, changed the course of history—or tried to.

The Fun and Laughter of Politics is a storehouse of jokes, stories, yarns, anecdotes, witticisms, retorts, and just plain political fun. It contains the deadly repartee of legislative debate, the humor of the White House, the campaign trail, and the vulcanized chicken circuit. The flashes and clashes of the great and the near great, their bulls and blunders, and their sense of humor are captured in this volume. The also-rans, the man-in-the-crowd, and the innocent bystander have a say as well.

Almost all men in politics and government seek relief from the strain of public office. Laughter has often provided that needed relief. Ben "Meat-Axe" Hardin, a Kentucky senator of long ago, once said in reference to the need for laughter, "If this Senate was made up of nothing but solemn asses, this government would fall apart in a month."

Much of the material in this book has been mined from the old veins of political humor, which are inexhaustible. Here and there an old chestnut surfaces again in a new form to increase the repertoire of contemporary political wit and humor.

Laughter is nature's defense against the world's burdens. Public men and women have found it the best medicine they know, better by far than roots, herbs, pills, and nostrums.

In a world that wants and needs desperately to laugh, *The Fun and Laughter of Politics* should provide just the right medicine for the reader who enjoys the great game of politics.

"If you lose your power to laugh,
you lose your power to think."
—Clarence Darrow

The Fun and
Laughter of Politics

1

A Few Appropriated Jokes

Political humor is ageless. No one can really tell who sprung the first political joke, or who made the first rib-tickling fluff during legislative debate. No one knows for sure who first crushed a political opponent with a swift, witty retort. It is certain, however, that it was a long, long time ago.

Ever since politics and government became a way of life for the people, wit, humor, laughter, repartee, mixed metaphors, cutting phrases, and political anecdotes have been as much a part of the scene as the bills and petitions put into law by public officials.

As with sin and sex, there is little in the field of political humor that can be considered new. The humor we hear today from the lips of our politicians can be traced to the ancient Pharaohs and, beyond, the market places and forums of Greece, the Roman Senate, the courts of England and France, the old parliaments and political gathering places of the centuries.

A humorous story is told, to prove the point, of the old Greek politician and statesman Solon, who lived some five hundred years before Christ. Suddenly, in the twentieth century, he was reincarnated. The whole world was agog that a man who had lived 2,500 years before had come back to earth.

Naturally, Solon was wined and dined in capital cities across the globe. Eventually, he arrived in Washington, where he was guest of honor at a majestic state dinner, attended by everybody from the President on down.

One of Washington's most brilliant storytellers was the toastmaster. He regaled his audience with political jokes and the banquet hall rocked with laughter. Everybody joined in except the old Greek politician.

Finally, the embarrassed toastmaster, who had noticed Solon's indifference to his stories, leaned over and whispered: "I'm sorry if these twentieth-century jokes are going over your head."

"No, they're not," was Solon's quiet reply, "but haven't you any new ones? You see, my good man, I started those jokes myself 2,500 years ago."

Solon's reply proved that political anecdotes and jokes never die. They simply pass through a thousand reformations and reappear century after century in newer, brighter, and more attractive form. They marry and intermarry among themselves and travel from language to language around the world.

A favorite joke in the Roman baths and market places at the time of Augustus concerned the great emperor himself. A simple youth coming to Rome from the country was observed to resemble Augustus so much that it was the subject of general conversation. The emperor ordered the young man to appear in court, and then inquired if his mother had ever been to Rome.

"No," answered the youth, as he looked Augustus straight in the eye, "but my father has."

How many times this story has been repeated in the courts of kings and among the followers of emperors, dictators, and other leaders will never be known. In one variation or another, it has surfaced periodically for two thousand years to be told slyly about the current leader of the people.

Age cannot wither a good political joke. It is perennial and immortal. Sometimes a splendid laugh-provoker, after going the rounds of the campaign trail and the banquet circuits, falls into the "old chestnut" class and disappears. A generation later, with a new twist, it suddenly flashes from the lips of an after-dinner speaker or a suddenly witty campaigner. The press eagerly gives space to the snappy "new" bons mots and the so-called "fresh new" anecdotes. Yet, if we could but trace the wit and humor of today, we might find it all on the crockery tablets of an Assyrian council, or emblazoned in the hieroglyphs of an Egyptian record.

When James Michael Curley was governor of Massachusetts, he was besieged by office-seekers. He had a common expression that always brought a few laughs from the press and a few lines in the papers to boot. "Whenever I make an appointment," said Governor Curley, "I make a hundred enemies and one cool friend."

The press treated the remark as an original humorous Curleyism until it was discovered that Lincoln, and before him Jackson, had said nearly the same thing. It was further discovered that Louis XIV had also made the same observation. As one researcher put it, "Louis wasn't that smart to originate the quotation. Chances are the remark was three thousand years old when Louis said it."

One of the most popular campaign jokes of all time was reborn during the Eisenhower-Stevenson presidential campaign of 1952. Madison Square Garden was packed to the rafters with a massive Republican crowd. The principal speaker convulsed the more than fifteen thousand present with the following story:

"A young woman was passing the corner of Broadway and Forty-second street, when she was attracted by the voice of a man selling puppies.

" 'Here's your Stevenson pups,' he was shouting at passers-by.

"It so happened the young lady was a devout Democrat and the novelty of possessing a Stevenson pup got the better of her judgment, so she purchased a little brown beauty.

"Two days later she was passing the same corner. The same man was there, but this time he was shouting, 'Here's your Eisenhower pups.'

"She pushed her way in and indignantly demanded: 'How is it you are selling Eisenhower pups now? Two days ago you said you were selling Stevenson pups.'

" 'They were then,' suavely replied the pup dealer, 'but you see, they've got their eyes open now.' "

Scarcely anyone who joined in the laughter when the joke rocked Madison Square Garden was aware that this story had served many gubernatorial and presidential campaigns as far back as the Buchanan-Frémont campaign of 1856. Political joke researchers agree that the puppy story is one of the best ever coined and sounds just like one the Greeks may have originated—and they probably did.

Abraham Lincoln was one of the few public men who admitted that his jokes and witticisms were resurrected or appropriated, then repolished and repackaged. Lincoln knew that anecdotes and stories are no man's property. They are common stock—an aspect of folklore—and tumble through the centuries, available for any man to use as he sees fit. If someone was bright enough to give the ancient stories a sharp new twist, the masses leaped to his side. Lincoln was aware of this and used jokes, anecdotes, puns, and witty remarks better and more effectively than any other politician who ever lived.

When a friend observed that every cell in Lincoln's brain had a funny story in it, Old Abe was quick to deny the assertion. He admitted that he knew a great many anecdotes, but he seldom invented one. He claimed that his sources were *Aesop's Fables*, the *Arabian Nights*, and the raw life of the frontier, along with the Bible.

"The people talk of Lincoln stories," said the President, "but I don't think that is a correct phrase. I don't make the stories mine by telling them. You see, I am only a retail dealer."

The anecdotes may be musty or timely, the wit an updated version of Cicero's puns, and the repartee and campaign trail humor, revived, borrowed or remolded, but without fun and laughter to lighten the burdens of office and oil the machinery of government, the whole business might very well collapse in total dullness.

As did Lincoln, Vice-President Alben W. Barkley understood the need for humor in politics and in government. Old Alben retailed humor wherever and whenever he could. He spiced his debates and after-dinner speeches with marvelous stories and bits of wit and merriment. The Kentucky senator was the best political humorist of his time and was much in demand as a political speaker. Barkley could cut, slash, and ridicule with the best and top it all off with sidesplitting yarns and stories. He was feared as an adversary and appreciated as a humorist.

One of Barkley's colleagues often remarked: "Ain't nobody goin' to fall asleep while Old Alben's talkin'."

Many of Barkley's jokes and stories were a bit hoary, but he passed this off by borrowing a few words from comedian George Jessel. "You see," said Barkley, "if your jokes are old enough and your audience is young enough, you're in good shape." Old Alben would then follow up with: "Hell, man, I don't need any new jokes. All I need are some new audiences."

Vice-President Barkley never boasted that he was an originator of jokes and stories. With a sly wink, Alben told a Washington reporter who had asked where he obtained his material: "Any politician worth his salt should never be at a loss for a few *appropriated* jokes."

2

Funny Things Happen on the Way to Public Office

Time has changed almost everything, including the procedures by which people campaign for public office. For centuries the people said of their candidates: "Never mind what they look like. What do they know?" Otherwise there probably never would have been a George Washington, Martin Van Buren, Andrew Jackson, Abraham Lincoln, Daniel Webster, Rufus Choate, John Randolph, Thaddeus Stevens, and a host of others.

These men and many more had all manner of physical deficiencies, but that mattered little to the electorate. In the rough (pre-TV) days of America's youth, the voters measured their candidates on what they knew and what they could do for a growing country.

In this modern age of Madison Avenue image-makers, professional molders of public opinion and high-powered campaign specialists, candidate approval very often depends on a simple turnaround of the old-time "what-do-they-know" attitude. Today the attitude is: "Never mind what they know. What do they look like?"

One consultant wrapped up modern electioneering by stating: "Any man with a fine shock of hair, a good set of teeth and a bewitching smile can park his brains and run for office." The end result places in high office, if not brainier public officials, at least people who are easier to look at. "Since television," said a Washington writer, "this Congress is 50 per cent prettier than it used to be."

In the simple, uncomplicated life of long ago, a candidate needed only a spavined horse, a rickety wagon, two jugs of corn juice, a plug of tobacco, a copy of the Declaration of Independence, strong lungs, and a sense of humor. He begged his meals as he campaigned and slept in his clothes. Drunk or sober, he entertained and informed the voters while damning every danger threatening America. It was vaudeville and politics and the best and worst of each. In any event, the voters saw and heard the "real" man in all his ability or stupidity and, if elected, he usually did a pretty good job.

Image and charisma are now the thing in big-time politics. If beetle-browed Daniel Webster, with his massive head and glowering eyes, were to ask the image-makers for advice on seeking office today, he might be told to run for the local school committee. Gaunt Rufus Choate, who looked like a ghost, would have been told to stick with the law. Matchstick John Randolph would be given the "save your money" routine, as would Thaddeus Stevens. George Washington's wooden teeth would get him in trouble on TV. And Andrew Jackson might be advised to try Western movies as the heavy.

Gangling Abraham Lincoln, with his hollow face and sad eyes, would have a hard time convincing the image boys of his potential as a presidential candidate. "I'll tell you, Lincoln," he might be advised, "if you insist on running, for God's sake, stay off television. Gear your campaign to the radio and take some voice lessons. Try a hand-shaking tour and some bumper stickers. And good luck."

To survive, the old-time political office-seeker needed spontaneous humor. He usually could manage to handle tomatoes, eggs, dead cats, fish heads, cabbages, and throat-cutting opponents with deadly wit and repartee. Very often the electorate measured their candidates on how they took down an opponent with a barb or a the earth, nature's own noblemen, what does he do? He plays the fiddle left-handed. He thinks that's good enough for you. He figures also that you won't know the difference."

The planter tried frantically to tell the voters he was naturally left-handed, but the damage had been done. The rumor spread and he was booed off the stump.

The modern television-oriented candidate has little opportunity to use humor. It is just not part of the package. Once in a while a carefully worded and well-rehearsed one-, two-, or three-liner creeps into the presentation, but with a few million dollars riding on a campaign, a candidate could sink the ship with an off-the-cuff humorous remark.

The campaign specialists know that ethnic and other minority groups are more sensitive than ever before, and a bit of misapplied humor could be bad news. Their advice to the candidate is simply this: "Look, Bill, if you've got to say something funny, spill it at a chicken barbecue and not on television."

The electronic age and the television tube have created a new politics. Today, it's the speech-writers, researchers, polltakers, tie straighteners, makeup artists, hair setters, and the image-makers who set the tone of a campaign.

Then come the advisers, slick or bearded young men and sharp young women, who flit around the candidate as he readies himself for the television performance.

A last-minute brainwash sharpens the candidate's wits as aides warn: "Don't forget to smile on camera. And by the way, I hope you brushed your teeth." "Don't wave your arms." "Watch the red light." "Don't rustle your papers." "Don't rub your makeup." "Don't muss your hair." "Try not to twitch your eye." "Don't stare." "Don't look shifty." "Talk in a moderate key and don't orate." "Don't be too humble and don't be too bold." "Remember—no jokes." All this is topped off with: "Here, take this pill. It will calm you down."

The litany of suggestions is such that the viewers very often see, not a relaxed candidate, but an unreal man—a political zombie, with a frozen smile, molded, plasticized, directed, and presented by the image-makers. "Hell," said a positive political strategist, "if the damn fool acts like himself on television, or throws in a humorous retort and on how they could handle hecklers in the audience. The people loved the man who could make them laugh. If he had a few words for the good of the country, so much the better.

Nothing in political history could compare with the Lincoln-Douglas campaign debates of the mid-1800s. During that marvelous time, the stumpy Stephen Douglas and the elongated Abraham Lincoln provided political fun and laughter without parallel in the history of the United States.

As the Lincoln-Douglas debates moved from town to town across Illinois, Douglas tried to humiliate Lincoln before the voters. This attempt by the "Little Giant" gave to the compendium of political humor the most telling response of one candidate to another ever recorded.

Mounting the platform in a small Illinois town, Douglas proceeded to inform the voters that Lincoln wasn't such a great man after all. "Do you know," said Douglas, "that this man at one time sold whiskey behind the bar in a saloon?"

When it was his turn to speak, Lincoln admitted that Judge Douglas was correct. "It is true," said Honest Abe, "that the first time I saw Judge Douglas, I was selling whiskey by the drink in a saloon. I was on the inside of the bar and the judge was on the outside. I was busy selling and Douglas was busy buying."

Another humorous and devastating response, which ranks with Lincoln's reply to Douglas—and which would never have made it on television—took place in Kentucky, where Bob Letcher was opposed by a prosperous planter for the governorship. Letcher's opponent, in addition to his wealth, also played the fiddle.

As the campaign progressed, the planter delighted the backwoodsmen with his fiddle playing. It looked bad for Letcher until he noticed that his opponent played the fiddle left-handed.

At the next stop, Letcher admitted that his opponent was a fine fiddle player. "But, did you notice," he told the yokels, "that he always plays the fiddle left-handed?"

Then Letcher went on: "When my opponent plays for his aristocratic friends in the Bluegrass, he plays right-handed. When he plays for the fine-feathered ladies in the cities, he plays right-handed. But when it comes to you people in the hills, the salt of joke, he might blow the whole package, and we don't get paid to let him do it."

The virtual disintegration of party politics has left the field wide open for personality politics. More and more, candidate glamorizing, cosmetics, Madison Avenue techniques, and sophisticated technology have pushed the county political chairman and the big city political muscleman into the background. The drones who did the dirty work of hanging signs or tearing them down and arguing in bars and taverns have become fewer and fewer. Politics has taken on style.

"It's enough to make an old ward heeler roll over in his grave," commented a veteran of the political wars. "Can you imagine sitting there in a big leather chair listening to a cold-faced thirty-year-old gun-for-hire consultant tell you how to win an election as he manicures his fingernails? And he don't even offer anybody a beer, tell a funny story or talk about doing little favors for the people. All he talks about are the issues and how he is going to present the best side of our candidate."

Then the veteran adds, with a note of surrender: "How the hell can you argue with it? This guy brings home political winners. But, God, how you have to pay for it!"

The electronic election reached its zenith in 1968 when Richard M. Nixon was turned over to the campaign specialists, bone, marrow, haircut, makeup, personality and all. What the voters saw on television was a packaged personality, making the right moves, saying the right things, smiling and affable, all under the direction of the high-powered consultants.

The old political arena, which Nixon loved, was ruled out. It was now the stage for candidate Dick. It became almost a puppet show, with the specialists pulling the strings. Nixon had become a captive of theater, whether he liked it or not.

"So what?" argued a public relations man. "Look, guys, the name of the game is to win, and dammit, we did, even though we created some illusions." Then he added, "Hey, they packaged Nixon all over again in 1972 and look what happened. He won forty-nine states. The boob tube is where the votes are, if you know how to use it. Any guy who doesn't take advantage of television has a potential loser on his hands."

Early in 1974, Senator Walter Mondale of Minnesota toyed with the idea of seeking the Democratic nomination for President. A serious, down-to-earth individual, Mondale looked forward to sitting down with knowledgeable people, pondering issues, and just meeting the folks.

As the Minnesota senator moved about the country, he came to the realization that he wasn't in a back-home contest, where you talked straight to the voters. Advice started to pour in. "Get a different suit." "Change your hair style." "Spend some time with a speech consultant." "Stop off in Hollywood for some video taping." "Get yourself a couple of know-how guys." And on it went. It started to get Mondale down.

Suddenly, Mondale withdrew from the race, commenting that he had lost his desire to be President. Said the harried Mondale: "I admire those who have an overwhelming desire to be President, which is essential for the kind of campaign that is required. But I have found that I am not among them."

Mondale further indicated that running for national office wasn't politics. It was theater, greasepaint and all. "I hated that," said Mondale. "Back home you don't have to pose, wear a new suit, or even make good speeches. All you have to do is talk straight and make a little common sense."

When Mondale withdrew from contention, he knew what he was leaving behind. The sturdy Minnesotan apparently wanted no part of the plastic politics, the personality remaking, the electronics, the lack of humor, and the demands that a candidate be all things to all people. He could not subscribe to the fact that in order to convince the voters, a man had to be ever-smiling, photogenic, and appealing to the voters in much the same manner as a movie star appeals to his audience.

Advised that Mondale had taken himself out of the presidential race, a campaign strategist observed: "In politics today, we want candidates who can appeal, like Burt Reynolds. We're in the business of selling political merchandise. The package is everything. It's as simple as that."

Then, with a nifty parting shot, the consultant paraphrased former President Harry S Truman's "heat-in-the-kitchen" remark, by declaring: ". . . and furthermore, as we look at it, we know what we want and how the candidate should be packaged. If the guy can't stand the greasepaint, he should stay out of the theater."

★

Shortly after capturing the 1976 Democratic presidential nomination, Jimmy Carter selected a surprised Senator Mondale as his vice-presidential running mate. Immediately Fritz set aside his earlier views on plastic politics, pressed his suit, restyled his hair, found himself a makeup artist and an image maker, and plunged back into the fray.

"Like I said," commented a consultant, "politics is no longer a baggy-pants business. If they want to win, they've got to do what we tell 'em!"

★

A candidate for Congress complained that he was groggy from television appearances and blinding lights. "When I got home one night, after four TV programs," he said, "I opened the refrigerator door to get something to eat. When the light went on I gave a ten-minute speech to a head of lettuce."

★

In an emotional appeal for votes, a young legislative candidate named Ruso said on television: "Don't forget, folks, Ruso is the name, spelled R-U-S-O. R stands for Righteousness, U stands for Unity, S stands for Service, and O stands for Honesty."

★

When William Jennings Bryan was one of the up-and-coming younger politicians in the Democratic Party, he volunteered to assist in the gubernatorial campaign in Nebraska. Bryan delivered some fifty speeches against the Republican candidate, who won just the same.

Sometime after the election, Bryan was scheduled to deliver a speech at a St. Patrick's Day program in one of the Nebraska towns. To his surprise he discovered that the newly elected Governor was to preside. Despite the fact that Bryan had talked against the Governor, he had never met him.

Finally, the Governor arose and said: "The next person on the program is William J. Bryan." As the latter stepped forward, the Governor grasped his hand and whispered: "Quick, mister. Tell me, do you speak, sing, or dance?"

"He had never heard of me," Bryan said later.

★

Nothing in present-day politics can compare with the old days when everything was tolerated on the campaign trail. One Texas candidate, referring to his opponent, said: "He's studying to be a half-wit, but I don't think he will make it."

★

An election battle for governor of Indiana found two newspapers in Crawsfordsville, one Democratic and the other Republican, taking sides with vicious effect.

The morning following a huge torchlight parade run by the local Democratic committee, the Democratic paper presented an account of the parade, calling it the greatest demonstration ever held in Crawfordsville; and claiming that it was so large it took two hours to pass a given point.

The evening Republican newspaper confessed that the parade was enormous, and then added that the given point was Mulholland's saloon.

★

Following his successful campaign for governor of Indiana, in 1908 Thomas R. Marshall boasted that he had given 169 speeches during the campaign. His wife, standing close by and having overheard the remark, said: "Oh, Tom, you know better than that. I was with you all the time. You gave one speech 169 times."

★

When Vice-President Spiro Agnew was riding high and cutting down everyone in sight, many national newswriters were appalled at what they said was Agnew's unsportsman-like conduct.

A weather-beaten Texas newsman scoffed at the criticism of the Vice-President, pointing out that the thin-skinned present-day writers should have been around in the old days when a politician would cut his opponent to the marrow of his bones, using every device available.

The old-timer then proceeded to relate a yarn about a candidate for governor of Texas, who told a backwoods crowd the following story about his opponent:

"They would have you believe," the candidate told the yokels, "that Colonel S—— is a Prohibitionist and never took a drink in his life. But they don't deny that he belongs to the exclusive Houston Club.

"Suppose you walked into the Houston Club. What would YOU order? Let's consult the menu (holding up a copy of the menu of the Houston Club).

"First, there's a fruit cocktail. You all know what a cocktail is. There's a manhattan cocktail and a martini cocktail, and they even squirt a little fruit juice in one and call it a fruit cocktail.

"Next, there is consommé, a French wine.

"Then, there is a filet mignon, a Russian drink, four times stronger than vodka.

"And the last thing is a demitasse, which has sent many a strong man reeling into an untimely grave.

"Not a chop or a single item of food on the list!

"Don't take my word for it. Step right up here and read it for yourself."

★

One of the most cutting responses of all time involved former Speaker Champ Clark and a burly opponent. At every rally, the big man made a great show of his strength. Thinking he had Clark on the ropes, he said at one political gathering, "And I'm hard as nails, and I'm tough, and in the business of politics you need a man who can take it."

When it was Clark's turn to speak he said softly: "Certainly my opponent is hard as nails and is tough, and I don't deny he can take it—no matter to whom it belongs."

★

An old and boastful Civil War general was aspiring to Congress and irked his opponent with fanciful tales of his military campaigns. Finally, when he had a chance to speak, the general's opponent said: "The general's sword was never drawn but once, and then in a raffle."

★

In the years following the Civil War, candidates for public office pleaded for election on the basis of all sorts of war-induced disabilities.

At a huge rally in Kentucky, the first candidate hobbled to the stand on crutches and with an empty trouser leg pinned to his belt. "When they called me I was ready," he boasted, "and they got me at Shiloh. It is for that reason I appeal for your votes."

The second candidate told how he had lost an arm in another engagement. The third candidate pointed to a patch over his eye, lost at Vicksburg.

The fourth candidate hobbled forth. "I never did get into the war," he said, "and I never did get wounded. But my fellow citizens, if physical disability is a qualification for this here office, I sure can tell you this: I'm the doggonedest most ruptured son-of-a-gun you ever saw."

★

"What happened?" a friend asked a disheartened politician who had just been walloped at the polls. "Well," said the loser, "I made the mistake of telling the voters I was a down-to-earth candidate and I guess they decided to plow me under."

★

Texas is Democratic country, but John Tower, whose family was also Democratic, made it through to victory for the United States Senate as a Republican. Tower was the first GOP senator from that state since Reconstruction days. Shortly after the victory announcement, Senator-elect Tower's father embraced him and remarked: "Son, the family's proud of you and I think most of them even voted for you."

★

Anything could happen at an old-time political rally. Once when a curious voter attended a raucous affair in a smoke-filled hall, he discovered to his dismay that his watch had disappeared. The voter sought out the man who looked like the leader of the affair, and told him that someone had stolen his watch.

The leader whispered: "Who were you standing next to last?" The victim looked out over the room and also whispered: "Next to that fellow with the plaid shirt." The leader replied, "Don't say anything—I'll be right back."

In a few minutes he was back and handed the citizen his watch, who thanked the leader and again whispered: "What did that pickpocket say?"

"Shh," was the soft response, "he doesn't know I got it."

★

An aspirant for the governorship in Texas said that an opponent who had made a great deal of noise on antitrust activities while Attorney General, reminded him of a dog he used to own.

"We'd build a fire out on the prairie and have supper. Then that dog would take out after a wolf," the candidate related. "And old Blucher knew just how fast to run NOT to catch up with that wolf."

★

A candidate for state office in Arkansas was accused by his opponent of merely posing as a "son of very poor parents." "As a matter of fact," thundered his opponent, "my adversary comes from the richest family in this county."

The candidate answered calmly, "It's quite true I wasn't born in a log cabin. *But we moved to one as soon as we could afford it.*"

★

On the stump or on the floor of Congress, Senator Ben Hardin of Kentucky was a tough adversary. Once during a vicious campaign, Ben's opponent turned on him and shouted: "You know you are telling lies about me."

Old Ben jumped to his feet and roared at the crowd: "I'm pretty generous with this man, only tellin' lies about him. Just supposin' I started tellin' the truth!"

Commenting on a candidate's extensive hand-shaking tour through the farm country, a courthouse politician observed: "If Blake had been milkin' instead of shakin' hands, he would have drained every cow in the county."

*

A veteran congressman found himself running against a young, fast-moving candidate. The youngster was one of the so-called "beautiful people." With a face like a Greek god, he naturally went for television in a big way. One of his TV programs showed the young man walking with his wife through a green pasture, looking upward toward the sky while the cows grazed peacefully in the background. It was an impressive program and designed to demonstrate that the candidate was an outdoorsman.

The elder congressman's answer to the TV advertisement was simple and devastating. He said: "I may not be as smart as my young opponent, but at least I have sense enough to look down when I'm walking through a cow pasture."

He won overwhelmingly.

*

Few men who ever sat in Congress could match Senator Theodore Bilbo of Mississippi when it came to verbal flame throwing. Strangely, one of those who could was Senator Pat Harrison, Bilbo's fellow senator from the same state. They hated each other and when Bilbo supported Mike Connor against Harrison in 1936, all hell broke loose.

In denouncing Harrison, Bilbo dug for every bit of dirt he could find. Harrison replied in kind by stating, "When Bilbo dies, the epitaph on his gravestone should read: 'Here lies Bilbo, deep in the dirt he loved so well.'"

*

Senator Bob Kerr of Oklahoma was a sharp-tongued politician, and out on the campaign circuit he "gave 'em hell," with a vengeance. Once his junior colleague from Oklahoma, Senator A. S. Mike Monroney, was opposed for re-election by Rev. W. H. Bill Alexander.

Out on the stump for Monroney, Old Bob made a devastating reference to Rev. Alexander. "Now, this fellow Alexander," said Kerr, "after communion with the Almighty, said he had decided to enter the Democratic primaries and run for the Senate.

"Well," continued Kerr, "soon after this announcement, Alexander switched over and won the Republican nomination.

"What I'd like to know," Kerr asked rather piously, "is this: If the Lord told Bill Alexander to run as a Democrat, who, then told him to run as a Republican."

★

A candidate for county judge was called one night over long distance by his manager, who said: "Bill, they're telling it down in this part of the county that you ain't drawd a sober breath since May 10 when you announced."

The candidate replied: "For God's sake, Bill, you didn't wake me up in the middle of the night to tell me that, did you? I can't pay any attention to such a statement. I'm too busy fighting *false* rumors!"

★

At a huge rally in his native Maine, Tom Reed was pounding away, driving home point after point. The crowd hung on every word as the Speaker of the House poured it on.

Just as Reed went into his peroration, a chair broke and dropped a constituent in a crash. A lesser man would have been completely confused, but not Reed. As soon as quiet again prevailed and the unfortunate listener had recovered his composure, Reed won the night with: "Well, you must at least credit me with making a knock-down argument here tonight."

★

During the great secession debates, emotions ran high across the land. A Southern Baptist minister got into the fray for Congress and a friend was asked to comment on his ability. "Ah think he'll be a right good man in Congress," was the response. "He's a pow'ful preacher. He has pounded three pulpits to pieces and banged the hell out of five Bibles."

In the days following the Civil War, Southern politicians made much political hay by emotional references to the magnificent fight of the Confederacy. When a new congressman arrived on the national scene, fresh from Virginia, he was asked how he managed his campaign.

"Wa'l," drawled the Virginian, "in every town in the district, ah had that fine Southern gentleman, Robert E. Lee, waist deep in Northern blood."

★

There are some candidates who offer honest answers to honest questions. During a race for Congress, a fellow who was running against a popular incumbent was asked by a voter: "I'd like to know your views on what the main issues of this campaign are."

"The way I see it," the candidate responded, "there's just one issue in this campaign. That so-and-so has the job—and I want it."

★

When presidential candidate Adlai Stevenson was campaigning in Oregon, he stopped by the office of Senator Wayne Morse. "Have you any advice for me?" said Adlai.

"Yes, I have," said the outspoken Morse. "Get that damned suit pressed."

★

A candidate for Congress, who was to speak in a small roughhouse town in the far reaches of the district, arrived early in the afternoon to get the lay of the land. He moved around town anonymously to find out what might be in store for him at the rally. He wandered into the general store and engaged the proprietor in conversation.

"Good afternoon, my friend," the candidate said cautiously. "What's going on around here tonight to help a stranger while away the time?"

The storekeeper, who had been moving the pickle barrel, straightened up, wiped his hands, and said: "I 'spect there's goin' to be a political speech on the town square, for I been sellin' eggs all day. How many do you want?"

"I think you'll be a great governor," a voter said to Jim Curley the day following his victory in Massachusetts. Never one to forgive an enemy and with the knowledge that the voter had not been on his side, Curley replied acidly: "Very nice of you to say that, Bill. Do say it behind my back someday."

★

Two voters met on the town square in a Western town and began discussing the coming election. Said one: "I don't want to vote for any of the candidates. I don't know any of them."

The second voter responded: "I don't know what to do either. You see, I know all of them."

★

Newspaper editors can be brutal and sarcastic. Referring to a certain candidate for Congress, one such ivory tower editor wrote: "Sam Grout is not very popular in this community. If he ran unopposed, he would still lose." Another editorial writer, who had had some words with a political candidate, referred to his enemy with a deliberate typographical error, calling him "a bottle-scarred veteran of the political wars."

An editor for the old Louisville *Courier*, who evidently had little use for politicians of any character, put it this way in his weekly column: "If you have a feeble minded individual in your community, put him in a proper institution and pay taxes for his support. Don't dodge the issue by sending him to Washington."

Still another editor poured on the vitriol when he wrote: "The highest praise that can ever be given the General Assembly of Maryland is that it might have been worse." Mark Twain once said that "the only way for a newspaperman to look at a politician is *down*."

★

Prowling the farm district for votes, a candidate for Congress stopped by a cow barn where a young maid was milking a cow. Presently a voice came from the nearby house, calling; "Who's there in the barn with you, Mirandy?" "A man," was the response. "What kind of a man?" "A politician, Mom."

There was a moment of silence, then a shrill cry came from the house. "Mirandy, you come right in the house this minute." Then, there was another silent moment and the voice again ordered: "And bring in the cow with you."

★

Years ago, a candidate for Congress in a Western state hung a sign on a burro, reading, "Vote for Smith for Congress." He then proceeded to lead the burro through a small mining town in the district. A crowd of miners gathered at the town square to survey the candidate and the donkey.

One of the miners, looking first at the sign hung over the pack and then at the candidate, and finally at the donkey, ventured: "Say, stranger, which one of you is Smith?"

★

"There are three things necessary for political victory," said Joseph P. Kennedy, father of the three Kennedy boys. "The first is money, the second is money, and the third is money."

★

A Midwestern governor, noted for his sense of humor, nevertheless had been clobbered at the polls. The next day he was invited to a press conference to explain what happened.

"I don't want you people to get the idea that being beaten in this election bothered me a bit," said the governor. "Oh, not a bit. After the election returns were in and I realized I had lost, I went to my apartment and had a good night's rest and a very hearty breakfast this morning. About nine o'clock, I said goodbye to my wife and strolled down the hall to the elevator as calm as I could be. I pushed the elevator bell and took a look at my profile in the hall mirror. I was still as handsome as ever and a picture of elegance in my tweed jacket and my well-shined shoes.

"Then I went back to my apartment and put on my pants."

★

A candidate for sheriff in a Western county distributed hundreds of placards with his picture, advertising for re-election. The candidate's wife went with her five-year-old son to the center of town, where the placards were prominently displayed.

After looking at a few of the placards in several stores, the youngster tugged on his mother's coat and whispered: "Gee, Mommy, I think Daddy is wanted, dead or alive."

★

When Jim Curley was running for mayor of Boston, a panhandler stopped him one day and said, "Well, if it ain't my old pal Jim Curley. Now, don't you remember me?" Curley shook hands and said: "I'm sorry I can't place your face, but I never forget a breath."

★

Many politicians find it difficult to remember names. One particular candidate for county office in Texas was so bad at remembering names that he wrote them on a small piece of paper and pinned it on the inside of his tie. He would then glance down at the notation from time to time.

The candidate was called upon one day to deliver a funeral sermon, which he did in this fashion: "Brethren and sisters, we are assembled to pay the last tribute of respect to our dearly beloved friend [glancing down at the note inside his tie] John Jones. Well do I remember back in [pause] 1897 when he came into our midst and soon afterward married [pause, and another look at the tie] Mary Smith. But after many years spent as a noble citizen, husband, and father, our good brother rests in the arms of his Blessed Saviour [pausing to look at the note], er—ah—Jesus Christ."

★

Congressman Dan Kuykendall of Tennessee had a favorite story about his first race for the House. Flushed with victory, he moved about the district receiving the praise of his soon-to-be-constituents. A crusty old voter moved into the circle of admirers in front of the town hall and thrust out his hand to Kuykendall and said frankly and without a smile, "If I'da knowed you wuz gonna win, I'da voted for ya."

Senator Tom Corwin once referred to an opponent as "a man who would never take a bribe—unless it was in cash."

★

A repeater was hired to go the polls during an Albany, New York, election a number of years ago. He had voted in a half-dozen districts and finally reached a precinct where the poll clerk asked him his name. The repeater, flushed with previous success, answered brassily, "William Croswell Doane."

"Come off it. You ain't Bishop Doane," said the poll worker.

"The hell I ain't, you SOB," yelled the repeater.

★

Sir Winston Churchill offered this comment concerning one of his bellicose opponents: "That man has a genius for compressing a minimum of thought into a maximum of words."

★

When the ever-frugal Calvin Coolidge was running for governor of Massachusetts, an aide introduced him one afternoon to an important ward leader. Cal was so impressed that he broke out a new bottle of Bourbon and poured each visitor a snifter.

Two days later the aide brought in another local big shot, but this time Coolidge only offered the big shot a drink.

"What about me?" the aide inquired.

Coolidge replied: "You had yours Thursday."

★

One of the problems Jack Kennedy faced during the 1960 presidential election was the Republican charge that he was inexperienced. Kennedy at the time was forty-three years of age and looked ten years younger.

As the charge of inexperience spread, Kennedy squelched it with a masterful response during a speech in Minneapolis. The witty candidate said: "The outstanding news story of this week was not the events of the United Nations or even the presidential campaign. It was the story coming out of my own city of Boston that

Ted Williams had retired from baseball. It seems that at forty-two he was too old. It shows that perhaps experience isn't enough."

★

"You're a liar and a fool," yelled a hostile voter to Private Johnny Allen during a wild political rally in the Old South.

"Don't mind him," said Allen coolly. "The poor fellow is always talking to himself."

★

After twenty-five years in Congress, the old-timer was facing one of the newer breed of political candidates, straight out of the state university.

One night they met on the same platform before a large audience. The young man spoke first and in a voice dripping with scorn he pointed his finger at the old-timer and charged: "You've never done anything for this district in all your twenty-five years in Congress. Not one school, not one bridge, not one road. You haven't helped us at all. I challenge you to name one thing you've done for this district."

The old congressman said nothing. The eager challenger then turned to the crowd and shouted: "Now I ask you people. Can anyone name one thing our congressman's done in this district?"

A string-bean farmer stood up, scratched his head, and said: "I don't know if he's done anything for this district, but I tell you, son, he has sure beat hell out of anybody who's tried to lick him for the last twenty-five years."

★

When a campaign is raging, the mimeograph machines in the candidates' press offices rotate ceaselessly, much to the chagrin of newspaper editors who have to contend with the avalanche. One editor put it this way: "We dig our way out of one blizzard of press releases, only to be hit with another snow job."

★

When asked what he would do if elected to Congress, a desperate candidate replied quite truthfully: "I'm not concerned about what I'll do if elected. My big problem is what will I do if I'm *not* elected."

★

While Richard Nixon always took the serious road in his campaign speeches, John F. Kennedy could not resist the witty remark. His approach softened hard-core voters and gained for JFK a great warmth and admiration.

Campaigning in Pennsylvania, he offered this: "I wonder when he [Mr. Nixon] put his finger under Mr. Khrushchev's nose whether he was saying: 'I know you are ahead of us in rockets, Mr. Khrushchev, but we are ahead of you in color television.' As for me, I would just as soon look at black and white television and be ahead of them in rockets."

★

Whether or not the charge is justified, a favorite Democratic accusation against Republicans is that they are a reactionary lot. Running for Vice-President during the 1964 presidential race, Hubert Humphrey chalked up one of the best remarks of the entire campaign. Speaking to a college audience, Humphrey told the Goldwater supporters: "I don't care if you do study ancient history, but for heaven's sake, don't vote for it."

★

As the 1936 campaign progressed, Republican candidate Alf Landon knew that Franklin D. Roosevelt was going to win. He hardly realized, however, that the win would be of landslide proportions and that he would capture only Maine and Vermont.

When the final returns trickled in, an assistant said to Landon: "Sorry, boss, but I guess the people have spoken."

"I know," said Landon sadly, "but did they have to speak so loudly?"

★

When Arthur Goldberg was a candidate for the governorship of New York, he returned home from a swing upstate to tell his wife of the various stops he had made on the campaign trail. Goldberg reported that he had made one speech at the AFL-CIO conven-

tion in Kiamesha Lake. "I spoke for forty-five minutes," said Goldberg, "and was interrupted twenty-three times by applause."

"Arthur," said Mrs. Goldberg, "anyone who speaks for forty-five
minutes *should* be interrupted twenty-three times."

★

When Robert Kennedy entered the race for the United States
Senate in 1964 as a candidate from New York State, he immediately made proposals involving the entire Eastern seaboard. His
suggestions for large-scale transportation, air and water pollution
projects, and whatnot prompted a comment from his opponent,
incumbent Senator Kenneth Keating. "As I see it," said Keating,
"he's either running for President of the United States, or is looking for some kind of federal job like High Commissioner of the
Northeast."

★

Candidates for the presidency often draw to their side supporters who lose all sense of rationality. Their man is "The New
God" and that's that. Teddy Roosevelt was one of those politicians. During the campaign, a backer insisted that Roosevelt was
the greatest man who ever lived.

"Oh, come on," said a doubter. "Do you think he's better than
George Washington?"

"He sure is," was the proud reply.

"How about Lincoln?"

"Teddy is head and shoulders over Old Abe."

"Now wait a minute. I suppose you think he's even greater than
Moses?"

"I don't know if he's greater," said the supporter, "but let me
put it this way. If Teddy had been leading the children of Israel,
it sure as hell wouldn't have taken them forty years to get out of
the wilderness."

★

New York Governor Thomas E. Dewey had the 1948 presidential election all wrapped up. Something backfired and, as we
know, Dewey lost out to Harry Truman.

In a grin-and-bear-it statement, Dewey said that he felt much like a man who had been drinking too much at a wake. Some friends laid him in a spare coffin in the funeral parlor and left for the night. When he came to the next morning and realized where he was, he asked himself: "If I'm alive, why am I in this coffin? And if I'm dead, why do I have to go to the men's room?"

★

A candidate for United States senator was extolling his virtues before a half-hostile audience when a heckler started wisecracking from the rear of the hall. The senator frowned and then lowered his voice and said: "When I was a lad back on the farm, my dad once gave me for my birthday a wonderful little donkey. He told me to treat it properly, curry it, feed it, bed it down, make sure it was warm and dry, and so forth. Then he reminded me always to lock the barn door.

"Well, gentlemen, there came one evening, unfortunately, when I forgot to lock the barn door. The donkey walked out and got hit by a truck and died. My father looked down at the dead donkey and said; 'Son, that animal's going to haunt you the rest of your life,' and my dad sure was right."

Then the senator pointed to the heckler and brought down the house with, "And there, my friends, sits that jackass now!"

★

Campaign specialists are hard-nosed people, and if you want to win you've got to do it their way. A campaign field man reported back to the chief image-maker that a United States Senate candidate made some very positive statements on a television show. "For C—— sake, man," warned the chief image-maker, "don't let him make that mistake again."

★

Following a hot South American revolution, a young escapee was interviewed on the career of his uncle, deposed president of the country. "Well," said the youthful Latin, "my uncle first ran for councilman in his village and he made it easy. Then he ran for judge and then district attorney and he had no trouble making those posts. Then he ran for governor of his province and he made it. Next he ran for president and he made that also. Then while he was president he made a run for the border, but he don't make it."

★

Campaign spending is a matter of growing concern to every candidate for public office. In referring to the amounts spent by Governor Nelson Rockefeller, Senator Tom Eagleton of Missouri said: "If the amount of money that Rockefeller spent on TV in New York State was put into balloons and the balloons were then filled with helium, they would lift New York State right off the map."

★

Running for re-election to the Illinois legislature, Abraham Lincoln was opposed by a side-winding orator named Forquer, a one-time Whig who had changed his party designation to Democrat. The change had given him a handsome appointment from President Jackson. On the strength of the appointment, Forquer had constructed a beautiful home, topped off with a lightning rod.

As the campaign warmed up, Forquer went at Lincoln with both barrels, ridiculing and insulting Honest Abe at every rally. Finally, Lincoln's friends prevailed upon Old Abe to fight back. The chance came the very next day. As usual, Forquer opened up on Lincoln, cutting him to ribbons with invective. Abe stood calm and pale, awaiting his turn to speak.

When Forquer sat down, Lincoln went at him with brutal sarcasm, stating: "Among other things," said Abe, "My opponent in this contest has said that 'this young man,' alluding to me, 'must be taken down.' I am not so young in years as I am in tricks of the trade of a politician, but," he continued, pointing a deadly finger at Forquer, "live long or die young, I would rather die now than, like the gentleman, change my politics and with it receive an office worth three thousand dollars a year, and then feel obliged to erect a lightning rod over my house to protect a guilty conscience from an offended God."

"Now, this is the way it will be," a hard-nosed congressman advised a group of eager young congressional candidates who had come to Washington for some sage advice on campaigning. "The opposition will spread all kinds of rumors about you. The press will ask you to comment on reports that you left college owing a tailor bill, or that you have a criminal record going back ten years, which might be only for passing a red light. They might ask you about a rumor that you are stepping out with one of the blond workers in your campaign. What you do is dismiss these charges with indignation, stating: 'Man, are they desperate, spreading rumors and nonsense like that.' Then you go out and pay the tailor bill and drop the blonde."

*

Hubert Humphrey arrived at a television studio in 1962 to prepare for a network presentation. An executive took him aside and advised him to relax. "Imagine," he said, "that you are speaking to a friend of average intelligence, education, and income."

Humphrey thought a moment and responded: "That's fine, but what about the unfriendly people, the dumb ones, the geniuses, the plumbers, the philosophers, the slum dwellers, and the fat cats in the audience?"

*

John F. Kennedy had the kind of ready wit that created an immediate communication response from the audience. Hammering his way across West Virginia in the crucial 1960 primary, Kennedy brought in his youngest brother, Ted, then a not-so-famous politician.

At one stop Ted took the microphone and went all out in an emotional speech about the coming presidential election: "Do you want a man who will give the country leadership? Do you want a man who has vigor?" and on he went.

Finally, Jack Kennedy got hold of the microphone and won the hearts of the voters by declaring, "I would like to tell my brother that you cannot be elected President until you are thirty-five years old."

Alabama politics can be as rough and tough as any. This was proved several years ago when a giant of a man was running against a diminutive opponent. At a big rally, the giant spoke first. After castigating the little fellow, he roared: "What this district needs is a *big* man . . . the bigger the better . . ."

Standing beside his opponent, the little fellow looked insignificant until he said: "My opponent has made a great show of his size here today, but if you'd let the booze and the hot air out of him, a pair of my pants would bag on him!"

★

It was a hot Democratic caucus in New Jersey and several candidates were vying for approval as candidates for Congress. All of the aspirants save one were young. During his plea for caucus approval the elderly candidate insisted that he still had his youth and could put up a good fight.

"He may still have his youth," said a delegate, "but we've got to find someone who hasn't had it quite so long."

★

Indiana farmers were tough to face in the old-time election campaigns. They loved to heckle candidates, and a man had to be pretty good to stand up under the hard shots from his audience.

During a congressional campaign, a candidate was reaching the heights of oratory when a booming voice from the center of the crowd bellowed: "Yer nuthin' but a two-faced politician."

There was a moment of silence as the candidate pondered the insult. Then he let go: "I leave it to the audience here. If I had two faces, would I be wearing this one?"

He won the day.

3

"I Accept the Nomination"

Down in Kentucky many years ago, Theodore Hallam, angered at the nomination of an enemy for governor, bolted the party convention choice and took the stump against the nominee.

The first gun in the campaign was to be fired in Bowling Green, where the Democratic ranks were split wide open. One could smell trouble brewing in the crowded courthouse where Hallam was to speak.

No sooner had Hallam started to talk than a rough-and-ready mountaineer jumped up on his chair and shouted: "I want to ask you a question, Hallam."

Cries of "throw him out" and "let him talk" came from all sides. Bedlam was in the making when Hallam held up his hand for silence.

"Let it be understood now and hereafter that this is no joint debate," said Hallam. "My friends have arranged for the use of this building and I intend to be the only speaker. However, it is a principle of our political faith that in a Democratic gathering no man who calls himself a Democrat shall be denied the right to be heard. If the gentleman will be content to ask his question, whatever it is, and to abide by my answer, I am willing that he should speak."

"That suits me," proclaimed the interrupter. "My question is this: Didn't you say at the Louisville convention four weeks ago that if the Democrats of Kentucky, in convention assembled, nominated a yaller dog for Governor, you would support him?"

"I did," said Hallam calmly.

"Well, then," snarled the heckler, eager to press his seeming advantage, "in the face of that statement, why do you now repudiate the nominee of that convention and refuse to support him?"

Hallam waited for perfect quiet in the room and then said: "I admit," he stated, "that I said then what I now repeat, namely that when the Democrats of Kentucky nominate a yaller dog for governor of this great state, I mean to support him—but lower than that ye shall not drag me."

★

When a newspaper reporter asked a certain senator why he did not announce for the presidency, he remarked: "Because, my dear friend, I don't believe I could get nominated. And if I did get nominated, I couldn't get elected. And if I did get elected, I couldn't fill the job properly. And if I did fill the job properly, I wouldn't get any credit for it anyhow."

★

When William Jennings Bryan was defeated in his third try for the presidency, he had this comment: "I am reminded of the drunk who, when he had been thrown down the stairs of a club for the third time, gathered himself up and said: 'I'm onto those people. They don't want me in there.'"

★

Lincoln loved to tell the story of a friend who had worked hard for his nomination for the presidency, and with great effect. "I went to him afterwards," said Abe, "and thanked him for his enthusiasm, but I also said: 'Colonel, when you spoke for me at the Convention, you prevaricated a little!'

"'Prevaricated, Mr. Lincoln?' said the colonel. 'Why, I lied like the devil.'"

On one occasion when Lincoln was going to a political convention, one of his rivals, a liveryman, provided him with a slow horse, hoping that he would not reach his destination in time. Lincoln got there, however, and when he returned the horse, he said:

"You keep this horse for funerals, don't you?"

"Oh no!" replied the liveryman.

"Well, I'm glad of that, for if you did you'd never get a corpse to the grave in time for the resurrection," laughed Lincoln.

★

Candidates for the legislature in Texas in the old days made no bones about why they were running for office. When Hick Halcomb announced for the Texas House, he declared he was running for two reasons:

"First," he said, "I want the ten dollars a day. It will be more money than I ever made in my life; and, second, because I want a free ringside seat at the world's biggest show, the Texas legislature in session."

A flock of candidates immediately descended on Halcomb. One of Hick's rivals eloquently erupted:

"Ladies and gentlemen, there's one man in this race whose position is indefinable. He says he's a-runnin' for the ten dollars a day. I don't care whether the place pays ten dollars or eight dollars or four dollars a day; it doesn't matter what the salary is—I'm a-runnin' for the opportunity to be of service to my fellow man."

The irrepressible Halcomb retorted:

"My opponent reminds me of a boy in my native village who applied for a job in a bank. The president said: 'But we don't have an appropriation for another salary.' He said, 'That's all right; I'm willing to work for what I can pick up around the place.' "

★

On her way to a political rally a young college student said: "I'm going with an open mind, a complete lack of prejudice, and a cool, rational approach to listen to what I'm convinced is pure rubbish."

A friend of James G. Blaine asked former Senator Roscoe Conkling if he would take the stump for Blaine in the campaign for the presidency in 1884. "I can't," said Conkling spitefully. "I have retired from criminal practice."

Blaine evened the score by telling a story about Conkling's considerable vanity: "One day," said Blaine, "when Conkling and I were friends, the proud New York senator asked Sam Cox who he thought were the two greatest characters America ever produced."

"I should say," said Cox solemnly, "I should say the two most distinguished men in America have been General Washington and yourself."

"Very true," said Conkling, "but I don't see why you should drag in the name of Washington."

★

During a bitter campaign Senator Tom Corwin was hammered hard at a rally by his opponent, who had appeared in a new suit of clothes in place of the scraggly outfit he normally wore.

When it was Tom's turn to speak, he first mentioned his opponent's new suit of clothes and then said: "Seeing my opponent all dressed up reminds me of the jackass who was peeved that he was not as popular as the family lapdog.

"So," continued Tom, "the jackass washed himself in the river, smoothed his hide until it shone, and then walked right into the house and began to lick the mistress' hand, put his feet on her and tried to climb onto her lap.

"Instead of kissing the animal and hugging it, the mistress screamed. Her husband rushed in and beat the jackass over the head and drove it out of the house.

"The moral of the story," laughed Corwin, as he nodded at his opponent, "is, that it is no use being anything but a jackass if you are one."

★

Lord Macaulay, the great British politician, once attended a political meeting, at which several other candidates shared the platform. During the proceedings, Macaulay was violently struck by a dead cat. The man who threw the cat immediately apologized, saying that he had meant it for Macaulay's opponent.

"Well, my friend," said the angry Macaulay, "I wish you had meant it for me and struck him."

*

A tenacious and brassy kid named O'Brien was running for state representative in a South Boston district. Closing out his campaign, he knocked one day on the last door in a battered apartment building, occupied by a Mrs. O'Toole.

When the door opened, candidate O'Brien went into his pitch, hoping to convince the lady who answered that he should be her man for the representative seat.

"Are you related to Mike O'Brien?" the lady interrupted.

"He's my father," replied the candidate, expecting to get a favorable response.

Instead, Mrs. O'Toole went into a rage, crying: "Get out of here, you scalawag. Your father is nothing but a drunkard, a cheat, and a bum, and so was his father before him. I don't think you'll amount to much either." As she slammed the door, Mrs. O'Toole shouted: "And furthermore, I'd never vote for anyone named O'Brien."

The young candidate stood in front of the door for a moment, rather stunned by it all. Then he demonstrated the confidence that all Boston candidates display when aspiring to public office. He shrugged his shoulders, took the voting list from his pocket, and searched out Mrs. O'Toole's name. Beside it he wrote: "Doubtful."

*

A Democratic candidate in the process of delivering a speech before a town hall gathering was interrupted by the loud cries of an infant in the audience.

Manfully, the politician tried to continue, but the shrieks of the baby grew louder and louder and the mother showed no inclination to carry it from the hall. Finally, the candidate's speech collapsed completely.

The embarrassed candidate was leaving the hall, when he heard a bit of dialogue between the baby's mother and a neighbor.

"Mary sure set up a racket, didn't she?" observed the neighbor.

"Yes, she yelled right brisk after she got started," replied the mother, "but do you know, I had to pinch that little child seven or eight times before she'd start up!"

★

Barry Goldwater was an ideal political target for the Democrats. The Arizona senator, on the campaign trail for the presidency, spoke out on issues that a normal candidate would leave alone.

Hubert Humphrey, prowling the hinterland for the Democrats, came up with a great crack about Goldwater: "Why, this man Goldwater," said Humphrey, "is living so far in the past and is so handsome that he was offered a movie contract by Eighteenth Century-Fox."

★

During the old frontier days, politics was a hard business. When a man took on an opponent, the sky was the limit. Usually, the two candidates lashed at each other with vicious effectiveness, exposing every tiny facet of life, looking for an advantage. One of the big issues was the amount of corn liquor an opponent consumed.

An old frontier judge named Sharkey was described by his opponent as "a man who obtained his inspiration from wine and whiskey. There is no sweeter music to him than the glug-glug-glug of the jug as he tilts it and pours from its reluctant mouth the corn juice so loved by his soul, unless it can be the same glug-glug-glug as it disappears down his capacious throat."

When it was Judge Sharkey's turn to speak, he wobbled to the platform and said: "Now, fellow citizens, during this ardent campaign, which has been so fatiguing, I have been drunk just once. Over in Simpson County, I was compelled to sleep in the same bed with my distinguished opponent, this delight of his party, this wonderful exponent of the principles and practices of the unwashed democracy. In the morning I found myself dead drunk on corn whiskey. I had lain too close to this soaked mass of democracy and I became drunk from absorption."

★

It is said that the press conference is a candidate's way of giving information without actually saying anything. Should he accidentally say something important, the press officer at his side immediately explains it away by "clarifying" it.

★

Old-time Chicago political campaigns were as rough as any in the land. Most of the candidates were Democrats, and since there was no difference in philosophy involved, the campaigns sank pretty low. Candidates hoping for an opportunity to serve the public found themselves defending some small misdeed of the past, a situation that drove many good men out of politics.

In any event, a number of citizens tried to get a young lawyer to run for a congressional seat. He refused, stating that it was a dirty business and he did not want to be dragged through the mud. The citizens persisted, and finally the young man weakened to the point where he said he would need to talk it over with his mother before making a decision.

At home, the young man said to his mother: "Ma, every group in the district wants me to run for Congress. I know how bad it is and that every little thing a man has done in his lifetime is magnified all out of proportion. Yet, I'm leaning to running. Before I do, can you think of anything I have ever done that the opposition might use against me?"

"I can think of nothing, son," said the mother. "You don't drink or smoke, chase girls, or stay out late. You are a good church member and support your mother."

"Gee, Mother," pleaded the son, "that's fine, but think hard. Did I ever do anything they could use against me in the campaign?"

"The only thing I can think of," responded the mother, "is that when you were a baby, you always wet the bed."

"Holy hell," cried the son, "that settles it. I'm not going to run."

★

When Calvin Coolidge was in the White House, a political bigwig came in to complain about a certain candidate for the Senate. "You ask me to tell him to withdraw," said Cal. "I can't do that, for this man has ability, and why would you want him out of the race?"

"He may have ability," said the visitor, "but he's a no-good SOB."

"Oh, well," said Coolidge, "there's a lot of no-good SOB's around. They're entitled to representation also."

★

Al Smith gave one of the best pieces of political advice when he commented: "Never roll in the mud with a pig. If you do, both of you will get covered with mud—and the pig will love it."

★

One of Barry Goldwater's best jokes (he told it nearly five hundred times on the presidential campaign trail) concerned an Arizona preacher and a tough cowboy.

It seems the cowboy had listened to a sermon by the preacher, then met him outside the church. The cowboy said, "That was a damn fine sermon, Mr. Preacher."

"Thank you," said the minister, "but there's no need to use profanity."

"Oh," said the cowboy, "what I meant was that the sermon was just great—so great in fact that I dropped a hundred-dollar bill in the collection plate."

"The hell you did!" said the preacher.

★

Once Robert Kennedy got going in the 1964 New York senatorial race, he drew the crowds by the thousands. In Buffalo one day, overenthusiastic supporters screamed and pushed, trying to get close enough to shake Kennedy's hand, touch him or pull at his coat. He was lucky to escape the pulling and tugging.

Later on in the evening, Kennedy was asked to speak at a quieter reception, and he quipped: "I've been all over the state talking Medicare today and when I came to Buffalo I thought I was going to need it myself."

★

When Pat Neff ran for governor of Texas on a "bone-dry" platform, he declared he was going to make Texas so dry "that a man will have to prime himself before he can spit."

★

Many years ago, a gubernatorial race in Kentucky found two old friends, Ed Morrow and Augustus O. Stanley, running against each other. Each ridiculed and flayed the other from all sides. When the rally was over, they covertly met afterward in a room back of the hotel lobby to pour a small libation on the altar of friendship.

One of their partisans happened to peer through a crack in the wall and saw the two convivializing. "Why," he exclaimed, shocked, "the two sons-of-bitches never meant a word they said against one another."

As the campaign progressed across Kentucky, it became hotter and hotter, but Stanley and Morrow still remained good friends. They debated such issues as dog taxes, school textbooks, and other incidental problems. One day, Morrow ventured some comments on foreign policy and Stanley was on him at once. "For Ed Morrow to talk foreign policy," Stanley intoned, "reminds me of a duck paddling about on the placid bosom of a bottomless lake, drawing two inches of water, and serenely unconscious of the fathomless depths beneath him."

One day Stanley cut Morrow dead on the street. Morrow ran after his friend, begging to know how he had offended. "Well, Ed," said Stanley, "you and I have been lying about each other for twenty years. Last night, you stood up at that damn rally and told the truth about me and I'm not going to stand for that."

Governor Eugene Talmadge of Georgia had a little story he used to tell about his opponents: "Ah nevah did say that mah opponent was a liah," shouted Talmadge on the campaign trail. "But ah will say he tells the truth inside out."

★

Well-established Mayor James Michael Curley of Boston was dumped out of office by handsome Maurice Tobin, later to become Secretary of Labor under President Harry Truman. Tobin was a handsome man, and his appeal to the ladies was irresistible, so Curley went down to defeat.

Later, Curley was elected to Congress. The first question asked of James Michael when he arrived in Washington was: "What happened in the last election, the one you lost to Maurice Tobin?"

"My good man," responded the unflappable Curley, "that was no election. That was a beauty contest."

★

One of the best stories out of the Truman-Dewey campaign concerned a posh school for young girls whose parents were among America's very rich. Home on vacation, one of the young ladies said to her father: "Guess what, Dad. We took a vote on the school bus the other day and Mr. Dewey won thirty-six to one."

The father beamed, "Remarkable, but who was the dolt who voted for Truman?"

Said the daughter: "Oh, only the bus driver."

★

Moving about his district, an up-for-re-election congressman approached an old hard-liner and immediately asked: "I hope you are going to support the party again this year, Sam."

"Not this year, I ain't," was the terse response.

"But," pleaded the congressman, "I thought you were a staunch party man."

"I am," grunted the constituent, "but the staunch is worse than ever this year."

A certain congressman had written a political joke book. It was very popular, but when the next election came around, a brash young candidate opposed the congressman and took the veteran down at every turn.

During a town hall rally, the young candidate charged that all his opponent had ever done during five terms in the House was to write a joke book.

When it was the veteran's turn to speak, he said: "It is true I have written a joke book about politics. Had I known this young man when I wrote the book, I would have included him as one of the best jokes I had ever heard."

*

The media from coast to coast hammered away at Barry Goldwater as he tried to move his campaign along during the 1964 presidential race. Solemn commentators stated that Goldwater, if elected, would involve the United States deeply in Vietnam and that he might be even crazy enough to send ground troops. It was brutal overkill.

Finally, Goldwater stated: "If I hadn't known Barry Goldwater personally, I would have voted against the son-of-a-bitch myself."

*

Old-time ward-boss politics gave rise to some unusual outlooks. In those hard and rough big city days, the ward boss was the unquestioned king of his turf. He fed, clothed, and cared for the people of his district and expected them to line up and vote right on election day, with no questions asked.

A reporter inquired of a longtime ward boss about tendencies of foreign-born voters. He received this honest reponse: "The Italians," said the ward boss, "are good voters; they know their friends and stand by them. The Greeks are nearly as loyal. But the Jews," bemoaned the boss, "oh, those Jews. You get them registered and do everything for them, then when the election comes around, what do they do? Why, they hold meetings and discuss the issues. That's the sort of ingrates they are."

Commenting on his campaign, a roguish big-city mayor confided to some friends: "There are a lot of people who think I chase around, drink all night, pinch pretty girls and all that stuff, and it bothers me."

"How's that?" asked a friend.

"Well," said the mayor, "the damn voters will get the idea I sleep all day.

★

A Philadelphia businessman had this to say about politics: "I have a lot of friends in the Democratic Party. I'd trust them anywhere—except in public office."

★

Congressman Ben Butler of Massachusetts was as tough a political animal as ever pounded a rostrum, and many stories were told of his adventures and misadventures. One of the best had Ben traveling through his congressional district when he met a young lady named Dora Butler, who said she had always wanted to meet the great Butler.

The young lady also added that wherever she went people asked if she was related to Congressman Butler.

"And what would you say?" asked Butler smoothly.

"Well," replied Dora, "depending on the mood they are in, I tell them I am either your niece or your sister. But, honestly, Mr. Butler, most of the time when they ask me if I am related to you, they are in such a terrible mood, I just tell them I never heard of you."

★

It is difficult to fool Midwestern farmers, as this story proves. Any farmer will agree that when a bull is brought in to mate with a cow, that is what is called "serving the cow."

"So," observed a stalwart farmer, "when you hear of some politician who says he wants to serve the public, you know exactly what he means."

It was a tough, violently personal battle in a Pennsylvania congressional district. Both candidates cut loose with every imaginable charge. When the votes were in, the Democrat had won handily. He boasted he had won in a landslide.

"That was no landslide," said the Republican loser. "Man, that was a mudslide."

★

Representative James P. Johnson of Colorado tells a humorous story of his first election victory. He called on his defeated opponent, who gave him three numbered envelopes, saying: "You're going to find times when the going will be rough. At such times, open one of these envelopes."

A few weeks later Johnson was under attack for an unpopular vote and because he hadn't solved every problem in sight.

"I opened the envelope marked 1," said Johnson, "and on a piece of paper were the words 'Blame me.'"

Johnson took the advice and blamed all the problems on his predecessor. It seemed to work and the criticism lessened.

A few months later, problems multiplied again and Johnson felt it was time to open the second envelope. The message read: "Blame the other political party." Johnson did and reported that it worked.

Finally, election time was nearing. Things got bad again. Nothing seemed to work for Johnson. The people and the press were down on him. Then he remembered the third envelope and opened it eagerly.

There on a sheet of paper were these words: "Prepare three envelopes."

★

Senator George Vest was a splendid wit. He told of an occasion when he invaded a town hall rally for his opponent. "They threw me out the back door," said George. "Then I told them who I was. They invited me in again, and threw me out the front door."

Billie S. Farnum ran for a House seat when he was still Auditor General of the State of Michigan. His schedule called for a door-to-door campaign in a certain upper-lower class section of the district.

Farnum knocked on one door, which opened wide enough to reveal a woman's face. "Good afternoon," said Farnum, "I am Billie Farnum, the Auditor General. . . ."

Before he could get a chance to tell the lady he was running for Congress, she said, "You're too late, I sent the check in yesterday."

With that she slammed the door.

★

Ebon C. Ingersoll of Illinois was one of the most powerful Republican spellbinders in the years after the Civil War. An enormous man, Ingersoll attacked Democrats and Christianity with equal vigor and always drew great crowds.

Witty and brutal in turn, Ingersoll once said: "There is good and bad in all parties, except the Democratic Party, and in the Democratic Party there are bad and worse."

During the Hayes-Tilden campaign, Ingersoll concluded, in one of his firebrand speeches, that the best that could be said about James Buchanan was that he was dead.

At that point, an Irishman shouted: "You lie, sir. You lie."

Without so much as turning his head, Ingersoll pointed a finger in the direction of the protestor. "Sit down, my Connemara friend," he said. "Sit down. I want nothing to do with you. I came to kill the Democrat dog tonight and I have no time to waste on fleas."

4

"The Country Needs Me"

One of the best and shortest political speeches of all time took place more than two thousand years ago, when an Athenian, noted as a poor speaker, faced a brilliant orator. The eloquent politician delivered a long and windy speech, promising great deeds if he were elected.

When the humble Athenian took the floor, he rose, fumbled with his robe, and then stated: "Men of Athens, all that my opponent has said, I will do."

Then he sat down and was elected overwhelmingly.

★

The classic political campaign speech was delivered by young Abraham Lincoln, when as a successful candidate for the Illinois Legislature, he said:

"Fellow citizens: I presume you know who I am. I am humble Abraham Lincoln. I have been solicited by many friends to become a candidate for the Legislature. My politics are short and sweet like an old lady's dance. I am in favor of the national bank; I am in favor of the internal improvement system and a high protective tariff. These are my sentiments; if elected, I shall be thankful; if not, it will be all the same."

A Kentucky legislative candidate made no bones about where he stood on the important issues of the day. His one-sentence campaign speech was simply: "My stand on taxes is this: If they are too high, we'll lower 'em and if they are too low, we'll hi'st em." He won handily.

*

Calvin Coolidge also wasted no words as a candidate for mayor of Northampton, Massachusetts. Canvassing the Democratic wards, Cal used a technique that was simple and to the point. All he said was: "I want your vote. I need it. I will appreciate it." The people understood that kind of language and Coolidge was elected.

*

The all-time successful campaign speech was uttered over and over again by Thomas Buckley, who served as Massachusetts state auditor for more than a generation. Wherever he went, Buckley would follow the long-winded spellbinders to the platform, look out over the weary crowd, and announce: "I am an auditor, not an orator." He then took his seat and the votes usually were tallied by weighing machines.

*

Another winning speech was delivered by a Nevada politician, who arrived at the town square and won the day with only eight words: "Fellow citizens," he said, "follow me to yonder liquor saloon."

*

Campaign oratory never impresses newspaper reporters, who are required to listen to so much of it. Said one cynical reporter when asked what he thought of political speakers: "Well, I'll tell you," was the observation. "No matter how long or short the campaign speech might be, I have concluded that most of those birds need the job much more than the country needs them."

John Nance Garner was never one to waste words. During one of his campaigns for the House, Old John came right to the point in announcing his candidacy. "If you elect me," he said, "I'll go up there and do the best I can for you as long as it is the best for the country as I see it.

"As to details, you'll have to trust my judgment. Don't write or wire me to support some bill just because the word has been passed around to devil your congressman. Even if you have read the bill, which is unlikely, you won't know what it will be like in the final form. I will know this and I will vote to do what I think is right for the Fifteenth District of Texas and for the country."

★

Franklin Delano Roosevelt brought down the fires of Republican hell upon his head when he announced for a fourth presidential term. FDR often told the story about a voter who explained his philosophy of politics. Said the voter:

"I voted Republican the first time you ran because I liked your opponent. I voted Republican the second time you ran because I didn't care about your thinking. And I'll vote Republican this time too, because I've never had it so good."

★

When the campaigning is rough and close, most politicians hit the middle of the road. They try to make bland statements sound like earth-shattering pronouncements. One Texas candidate, involved in the fight of his life for the governorship and scared to death to boot, came up with this gem of frankness and courage: "My friends, I will make this assertion: I will defend it on every stump and I will risk my entire political future upon it—that Texas, my fellow countrymen, is the biggest state in the American Union!"

★

Soon after drenching rains ended a Texas drought, this advertisement appeared in the Stanton *Times*: "J. H. Hones withdraws his candidacy for Treasurer of Martin County. It has rained sufficiently for Mr. Hones to return to farming."

Down in Kentucky a young man gave his first political speech in the county seat. Telling the story later, he said: "Ahead of me on the program was a long-winded orator. The crowd started to hiss and boo until he could no longer continue. Then I came on for my speech. I was doing fine for about three minutes. Then, would you believe it, right in the middle of my speech, they started in booing the first speaker all over again."

★

Congressman Howard W. Smith had a formula for new candidates for public office, which he contended would guarantee success at the polls: "Run on a platform with only four planks," he said. "Claim everything, concede nothing, allege fraud, and demand a recount."

★

Texas has produced many wild and woolly political campaigners. One of these showed up in a small southeastern Texas town, and, mounting the courthouse steps, he shouted: "They're wastin' yore tax money a-teachin' Latin and Greek in the schools. That ain't necessary. If English was good enough for Jesus Christ it ought to be good enough for Texas."

★

During the course of a tough campaign, Louisiana Governor Huey Long was advised to find a way to appease both the Catholics and Protestants, and the Kingfish found it.

Speaking before a Catholic group, Huey would say: "Every Sunday I'd hitch up my horse and take my Catholic grandparents to mass. After I brought them home from mass, I'd drive over to my Baptist grandparents and pick them up and drive them to the Baptist church."

This seemed to handle the situation and cut Huey across religious lines, until a friend said to Long: "I didn't know you had any Catholic grandparents, Huey?"

"Don't be a damn fool," said Long, "we didn't even have a horse."

When someone asked Lincoln what he considered the most valuable asset a politician could have, he thought a moment and then commented: "Well, it is my opinion a good politician is one who is able to raise a cause which will produce an effect and then to fight the effect."

★

They never proved it was so, but the story persists in Louisiana that Huey Long found a most effective way to raise money for his various political campaigns. Following a plea for votes Huey would importune the crowd in this fashion: "All those who wish to contribute to my campaign, please stand up."

Then quickly, Huey would turn to the band and whisper, "Hurry up, play the *Star-Spangled Banner!*"

★

Public service was put in its right perspective by the outgoing mayor of a large, deficit-ridden Eastern city. As he walked out of City Hall after four hard years as mayor, and happy to leave to boot, the chief executive said woefully: "The day they swear you in, it's champagne all around. The day you leave it's Maalox on the rocks."

★

It was said of Johnny Allen when he was in Congress that he could talk a crow out of a cornfield. When someone reminded him of this, Allen responded: "Why, only last night I talked to a group of farmers for two hours and fifteen minutes."

Allen's friend then said: "Gosh, weren't you awfully tired at the end of your speech?"

"Hell no," laughed the irrepressible Allen, "but you should have seen the audience."

★

The famed G.O.P. slogan, "A chicken in every pot," was at best a warmed-over chestnut. Back in 1840 the Whigs boomed Harrison over Van Buren by shouting: "Van's policy: 50 cents a day and French soup; our policy, $2.00 a day and roast beef." Then along came McKinley, who tom-tommed "The Full Dinner Pail," and it's been going on ever since, with one party or the other appealing to the voters' stomachs. As one old pro put it: "Why not? The stomach is where the votes are. You'll get nowhere appealing to their brains."

★

Presidential candidate Barry Goldwater was a good man with a quip. One of his best concerned the spending programs of the Johnson administration. Said Goldwater: "The immediate task before us is to cut the federal budget down to size . . . we must take Lyndon's credit card away from him."

★

Years ago election day was a time for brawling and fighting in the lower wards of the city of Cleveland. Partisan politics brought out the worst in the voters.

During one election, the police were called in to quell a near-riot in front of a certain precinct. When the fracas had been broken up, a police captain approached a bloody and battered ward worker and asked: "How did the fight start?"

"Well, I'll tell you, Captain," said the worker. "It all started when a Republican son-of-a-bitch hit me back."

★

Many years ago a famous orator, in need of money, was hired by Tammany Hall to make street-corner speeches for the Democrats. For a few nights the spellbinder extolled the virtues of the Democratic Party on various street corners.

Tammany Hall officials were shocked a few days later when it was reported that their orator was also speaking on street corners for the Republicans. A Tammany leader rushed over to where the fellow was talking. "What do you mean?" he demanded. "We Democrats are paying you to speak for us and now we find you also speaking for the Republicans. What's the big idea?"

"Well," the defendant shrugged, "there's much that can be said on both sides."

When a reporter asked a defeated congressman to explain his loss at the polls, he was treated to this reply: "I was a victim."

"A victim?" exclaimed the newsman. "A victim of what?"

"Accurate counting, I guess," was the glum reply.

★

William Jennings Bryan was at his best during a campaign address in a little South Texas town. His speech was received with wild enthusiasm. When he had finished, an excited young woman rushed up and asked permission to kiss the orator.

Bryan declined the salute, politely but firmly. When they were back in the hotel, the campaign manager took Bryan to task for his lack of gallantry. He also said that the Texans might be offended by Bryan's action.

"Well," said the silver-tongued orator, with a glance at his wife, who was a very pretty woman, "I shall be in Texas only a few days, but I shall be with Mrs. Bryan all my life."

★

Wearied after a long day of campaigning for re-election, a congressman stopped by a small drugstore to quench his thirst. He seated himself next to an elderly lady who was sipping a soft drink. Nothing was said until the congressman had finished his drink. He then placed a dollar on the counter and said to the clerk: "I'll pay for this lady's drink also."

The lady turned and looked at the congressman and asked: "Why do you want to pay for my drink?"

"Oh," said the congressman, with his best political smile, "you know, it's election time and I'd like to get your vote for Congress."

"You bet I'll vote for you," said the lady, "that damn fool who is in there now is no damn good."

The humbled congressman left without waiting for his change.

★

Calvin Coolidge's campaign train rolled into a small Midwestern town. Cal walked out onto the platform and noted that the crowd was very small. Silent Cal studied the people for a few minutes then returned to his private car.

When a reporter asked him to explain his action, Coolidge responded: "That crowd out there is too big for an an anecdote and too small for an oration."

★

When Robert Kennedy descended on New York to run for the United States Senate, he was accused of being a "carpetbagger." Kennedy took it all in good humor and won lots of votes one night at a dinner when he said: "I can't tell you how happy I am to be here in the great state of . . . ah . . . ah . . ."

★

Senator Everett Dirksen used to tell the one about a candidate for county coroner and a neighbor who was asked about the office-seeker's honesty. "Well," said the neighbor, "I'm not one to throw the first stone, so I wouldn't exactly call him a liar. But I heard when he wants his hogs to come for feed, he has someone else call 'em."

★

When Ted Kennedy was invited to appear on "Meet the Press" during his campaign for the United States Senate, his brother, President John F. Kennedy, warned him not to appear on the television show. Ted went on anyway and after the show Lawrence Spivak received a telephone call from the President who asked for his opinion of Ted's performance.

Spivak remarked that Ted's answer to a question about federal aid to Catholic parochial schools was vague and fuzzy.

"Yes," said JFK, "he was very good on that one."

★

"The Republican Party," said Al Smith to a New York audience, "is like the man riding backwards in a streetcar. They never see anything until they have passed it."

Sly comments about both political parties abound in every political campaign. Once an observer had this to say about the Democrats: "Ten per cent visible, 90 per cent submerged, and 100 per cent at sea."

★

One of the candidates for sheriff in a small South Carolina town was notorious for his dishonesty. When a certain lady said she was going to vote for him, a fellow citizen asked why, pointing out that the candidate's opponent was a man of unquestioned integrity.

"Well," said the lady voter, "I look at it this way—if a man ain't ruint when he goes into office, he's ruint when he comes out. And there ain't no use in ruinin' a good man!"

★

The deeper he got into the 1964 election campaign, the more Barry Goldwater found himself in trouble. Some of his statements made Republicans wince. As the campaign progressed it became apparent that Barry would be lucky to get his own vote. The polls indicated that Lyndon Johnson was heading for a landslide.

With the handwriting on the wall for Goldwater, a staunch Republican commented wryly: "What the hell, Barry knows he ain't going to be President and so he might as well be right."

★

Gimmicks are always part of election campaigns. When Colleen O'Connor ran for the House in California, she took a swim in San Diego Bay, declaring: "If I can handle the sharks in the Pacific, I can handle those jellyfish in Washington."

★

Lyndon B. Johnson was the greatest handshaker who ever held the highest office in the land. Countless stories have been told of LBJ's hand-shaking tactics, including one which had him arriving in a small Southern town during the race against Barry Goldwater.

When Johnson finished speaking in the town square, he waded into the crowd, reaching for hands in every direction and enjoying it. "And you know something," said a newsman, "the son-of-a-gun shook hands with everybody in sight, including the Confederate soldier on the town monument."

On another occasion, Johnson was reported to have moved into an airport crowd, pressing flesh as fast as he could reach it. "And, as I watched," swore a reporter, "he reached in and took a man's hand out of his topcoat pocket, pumped it a couple of times, and then put it gently back in the guy's pocket. Now that's campaigning."

★

When Governor Jim Nance McCord was running for re-election in Tennessee in the late 1940s, he found himself addressing a large crowd of mountain folk at Roan Mountain in the high Great Smokies. At that time there were no interstate highways, which meant that, to get to the place where the rally was held, the governor's car had to pick its way along a rutty, battered, almost nonexistent road which severely tested both the car and the governor's sacroiliac.

Warming up to his audience, Governor McCord told them that the next time he returned to Roan Mountain he would ride up the mountain on a brand-new four-lane highway. The natives applauded loudly and stood in line to shake the governor's hand.

On the way back down the narrow road, the governor's aide reminded him of the poor condition of the state highway budget and asked him if he could afford to promise the people a new highway.

"I'm sure you misunderstood me," the governor said. "I didn't promise them any such thing. All I said was that if I ever come back up this G—— d—— mountain, it'll *BE* on a four-lane highway."

★

It was the day after the election and a voter met the defeated candidate in an optometrist's office. "What are you doing here?" asked the citizen.

"I'm having my eyes tested," responded the loser.

"Is there something wrong with your eyesight?" queried the voter.

"There must be," sighed the candidate, "the handwriting was on the wall and I guess I didn't see it."

★

In his quest for the presidency, Barry Goldwater advised his workers to go out and get the vote. "We can win this election," said Goldwater, "and we can fulfill our campaign pledge to elect Goldwater, if we can just find more of those districts such as the one the New Frontier found in Cook County, Illinois—the one that had twenty residents and came up with seventy-five votes."

★

In the political long-ago, it was a ritual for candidates to talk about their poverty-stricken backgrounds. This always appealed to the masses and was a great vote producer. However, Al Smith of New York could not work the born-in-a-log-cabin routine, so he came up with something even better.

"In the part of Manhattan where I was born," Smith told the electorate, "BOTH sides of the tracks were the wrong side."

★

A bitter congressional campaign found the two candidates firing charges left and right and making promises as fast as they could think them up.

"They sure are dueling each other," observed a citizen to a local reporter.

"Dueling is right," responded the reporter, "only in this duel they should be using manure scoops at thirty paces."

★

Independents very seldom are elected to the Massachusetts legislature. Whenever one does make it to the House or Senate, he generally is like a fish out of water in a strong party state, and most of the time doesn't know which way to turn.

When the Dukakis-Sargent gubernatorial contest was raging

and seemingly close, a reporter asked an independent House member if he was supporting Dukakis or Sargent in the November election.

"I am," was the quick response.

★

When George Romney first tried for the governorship of Michigan, he charged like a white knight from precinct to precinct, getting the message across no matter what the issue. "Hell," said a Democratic county chairman, "this guy Romney stands four-square on every side of every issue and that's a hard platform to beat."

★

Said a candidate for county office in West Texas: "I ain't a-runnin' on my opponent's demerits—I'm a-runnin' on my own demerits."

He was elected, too.

★

Prior to his nomination as the Democratic presidential standard-bearer in 1924, John W. Davis presided over a meeting during which he cast aside the rules to present a motion he wanted to have passed. He jammed it through, declaring that there were no contrary votes.

Questioned on the tactic, Davis said simply: "Back in the mountain region from which I come there is a citizen who is a man of some parts in his community. When he was in charge of a meeting it ordinarily ran as he wanted it.

"At one such meeting, he put the question as follows: 'All in favor, say aye. The ayes have it. Motion carried!'

"Someone said to him, 'Sam, you didn't put the noes, did you?'

" 'No,' " said Sam, " 'I did that once and it taught me a lesson.' "

★

A certain Midwestern hopeful had run for office in six straight campaigns without success. Finally, the voters elected the man to Congress.

The newly elected congressman was beside himself with joy over his narrow victory and moved about the election head-quarters shaking hands with gusto. At last, he mounted a chair and delivered a rousing victory speech.

Standing in the crowd, a worker turned to a companion and remarked: "Boy, that was a great victory speech."

"It should be," was the smiling response, "for after all, Chet has been practicing it for twelve years."

5

The Grass Roots

No matter what office a person might seek—particularly at the lower levels—he or she feels that to come out ahead, they must take their campaigns to the grass roots, where one meets the voter face to face. The adrenalin many candidates need to drive them on comes from moving among the people, communicating voice to voice, eye to eye, and hand to hand. While it is hard work, many office-seekers feel justly rewarded after a day of "pressing the flesh."

Unable to finance glossy election productions, blitz media campaigns, and big mailings, many candidates grind it out on the sidewalks, kissing babies, hugging mothers, and bending their ears to the day-to-day gripes of the citizens.

Abraham Lincoln once advised a fellow office-seeker thus: "Billy, don't aim too high—aim lower, and the common people will understand you. They are the ones you want to reach—at least, they are the ones you ought to reach.

"And," continued Old Abe, "the educated and the refined people will understand anyway. If you aim too high, your ideas will go over the heads of the masses and only hit those who need no hitting."

Former House Speaker John McCormack once offered some sage advice to a young aspirant. Said McCormack: "Stay down there with the people. It's all right to get your head in the clouds, but remember to keep your feet on the ground, right where the grass is lush and green."

Author Ed Lowry once wrote his observations of the Washington scene and the men who were there: "Politicians," said Lowry in his book *Washington Close-Ups*, "are great men in Washington and get their names in the newspapers, and hold their jobs just so long as they remember their home towns. When they forget their origins, when they begin to think of themselves as 'big men,' in and of themselves, rather than as delegated spokesmen for their constituents, they wither and die.

"I often think of Washington as being like a flower show. Nothing grows here, but every community sends what it deems at the moment to be its choicest product. So long as these budding, flowering plants remember that their tap-root is in Augusta, Maine, or Terre Haute, Indiana, or Red Oak, Iowa, and must be watered and nourished there, they thrive: but when they forget it, they become just cut flowers and their end is at hand."

Few men in politics appreciated the "grass roots" more than John Nance Garner, who rose from House member and Speaker to the vice-presidency. Old John knew the hollowness of Washington and what it did to people. His observation could well be the motto for any Washington-addicted public servant. Said Garner: "Some people would stay in Washington if they had to live in trees. I always took the last train that would get me there for whatever business there was, and I took the first train out when it was finished."

The voters like to see and hear their elected officials. Moving around among the people is the hardest work a politician encounters. He must be on guard against hostility, pushy people, hecklers, buttonholers, complainers, favor-seekers, job hunters, bone-cracking handshakers, pyschotics, enemy partisans, and whatnot. The experienced politician learns to read eyes very quickly and almost instinctively can tell if a voter approaching him wants a favor, is going to give him a hard time, or is just going to say "Hello."

The advent of television has cut down on personal appearances of the so-called "big-time" politicians. The big boys get much of their public contact via the tube, knowing that they can reach vastly more people than is possible through the grueling method of beating the bushes. John F. Kennedy introduced the sophisticated use of television on a wide scale during the 1960 campaign, placing particular emphasis on personality and image, and it saw him through.

Kennedy once said: "This business of going to plant gates at five o'clock in the morning is the bunk. I can expose myself to twice as many people in other places. But it gives me the appearance of activity, of being up at five o'clock, hustling for votes."

Sliding down the political scale, the so-called "little" politician still has to slug it out door-to-door, house-to-house, and town-to-town. This little fellow knows that the grass roots for him are where the glory begins and ends. The people have amazing instincts, and when they feel a man is getting his feet too far off the ground, they shoot him down.

What can happen to a man campaigning at the grass roots level was never expressed better than by Harry T. Hartwell of Alabama, a candidate for Congress many years ago. In filing his statement with the Secretary of State, Hartwell noted that the expenditure of money was the least of his election problems. This is what he filed:

"I lost 6 months and 10 days campaigning, lost 1000 hours of sleep worrying over the results of the election, lost 20 pounds of flesh, kissed 500 babies, kindled 100 kitchen fires, put up 10 stoves, cut 11 cords of wood, carried 50 buckets of water, pulled 400 bundles of fodder, walked 1100 miles, shook 27,000 hands and talked enough to fill one month's issue of the New York *Daily World*. I was baptised on 5 different occasions, made love to 9 grass widows, got dog-bit 8 times—and then, damn it, I got defeated."

★

According to former Governor Robert Bradford of Massachusetts: "To survive in the toughest game known to man, a politician needs the hide of a rhinoceros, the memory of an elephant, the energy of a draft horse, the persistence of a beaver, the friendliness of a mongrel pup, the tenaciousness of a bulldog, the health of a sea turtle, the stomach of an ostrich, the heart and courage of a lion, the speed of an antelope, the kindness of a St. Bernard dog, the nervous system of a mountain goat, and the humor of a crow.

"And," said Bob, "all of these things combined are not enough, unless, when it comes to matters of principle, a man also has the ornery stubbornness of an old army mule."

★

When the Illinois Republicans named Lincoln as their choice for the presidency, an old Democrat approached Mr. Lincoln and said: "So you're Abe Lincoln."

"Yes, that's my name."

"They say you're a self-made man?"

"Well, yes; what there is of me is self-made."

"Well, all I've got to say," observed the Democrat, after a careful survey of the lanky Lincoln, "is that it was a damned bad job."

★

Governor John A. Volpe, later Ambassador to Italy, was one of the best handshake campaigners in Massachusetts history. His staff boasted that Volpe could shake hands like an automatic machine.

A confident and relentless campaigner with class, style, and a great statewide image, Volpe always figured that everybody knew him, until one day he approached a local merchant in a small town.

Moving in on the merchant with a broad smile and a big handshake, Volpe said: "Haven't I met you someplace before?"

"You could have," said the unimpressed merchant. "I meet a lot of people and damned if I can remember them all."

★

Traveling across the State of Illinois one day, Abraham Lincoln was asked by the driver of the stage to "treat" him. Lincoln replied that he never used liquor and would not induce others to use it.

"Don't chew either, I suppose," said the driver.

"No, sir," said Lincoln. "I never use tobacco in any form."

"Well," remarked the disgusted driver, "I hain't got much opinion of those fellows with no small vices; they usually make it up on the big ones."

Old Abe smiled and said no more.

★

During a question-and-answer period following his speech, a veteran Midwestern congressman said to his audience: "More people should go into politics and government." From back in the hall a shrill voice screeched: "Not me. There are too many crooks in politics."

He was shot down immediately by the sharp congressman, who said: "There's always room for one more."

★

The candidate had poured it on for about an hour, despite the fact that the seats were hard and the hour was late. Finally he drove home his last statistic and confidently asked: "Now, are there any questions?"

"Yes," came a voice from the rear. "Who else is running?"

★

When Senator Jonathan P. Dolliver of Iowa returned from a campaign speech, he was asked by his secretary: "How did it go, Senator? Did you kill them?"

"No," said Dolliver wearily, "I didn't have to. They were dead when I got there."

★

Senator Carter Glass was a rough man in debate, but like all politicians he was rebuffed more than once. Glass admitted that the worst setback he had ever received was not on the floor of the Senate, but at a farmer's meeting in a little village in his home state.

"I was addressing the gathering on a live issue that had an important bearing on local agricultural interests," said Glass. "In the midst of my speech a man arose and said:

"'I'd like ter ask yer a question about that.'

"I was in the midst of an important point and did not want to be interrupted, so I said: 'If you will kindly wait until the close of my talk, I will do my best to answer you.'

"The man persisted in forcing his question, which brought another man to his feet shouting: 'Sit down, you ass!'

"An altercation of a wholly personal and uncomplimentary character followed between the two men, when a third man got up and said: 'Sit down. The two of yer; both of yer are asses.'

"And, here," said Glass, "is where I blew it. I turned to the three of them and said, "There seems to be an unusual number of asses here tonight, but for heaven's sake let's hear one at a time.'

"Whereupon the first gentleman, pointing a long finger at me, replied, 'Well, you go ahead, then.'"

★

It is well known that Calvin Coolidge was extremely shy and retiring. Neighbors who lived on the same street in Northampton, Massachusetts, for twenty years knew him only "by sight." One of them, exasperated, finally approached the great man and said: "I didn't vote for you."

"Somebody did," was the prompt reply.

★

In the old days of big-city politics, Irish and anti-Irish speakers were prominent in every election. During one New York rally, a street-corner orator roared at the crowd: "Show me an Irishman and I'll show you a coward."

There was a brief lull, and then suddenly from the side of the crowd, a huge, ham-fisted Irishman shouted: "What did you say?"

The orator repeated his statement but seemed considerably subdued. "Well," shouted the big man as he approached the bandstand, "I'm an Irishman."

"And I'm a coward," said the deflated orator with a thin laugh.

In the rough days of Southern politics, a congressional aspirant ascended the platform and prepared to launch his address. Just at that moment, a ripe tomato smacked him squarely in the face.

Angrily, the candidate wiped away the debris, and then bellowed: "My fellow citizens, for the next thirty minutes, I'm goin' to deliver a pow'ful discourse on the evils of war, and ef you'll stick around after that, you ah goin' to see the damndest fight you evah witnessed."

★

At a hot Chicago rally, William Jennings Bryan was holding forth in his best oratorical style. "While we are meeting here," he said, "Mrs. Bryan is sleeping in a humble boardinghouse down by the stockyards. But that's all right, come next March she'll be sleeping in the White House."

That was too much for a heckler in the crowd, who promptly piped, "If she's in the White House in March, she'll be sleeping with McKinley."

★

John Sherman Cooper was campaigning for the office of United States senator. He went into a fiercely Democratic area of Kentucky, where Republicans had previously feared to tread. As usual, the affable Cooper shook every hand in sight. One old man seemed reluctant.

"I'm John Cooper," the senator said.

"You're a Republican, ain't you?" the man countered guardedly.

"Yes."

"Well," drawled the man, extending his limp paw, "just press it light."

★

The candidate closed out an hour-long oration with, "And now, are there any questions from the audience?"

"Yes," came a thick voice from the rear. "What is the difference between a liberal and a conservative?"

The candidate paused and then answered: "If you will ask me that question when you are sober, I will be happy to tell you."

"Look, mister," the drunk responded, "when I'm sober, I don't give a damn."

"Ten years ago," shouted the bald headed candidate for Congress, "my head was grazed by a bullet at Chickamauga."

"Not much grazing there now," was the retort from someone in the crowd.

Senator Ted Kennedy tells the story of his visit to a factory in central Massachusetts during his re-election campaign. One of the blue collar workers came up to him and said: "Senator, I understand you've never worked a day in your life. Let me tell you, Senator, you haven't missed a thing."

A Tammany Hall bomb thrower demanded of his audience: ". . . and I ask you people. Who built all the bridges?" "The New Deal," cried the hired shouters.

Then the orator went on: ". . . and who built all the new public buildings?" "The Democrats," came the chorus. Then the speaker went up another notch: ". . . and," he roared, "what about the parks, the lakes, the grassy slopes? Who gave us those?"

Before the hirelings could reply, a shrill voice came whistling across the hall and the cry was: "God did."

The hall went quiet for only a moment. Then a quick-witted Irishman saved the night when he shouted: ". . . that's a lot of cheap Republican propaganda."

One of the most humorous stories out of old-time Texas politics involved a Jewish merchant. An announcement was made that a certain noted politician, whom we shall call Joe Zilch, was coming to town. The reception committee had decided to close down the town for the occasion.

While the chairman was introducing the famous politician, who had rather a spotted record, one of the committeemen noticed that the tiny shop run by the Jewish merchant was open. He dropped off the platform, hurried over, and said:

"Sam, why aren't you closed?"

"For vy should I close?" was the response.

"Joe Zilch is in town."

"Vell," shrugged Sam, "he von't hold me up in broad daylight, vill he?"

★

Peter Doherty, an old-time, hard-nose Boston Democratic politician, was in the midst of a hell-raising speech in Faneuil Hall, when a heckler interrupted him with a question. Doherty replied and then proceeded to mount another oratorical assault. Again he was interrupted by the same man. This went on each time Doherty tried to restart his speech, and it was becoming embarrassing.

Finally, after he had practically demolished Doherty's address, the man shouted: "I've had enough of your blarney. I'm getting out of here and going home."

Red-faced, Doherty watched the man as he started up the aisle for the door. Then in a booming voice Doherty roared: "And when you get home, buster, don't forget to throw your mother a bone."

★

A candidate for re-election to the Missouri legislature was intercepted by a voter who said he would no longer support him.

"You spent too much money," he noted, "like building that palace for the Highway Patrol Headquarters."

"We must have a good patrol," the legislator protested. "Look at all the good they do. Think of the accidents the patrol has prevented!"

The complaining voter quickly moved in, raised his eyes, and ordered: "All right, name one."

The prohibition battles between the wets and the drys brought out the best in the orators of the period. A Midwestern town was the scene one day of a speech by a famous "dry" orator who spoke eloquently on the evils of drink.

As the orator was reaching his highest plateau, a grizzled old man interrupted. "All this talk about prohibition is the bunk," declared the old man. "It was whiskey that saved my life once."

"Snakebite?" inquired the orator.

"Snakebite, nuthin'," exclaimed the native. "I was diggin' a well and came up for a drink, and while I was gettin' it, the well caved in."

★

A candidate wound up his speech with a real patriotic flourish, declaring: ". . . and we should all be proud to be paying taxes in the United States of America."

A squeaky voice from the rear announced: "We could be just as proud for half the money."

★

A heckler chided a well-known politician during a midday rally. The officeholder thought he would cut him down by saying: "My car is just outside the hall. Would you like to breathe the exhaust fumes for a few minutes?"

The heckler shot back: "Where's the car parked? Anything is better than your speech."

★

Political speeches in Texas are not known for understatement. One Texas orator climaxed his speech with the following bit of grandiloquence. "No planet in the universe has contributed as many notable figures to history as Texas," he shouted. "Ma Ferguson, Sam Houston, Abraham Lincoln, George Washington, Charlemagne, the twelve Apostles . . ."

Here he was interrupted by a voice from the edge of the crowd. "Excuse me, pardner," a big Texan drawled, "but only nine of them twelve Apostles was from Texas."

Campaigning for House seats in Boston's Irish wards was hard and brutal work. Candidates left no stones unturned to grab a few votes. An old-time election story in South Boston involved a candidate who went to mass every Sunday at a different Catholic church in the district.

This particular Sunday after mass, the candidate sought out the pastor and gave him twenty-five dollars, along with the words: "Father, I hope you won't forget to say a few prayers for my election victory next Tuesday?"

"Thank you," replied the priest as he pocketed the donation, "but I think you ought to know that your opponent gave me fifty dollars for the same prayers at the early mass."

★

With arms flailing to get across his point, the puffy politician shouted: "Let me tell you, ladies and gentlemen, it is the working man who has made this country what it is today."

From the middle of the hall came this shrill rejoinder: "That's the trouble with you politicians. You blame everything on the poor people."

★

Al Smith was telling a rapt audience about some of his adventures and misadventures as a public servant. From the back of the hall a thick voice called out: "Well, Al, I guess experience teaches fools."

"I'm aware of that, my friend," returned Smith at once. "That's why I want you to profit from my experience."

★

During a big rally in Massachusetts many years ago, James Michael Curley, running for re-election as mayor of Boston, was under verbal fire from a crowd of back-row hecklers.

Finally, one individual made his voice heard above the others and offered a wild suggestion for better municipal services. Curley eyed the man for a moment and then won the night when he said: "I'm glad to see you using your head, mister. It's the little things that count."

When a losing candidate was asked what happened, he explained: "Well, the people just wouldn't re-elect me because of my youth."

"But you are over fifty years of age, and your youth has been spent," said the puzzled voter.

"That's the trouble," said the candidate. "They found out how I spent it."

★

Nosing around for votes through the Maine potato country, a candidate observed a farmer near an apple tree. "This tree seems to be loaded with apples," he said. "And are all your trees as loaded with apples as this one?"

"Nope," said the farmer, "only the apple trees."

★

The speaker for a candidate for Congress in Arkansas spoke in glowing terms about his man's ability. ". . . and I'm telling you voters," he concluded, "that Sam Brown is a politician worth watching."

From back in the hall came the inevitable: "Yes, night and day."

★

An opponent of Iowa's Senator Bourke Hickenlooper was having a hard time getting across to an old farmer. To every argument the farmer replied: "I don't care what you say, Hickenlooper is a God-fearing man and I'm going to vote for him."

Exasperated, the challenger asked the reason for the farmer's belief and was told that Hickenlooper's airplane had gone down in the ocean and for thirty days Hickenlooper had prayed and prayed and finally was rescued. "That proves he's a God-fearing man," said the farmer.

"But," was the challenger's argument, "it wasn't Bourke Hickenlooper that was lost at sea and prayed and was rescued. It was Eddie Rickenbacker."

The farmer replied stubbornly: "Hickenbacker, Rickenlooper,

what difference does it make how you pronounce his name? He's a God-fearing man and I'm going to vote for him!"

★

Words flowed from Senator Tom Connally of Texas like honey from a jar. He had few peers when it came to speaking of the glories of Texas.

Once at a political rally, Connally started his speech with the rolling waves of the Gulf of Mexico, and waxed eloquently for fifteen minutes on the subject. He then swept across the bluebonnet plains, climbed the mountains, swung around the hills, and dipped into the Gulf again.

Catching his second wind, Old Tom started to move into the second hour of his speech and another oratorical tour of the state, when a little man in the rear of the hall stood up and shouted: "Hey, Tom, the next time you get to Lubbock, how about leaving me off?"

★

In an upstate New York community, a political speaker ended his oration with this bit of advice to the voters: ". . . and now, don't forget to vote for Taylor and good government."

From somewhere in the middle of the crowd came the crusher: "How the hell can you vote twice?"

★

A Republican candidate for Congress in a tough Democratic district hired a consultant to help with the campaign. "As I see it," said the consultant, "the registration odds are so great that if you expect to get anywhere you've got to start out by dropping four words from your vocabulary: breakfast, lunch, dinner, and sleep."

★

Some years ago, a candidate for local selectman told his constituents that if elected, he would make sure they had any kind of weather they liked best.

It was a great inducement to the farm vote and they could not resist voting for him. He won in a landslide.

Soon after the election one of his constituents visited the selectman and requested some rain. "Well, my good friend," said the selectman, "and what do you want with rain? Won't it spoil your hay?" The response was: "Why, it will be very serviceable to the wheat, and as for my hay, I just got it in."

"But," persisted the selectman, "has your neighbor got his hay in yet? I should suppose rain would do him some mischief." Scratching his head, the farmer agreed. "Gee, I guess the rain would do him some harm at that."

"So you see," said the cagey politician, "I have promised to get any kind of weather you like; but if I give you rain, I must disoblige your neighbor; so your best way will be, I think, to meet together, all of you, and agree on the weather that will be best for you all—and you may depend upon your having it."

MORAL: There's a way around every campaign promise.

★

One of the funniest stories about Kentucky campaigns concerns a big rally held by the Republicans in one of the small mid-state towns. Brass bands, all kinds of floats, and hundreds of men, women, and children paraded down the streets. A young girl claimed that while on her vine-covered front porch she was repeatedly hugged and kissed by a young man she hardly knew.

A warrant was issued for the arrest of her assailant. He was apprehended and brought before the court for prosecution. A man named John D. Carroll was employed by the Republicans to defend the young man. When the prosecutor had finished his examination of the girl, she was turned over to Carroll for cross-examination.

"What night did this happen?" thundered Carroll.

"Thursday night," answered the witness.

"Thursday night, you say? What time of night?"

"About eight o'clock."

"That was about the time the Republican parade was passing your house?"

"Yes."

"Did you cry out or scream?"

"No, sir, I did not."

"Will you tell this jury," asked Carroll with rising voice, "with the streets thronged with people, and this man hugging and kissing you against your will, as you claim, why you never uttered a single cry for help or assistance?"

"Yes, sir. I will tell the jury, and everybody else, that you'll never ketch me hollerin' and screamin' at no Republican gatherin'!"

★

A Midwestern congressman took his family to a big rally in one of the counties. At the conclusion of his speech, he asked the audience if they had any questions. Then for about a half hour he proceeded to rattle off answers. Finally he noticed his eleven-year-old daughter with her hand raised and snapping her fingers with enthusiasm. The congressman ignored his daughter's repeated attempts to gain his attention until he had run out of adults with questions.

Then he turned to his daughter and said: "All right, one final question from the little girl in the back wearing the white dress."

Right here the little girl broke up the crowd by asking: "Daddy, when are we going home?"

★

One of the good jokes out of New Mexico concerned the Indian who went to a political rally. When it was over, he was asked how he liked the speaker. The Indian responded with a shrug of his shoulder: "High wind, big thunder, no rain."

★

A candidate for Congress trudged into the back hills of Virginia in an attempt to dig up some votes for re-election. He arrived at a country store and proceeded to ask the storekeeper: "How are things up here for me?"

"There just ain't no interest around here," replied the storekeeper.

The candidate continued to press, hoping for a favorable expression. Finally, in exasperation, the storekeeper said: "I said there ain't no interest up here, and ain't none of them comin' out to vote, and you should be happy 'cause the more of them that stay home the better off you'll be!"

★

A staunch old Republican invariably managed to show up at all the Democratic rallies. A friend suggested that perhaps he was thinking of switching sides. The diehard snorted indignantly. "Change parties? Never," he snapped. "I just go to the Democratic meetings to keep my disgust fresh."

★

The mother of six sons had raised them to be straight-ticket Chicago Democrats, so, when one of the lads announced that he might vote Republican, his mother became very upset.

"Mom," the son said, "if the Good Lord himself was running on the Republican ticket, I don't think you'd vote for him."

"Of course I wouldn't," she replied quickly. "He'd have no business to change now."

★

Like everything else, politics must continually develop new techniques. A Midwestern congressional candidate came up with a new procedure: "As I tour my district," he said, "I shake hands with the baby and kiss the mother. If I lose, at least I'll have some happy memories."

★

Senator Pat Harrison of Mississippi had a favorite story about an invitation that had been extended to William Jennings Bryan to speak at Tupelo, Mississippi. Bryan demanded seven hundred dollars for the engagement, and also stated that he could not stay around town long after the speech, for he had to catch a train for Washington.

The local committee thought seven hundred dollars was a great deal of money but nevertheless went ahead with the arrangements. They invited a well-known powder keg orator to introduce Bryan. The old orator practiced for a week on his introduction, adding new phrases every time he practiced.

When finally the day of Bryan's appearance arrived, there was a great crowd at the town square. The old orator went into his spiel. For ten minutes he spoke about the greatness of Mississippi, then he moved to other matters for fifteen minutes more. By this time, Bryan was mentally reducing his speech, knowing that he had to catch a train. Still the introduction went on. The orator dwelled on the greatness of Tupelo for another fifteen minutes. Bryan again mentally cut down his speech. At the end of about an hour, the orator wrapped up his introduction of Bryan and received a tremendous hand.

Bryan was left with about ten minutes of speaking time before he had to leave. He did the best he could under the circumstances, jumped down from the platform, and headed for the train station.

As Harrison told the story, the arrangements committee thought there would be resentment among the crowd that seven hundred dollars had been spent for a ten-minute speech. A committee member asked one of the crowd how he liked Bryan's speech. His answer was simply this: "The greatest speech I ever heard, and that old bald headed guy who spoke last wasn't so bad either."

★

A reporter once asked Senator Chauncey Depew if he objected to hecklers. "Not under certain circumstances," said the senator. "They are a great help if you meet them beforehand and have them rehearsed."

★

A man approached a politician and angrily shouted: "Remember me? You beat up my father, broke my mother's leg, accused me of drunkenness, ran my relatives out of town, ruined my business, burned down my house, seduced my wife, and all because I ran against you for Congress."

"Go away, man," said the winning candidate. "I hate sore losers."

★

The candidate was rolling into his second hour of oratory. The room was stifling hot and the people in the back rows were starting to fall asleep. Still the candidate roared on. Noting the dozing voters, the orator shouted: "I want you to know I'm speaking for the future citizens of South Carolina."

A man in the rear of the hall was aroused by the loud outburst. He shook his head and cried out: "Well, brother, if you speak much longer they'll be here."

★

The mayor of an upstate New York city was standing for reelection. The hall was crowded as he extolled the virtues of his administration. "Why," said the mayor, "look at the roads we have now, and the schools, the water system and the general improvements . . ."

Just as he reached the three-quarter mark in his speech, a voice wafted out from the rear of the room in challenge to the mayor's blasting: "I don't believe you have done all that much good," said the voice.

The mayor, obviously flustered, shouted back: "That's all right for you to talk, but let me ask you this: What have you ever done, mister, that's been good for the city?"

There followed a few seconds of deadly silence, then came the demolishing retort: "Only one good thing, Mr. Mayor. I voted against you every time you ran."

★

A candidate for Congress was raving away before a considerable crowd in a southern Illinois town hall. Halfway through his oration a voice rose from the back of the hall: "I can't hear you."

An old farmer stood up in the front row, turned, and said: "Mister, you can have my seat."

A stranger walked into a political rally in the town hall while a well-known local office-seeker was firing away. The stranger took a seat in the back row, listened for a while and then began to fidget. Leaning over to a man in front of him, he whispered:

"How long has this guy been speaking?"

"Ten or fifteen years, I think," the old man answered.

"I'll stay, then," decided the stranger. "He must be nearly through."

★

During a question-and-answer program, a candidate for re-election to the Senate said, "All I want is a chance to complete my program."

"And what is your program, Senator," asked a member of the audience.

"To stay in office another six years," was the candid response.

★

It was a bitter battle for a Louisiana House seat, and both candidates were reaching for the bottom of the barrel in order to gain votes. Finally, one candidate announced at a huge outdoor rally: "I hate to say this, but my opponent has a bad reputation. He not only steals money, but he drinks heavily and chases around after women."

"That's great," piped a voice from the rear of the crowd, "we won't have to break him in."

★

Almost to a man or woman, politicians worry about what the people back home will think. Rare is the congressman who "doesn't give a damn." Congressman Silvio Conte of Massachusetts summed it up several years ago when he observed that constituents are sensitive to almost everything that a man does in office. Conte put it this way:

"When I returned to my district office, there were long and loud complaints that I was spending too much time in the district and should be in Washington. Then when I didn't come home for several weeks others said: 'Who does that guy think he is? We only see him during elections.'

"When I came home shortly after being sworn in, driving my old car, they were upset because it looked like something farmers use to haul trash. But, by gosh, when I bought a new one they were sure the lobbyists had gotten to me already.

"The first time I came home wearing an old suit, I heard: 'Look at him. Just an old bum.' Yet, when I bought a new suit, I heard: 'He's gone high-hat with that Ivy League suit of his.'

"One Sunday I missed church because I was tied up with constituents, and some people said being down in Washington had made an atheist out of me. Several weeks later, when I was back home again and did get to church, they said, 'Why that pious fraud, he's just trying to dig up votes!'"

★

One day a congressional candidate from Brooklyn was getting it from a street-corner heckler who finally shouted: "You don't even know me."

"Oh yes, I do," said the candidate. "Your father was a bachelor."

★

One of the good little stories out of West Virginia had a native running for a minor office. However, on election day, he was unable to get to the polls because of illness. When the election results were announced, the candidate noted that he had received but one vote.

Annoyed by the accusation that he had voted for himself, the candidate announced that, if the person who had voted for him would come forward and make a sworn statement to that effect, he would reward him with a new suit of clothes.

A few mornings later, a rather stupid-looking townsman called upon the candidate and abruptly declared that he was the man who had voted for the candidate and was entitled to the suit of clothes. He also agreed to sign an affidavit.

Following the signing of the affidavit before the justice of the peace, the candidate stated that he was delighted to be relieved from the embarrassment of the situation. He stated for all to hear that he was pleased there was at least one righteous person in the community who believed in what the candidate stood for.

Just as the meeting broke up, the candidate said to the voter: "Now, my friend, you have your suit of clothes, just answer me one question—why did you vote for me?"

"You won't take back the suit, will you?" pleaded the townsman.

"Certainly not."

"Well, I'll tell you," was the meek reply. "I made a mistake and marked the ballot wrong."

*

A House incumbent, speaking before a rally in his hot, arid West Texas district, said: "What we need down here is more good people and more water!"

A voice from the audience shot back: "That's all they need down in hell!"

*

Clever as he was at handling a hostile crowd, Congressman Johnny Allen was often sacked by someone in the audience. Once as Johnny was speaking, a farmer in the front row got up and started to leave. "Hey, you," Allen shouted after the farmer, "I've got lots more to say on the subject."

"I know," said the farmer, with a shrug of disgust, "that's why I'm leaving."

*

Thomas E. Dewey was in full swing on the presidential campaign trail. In a Southwest town, he commenced his speech by expounding on a favorite theme of the Republican campaign: "The Democrats have been in power too long."

"We must remember," warned Dewey, "that our party system has two wings."

Instantly a voice rang out, sharp and clear: "And one ain't got no feathers on it."

The orator was thundering on in town hall while a heavy rainstorm was raging outside. Safe in the conviction that he had held his audience enthralled for the past hour, he wound up his speech with: "And so, my friends, I feel that I have bored you with these trivial matters far too long."

And the customary voice from the rear piped: "Oh, you might as well go on, Senator, it's still raining like hell outside."

★

Campaigning in Bristol, Tennessee, during the 1960 presidential race, John Kennedy floored the locals with the following story. He reminded the audience that the last presidential candidate to campaign in Bristol was Herbert Hoover in 1928. "It was here," said JFK with a smile, "that Hoover initiated the slogan 'Two chickens in every pot,' and it is no accident that no presidential candidate has ever dared to come back to this community since."

★

Congressman Thomas B. Reed was addressing a meeting in Biddeford, Maine, one night, when a large group of Democrats moved noisily into the hall. Reed knew they would start some trouble, so he beat them to the punch by saying: "If a photographic snapshot could be taken of the Democrats at any time or any place, it would reveal them in the art of doing some mean, low-lived, and contemptible thing."

Immediately the Democrats in the audience started banging chairs, whistling, booing, and cackling, among other things.

Republican Reed rose to his full height and roared out over the audience, "There, I told you so."

★

Every political candidate has his own style as he presents his case to the voters. Some aspirants stand stiff as a board. Some barely move their arms. Still others pound the table with a vengeance, or pump their arms up and down as they try to make points.

One such candidate was blowing full blast about the evils of the country and what he would do about them if elected. At the end of every sentence his arm would go over his head and come down to his waist in a pumping motion.

The candidate had made this gesture no less than fifty times when a voice from the audience cried out: "Hey, mister, when you're through pumping, let go of the handle."

★

Veteran Congressman Emanuel Celler of New York stopped a heckler cold one day on the campaign trail. When the heckler persistently challenged Celler, the congressman buried him with: "If I were an undertaker or a hangman, there's no one I'd rather see than you."

★

Representative Bill Hungate of Missouri loved to tell a little story about meeting people on the campaign trail. "When you are campaigning in a large rural area, meeting voters, it is easy the first time around. You simply state your name, shake hands, and they state their name. The second time it's different. They know your name, but in most cases you cannot remember theirs.

"So," continued Hungate, "you develop a friendly ambiguous greeting like: 'It's good to shake hands with you again.'

"One night at a meeting of some seventy-five or more people, I spotted a man I had met before but whose name I could not remember. Confidently, I said: 'It's good to shake hands with you again.'

"The voter dourly replied: 'I guess so. That's the third time tonight.' "

★

When a politician is out among the grass-rooters, he never knows what will be coming at him. During a campaign visit to a country fair, a Maine congressman, was approached by two elderly brothers who appeared to be slightly deaf.

One of the brothers sidled up to the congressman and shouted: "I'm proud of you, Mr. Congressman."

The other brother cocked his head, adjusted his hearing aid, and floored the congressman with these words: "Yes, and I'm tired of you too, Sam."

★

All candidates find the going rough in a cross fire with a voter bent on having the last word. Once during a question-and-answer period at a town rally, a Massachusetts state senator reminded the group that the legislature had passed a bill granting free hunting and fishing licenses to persons of age seventy and over.

From out in the crowd came this gruff response: "Ya shoulda made it sixty-five years of age."

Just then the senator's aide leaned over and whispered in the senator's ear: "We did pass a law for sixty-five years and not seventy."

With a beaming smile, the senator said to the voter, "I'm sorry about that. I had forgotten that we reduced it to sixty-five this year for those hunting and fishing licenses."

Without batting an eye the voter growled back, "Ya shoulda made it sixty!"

★

Running against a rather eccentric opponent, a Midwest congressman became increasingly miffed at his antics. Finally, the congressman told an audience: "My opponent may talk like a fool and act like a fool. But do not be deceived, my friends. He really *is* a fool."

★

A candidate for re-election to Congress was pouring out the fire and brimstone at a town hall rally, when he was interrupted by a listener who yelled: "The only reason you're in politics is you're too lazy to get a decent job."

The congressman stopped his speech, eyed the heckler, and hissed: "Okay. What kind of a job has a smart guy like you got?"

"I'm a garbage collector," responded the heckler, "and it's a better job even than my father had."

The politician shook his head, and snickered. "Well, at least you're honest, admitting you have a better job than your father had. By the way what did your father do?"

"He was a cheap politician," was the verbal deathblow.

★

For decades on end it was known that Southerners were solid-as-granite Democrats, with no deviation. This was proved one day when a parishioner said to his minister: "Reverend, you are so partisan I believe you would vote for the devil himself if he were on the Democratic ticket."

The dyed-in-the-wool Democratic minister thought a moment and then responded: "Well, not in the primary I wouldn't."

★

Senator Dale Bumpers of Arkansas rose in less than five years from an unknown small-town lawyer to governor, then on to the United States Senate. Commenting on Bumper's meteoric rise, a newsman said: "And he did it with only one speech, a shoeshine, and a smile."

★

In a tough Chicago congressional district some years ago, an individual had been assigned the task of raising campaign money. One day the candidate met the fund-raiser in a drunken state. "For God's sake," cried the candidate, "why do you have to get so drunk?"

"Well—hic—hic, sir," mumbled the fund-raiser, "every place I go to ask for a contribution they bring out the booze."

"But," noted the candidate, grimacing, "surely all the people in the district aren't drinkers. There must be some abstainers who are good for a contribution."

"There are," responded the inebriate, "but I'm soliciting them by mail."

★

A congressional candidate in Alabama arrived at a country store one day and noticed a hound dog howling his head off.

"What's wrong with the dog?" the congressman asked the storekeeper.

" 'Tain't nothing," said the stoprekeeper, " 'cept he's sittin' on a cocklebur."

"Why doesn't he get off?" came the question.

"Well, he's a politician dog," responded the storekeeper. "He'd rather just holler than move."

★

In a certain Mississippi town many years ago a Republican vote kept cropping up election after election. Everybody figured it was cast by an old Union soldier who had been wounded and left behind during the War Between the States.

When the old-timer died, the town gave him a fine funeral. Everybody then breathed a sigh of relief that its one Republican vote —that great black mark against its Democratic honor—had been eliminated.

But that fall, when the votes in the presidential race were being counted, a sudden commotion arose.

"That Republican vote has showed up again!" one of the tabulators yelled. "G—— d—— it, we buried the wrong man!"

★

A crusty old Democrat told the chairman of a local Republican committee that he was thinking seriously of changing his party affiliation to Republican because the Democrats were making him sick.

A few weeks later the Republican chairman met the Democrat and inquired if he had in fact changed his registration.

"No, I didn't," the Democrat responded. "I'll agree the Democrats make me sick. But the more I thought about becoming a Republican, I got even sicker."

6

They Die but Do Not Resign

Every crop of fresh young congressmen, puffed by victory in their districts, sets out for Washington, ready to move everybody to the rear and take over the government, lock, stock, barrel, bills, and statutes. Upon arrival at the Capitol they generally find that they are small frogs in a big pond. Those with long service have all the good committee assignments, the best offices, the entrees around town, the attention of the national press, and about everything else worthwhile. The halls of Congress reek with the incense of tradition and no bushy-tailed upstart is going to fumigate the place, as far as wary veterans are concerned.

When a peppy new congressman realizes that the system is against him and that a little gray in the hair is necessary before he can wind up with any committee or other influence in Washington, he very often rebels.

The first thing he does is to clan up with other disgruntled freshmen. Together they attack the system, the rules, the seniority that prevails. They grumble that veteran committee chairmen and members are too old to know what's going on and that sev-

eral of them have to be pointed in the direction of their committee rooms.

The battle of the young for power has long been a staple of
life in Congress. Every batch of eager freshmen has assailed the
system that gives power to those with long service. Mostly, these
Sir Lancelots wind up with bloody ears and broken lances. They
then lick their wounds, accept the situation, blend into the system, and look forward to the day when they too will be called
"veterans." Among other things, to be called veterans would give
them the same opportunity to scoff at every new crop of congressional upstarts.

The Seventy-eighth Congress was no different from others before it. Freshmen were given short shrift by the system. As usual,
resentment set in and the ninety-six freshmen fired off salvos, verbal rockets, and plain ordinary steam, in an attempt to gain some
sympathy for their cause. It all fell on deaf ears as time-hardened
House members waddled along the corridors laughing and joking,
unmindful of the tempest around them and knowing full well it
would blow away.

During the height of the battle to crack the seniority system,
Representative Walter E. Brehm of Ohio put together some
plaintive verse, setting forth the plight of the freshmen as they
cracked their lances against the armor of the congressional chieftains. This is what Representative Brehm wrote:

> On behalf of 96 freshmen,
>   Who came here with hopes so high,
> But now find ourselves hanging,
>   Like clothes on a line to dry,
> I'd like to remind you old timers—
>   You may take it for what it is worth—
> There never can be growth without moisture,
>   Even though you have good earth.
>
>   * * *
>
> We have learned after sticking around,
>   The committees really handle the ropes,
> You old boys get pooped, go home for a rest,
>   And the people back home are the goats,

> While we with the excessive moisture,
>   Feeling and wanting to try,
> Are buried in arid committees,
>   Until we are thoroughly dried.

In Washington, becoming "thoroughly dried" always meant attaining the statics of "veteran." It was the number-one accolade on Capitol Hill. To be called a veteran meant that a man had arrived. He had authority through the seniority system. He was somebody to be looked up to. He demanded respect and got it.

Everett Burkhalter, a California congressman during the mid-1960s, saw how high the wall was during his first term in the House. Shortly after completing twelve months in Congress, Burkhalter announced his retirement. Sourly he observed: "I could see I wasn't going anyplace. Nobody listens to what you have to say until you've been here ten or twelve years."

Every young congressman over the years has gone back to his district telling mouth-opening stories about power and its use in Washington. If they look young enough they always come up with a story about being mistaken for a page and asked to run an errand by a longtime member. Whether or not it is true, the story is always good for a few home-town laughs.

The boyish congressman might have believed that the elder House member was mistaken in his identity, but often it was not so. The oldster was just getting the message across. A tough House tiger of long service freely admitted that he used this approach on young newcomers. "It kinda puts 'em in their places," he laughed impishly.

Whenever a freshman approached Texan John Nance Garner, during his years as a House member and Speaker, to ask for advice on how to get ahead in Congress, Cactus John had this to say: "Son, the only way to get anywhere in Congress is to stay here and let seniority take its course."

When the youngster would mention Garner's words to an older colleague, he would be squashed still further with this observation: "And furthermore, son, those words are in granite."

The full impact of seniority and the tendency of older members to guard it jealously and vehemently was made evident during

Senator William E. Borah's time in the upper branch. The cranky Idaho senator was a stickler for seniority, and woe to the one who tried to get around it.

Borah's hatred of youngsters who tried to be heard as well as seen surfaced one day when Borah's colleagues took the floor to compliment the longtime veteran on his birthday.

One after another his colleagues praised Borah for his accomplishments, and the Idaho senator's face glowed with appreciation. Suddenly, a new young senator rose and asked for recognition. He was a good speaker and his eloquence was impressive as he enlarged on Borah's service in politics.

No sooner had the youngster started to speak than a frown crossed Borah's brow. He slumped in his seat and all the time the freshman senator was talking and praising his record, Borah was muttering under his breath: "The son-of-a-bitch . . . the son-of-a-bitch . . . the son-of-a-bitch."

In Borah's mind, no matter how high the praise, the new member was breaking the unwritten rule of the Senate: "You ain't nobody until you've been here awhile."

The Ninety-fourth Congress, sworn into office in January, 1975, was loaded with fast-talking, gung-ho, crack-the-system members. The ninety-two freshmen insurgents—the largest and most independent crop in many years—appeared to present a formidable front against the venerable congressional establishment.

Crying reform, the fuzzy-beards served notice that they were not about to accept John Nance Garner's "go along" philosophy. The newcomers were mostly heady liberal mavericks, at least on the Democratic side. They boasted that they were beholden to themselves alone. During their campaigns many had virtually ignored their party label. "I just used that old 'D' for what I could get out of it," said a brash Democrat. "But I don't think like those old-line party loyalists. I have no commitment to the political structures, either back home or here in Washington. I am my own man and I am proud to be labeled a maverick."

Many of these new members rode into Washington high in the saddle and with both guns blazing. They had made lots of points with the electorate by promising to shoot up the place. The tyrants would be led to the guillotine. The entrenched congressional seniority system would be dismantled. The winds of change would ventilate the Capitol.

It all seemed like the old cry of the young for a piece of the action. However, in 1975, the threat to the seniority system became a reality. The seventy-five-member Democratic freshman class was determined to get along by not going along and was brilliantly molded into a battering ram that through the caucus procedure crashed down the gates of committee feudalism.

There was no way, according to freshman spokespersons, that they were going to be buried in arid committees or mistaken for pages. Despotic chairmen of standing committees were hauled before the caucus of seventy-five callow new Democrats to suffer the indignity of interrogation.

The solid cement of seniority cracked and broke under the pressure of liberal hotbloods, aided and abetted by other idealists of longer standing in the House. The pieces fell on the heads of three powerful House chairmen, who were unceremoniously dumped from their thrones of authority: Representative F. Edward Hebert of Louisiana, Representative Wright Patman of Texas, and Representative W. R. Poage, also of Texas. Representative Wilbur Mills of Arkansas, powerful chairman of the House Ways and Means Committee, probably would have been dethroned also, but this had been previously taken care of through Wilbur's indiscretions with Fanne Fox, a stripteaser.

When someone asked a Northern liberal maverick what he thought the three Southern House chairman would do now that they were out of their powerful posts, he commented: "It looks like all they can do is whistle 'Dixie.'"

Sitting in the House cafeteria, sipping his soup, a shaky chairman observed: "When these young guys start talking about reform, all they are saying is they want our jobs. They don't want to wait. Christ, some of them don't know yet where the front door is."

A reporter asked a longtime House member what he thought of the expulsion of the three chairmen and could he give a reason for it. "I don't think much of the knife job," said the member, "but the reason is very simple. They got caught growing old."

Not every new member was a bowl-'em-over representative. Despite the awesome attrack that dropped the three chairmen and made other changes, the system had not completely become unstuck. It still had weight and power, based on the seniority of older members, and the new congressmen knew it.

Martha Keys of Kansas, one of the bright fledglings, stated that she just wanted to be an effective member of Congress. The tip-off of her recognition of the system came when a newsman asked: "What specifically do you plan to do?" Mrs. Keys responded: "Oh, do my best, I guess."

Another freshman came up with this observation: "Well, we gave it a great try and we opened a few big cracks. At first, I thought we'd blow most of the old fogies out the door. It really didn't happen, but boy, did we make some inroads. Now, I hope some of the other chairmen aren't too mad at us. You see, I've got a couple of bills coming before a certain committee. I need them for my district. Do you think I should run a couple of errands for the chairman, or take him to lunch, or what?"

An inquiring columnist picked up a conversation with a newcomer and asked his views on the fight for power. Casting glances over his right and left shoulders, the youngster said uneasily:

"Look, mister, I'm not looking for trouble. I'm lucky to be here and if it wasn't for Watergate, I'd still be chasing ambulances trying to earn a living as a lawyer. I never thought I'd win, and the only reason I ran is because I figured they were going to throw out the ins and they did.

"I never made a hell of a lot of money as a lawyer and I don't intend to blow this job by shooting off or fighting the system. An old-timer told me only today that if I play my cards right, I will have found a home here in Congress. Frankly that sounds good to me and I'm going to try and go along."

★

Representative F. Edward Hebert of Louisiana pulled no punches when it came to evaluating members of Congress. "This is the most unstable Congress in our history," he said, "and irresponsibility is so widespread that if the Ten Commandments came before it, they would be amended."

Taking note of the new breed of young congressmen, some of

them insatiable publicity hounds, Hebert observed: "Their claim to fame is that they are the fastest people on Capitol Hill with press releases."

(NOTE: Many of this newer breed of congressmen remembered Hebert's remarks and helped to dump him from his prestigious position as chairman of the Armed Services Committee.)

★

A cagey politician gave some advice to a group of political science students who were interested in running for public office. "I'll tell you," he said. "If you want to get elected, learn how to speak. If you want to stay elected, learn to keep your mouth shut."

★

When a particularly difficult congressman opened up on a newer member of the House, a colleague warned: "Getting into a debate with him is like wrestling a skunk. The skunk doesn't care; he likes the smell."

★

Senator Charles Sumner of Massachusetts was haughty and dictatorial. The longer he served in Congress the less use he had for the new senators who were being elected. He was quick to cut them down whenever they approached him with a question.

One bright young senator moved in on Sumner and asked for some advice on a speech he hoped to deliver. "I've got to talk to a group of ladies," said the youngster. "What should I talk about?"

Sumner drew himself up to full height, looked down his nose at his colleague, and sneeringly responded: "Well, what do you know?"

★

The newly elected young congressman, who had been swept into office on a campaign condemning dishonesty in government, arrived in Washington and was sworn in. He carried his campaign right along with him and, much to the embarrassment of House colleagues, he started to intimate that honesty was a dead trait in

Washington. A veteran congressman figured that it was about time to straighten him out, so he went to the youngster's hotel room for a talk.

"Do you know, Henry," said the visitor, "that the underground railroad bill will be on the docket tomorrow? Are you going to vote for it?"

"Well," responded the youngster, "I haven't made up my mind. I am inclined to think it is a good bill, but why do you ask?"

"I thought you were in favor of it," said the cagey graybeard, "and inasmuch as you have decided to vote for it, I should tell you the backers of the bill are paying a thousand dollars for each vote. You're going to vote for the bill, so you might just as well take the money."

Taken aback, the new congressman jumped up and roared: "I'll be damned if I'll vote for the bill now. After what you told me, you can put me down as voting against the damn bill."

"Oh," said the veteran, "I don't care what you do. I'm only trying to do you a favor. To tell you the truth, the opponents of the bill are moving heaven and earth to defeat it. They are paying a thousand dollars also for votes against it, so you can pick up a thousand dollars either way."

"My God," screamed the perplexed freshman, "is there no justice? A plague on both their houses. I won't vote at all. Nobody's going to buy my vote. Mark me absent when the vote comes up."

"All right," said the visitor, with an inward smile. "I'll get you a thousand for staying away. They are paying the same amount to the congressmen who want to be marked absent."

With that, the elder congressman walked out, leaving the freshman with his worries. The whole act by the veteran was only a joke, but it completely cornered the youngster and set him up for a sleepless night. When the veteran told his colleagues the story, they could hardly wait for the next day to see how the freshman voted or marked himself absent. Whichever way he went he was going to get a knowing glance from other House members.

When the vote on the bill was called, the newcomer voted yes, but his face was red and he sneaked out of the chamber as soon as his named was called. From that point on there was little said about dishonesty in Congress.

★

When John F. Kennedy first went to Congress in 1947, he was under thirty years of age and as skinny as a rail. A story is told that the boyish-looking Kennedy approached a committee chairman and said: "I have a letter of introduction to you."

The chairman looked up at the young congressman, did not recognize him, and then responded: "I can do nothing for you, son, all the messenger positions are filled."

★

A sharp young former congressman was elected to the United States Senate. He sought out a veteran for some advice. "What do I need to do," the young man asked, "to become a good speaker in the Senate and gain the ear of my colleagues?"

"Practice, my son," was the response, "and if you live near a graveyard, practice upon the tombstones. You'll get as much attention there as you will here."

★

When a new covey of congressmen started to throw their weight around the House and fouled up several bills in the bargain, a white-haired chairman commented: "You can lead men to Congress, but you can't make them think."

★

Senator Tom Connally was a tough man in debate. Few senators were willing to take him on. When a bright young senator first took his seat, he approached the senior senator from his state and asked for some advice on tackling Old Tom. "How would you debate Connally?" he asked. Moving his glasses down on his nose better to squint at the upstart, the member said: "Reluctantly, son, reluctantly."

One of the best cracks of the year came from a young congressman's wife, who, when her husband asked her how the baby was making out, smiled and said: "Look, dear—he takes after you. He's got his foot in his mouth."

★

Representative Brooks Hays had just made his first speech on the House floor. "I worked long and hard on that maiden speech," he said, "and really put everything into it when I delivered it. The next day I eagerly opened the *Congressional Record* and there was my speech, word for word, just as I had given it. There was just one thing wrong. The *Record* had given the credit for the speech to Representative Oren Harris.

"I stormed down to the *Record* office and gave them a good talking to. When they apologized I felt ashamed and told them I was sorry for blowing my top."

"'Oh, that's all right, Mr. Hays,' the printer said. 'It's really nothing. You should have heard what Mr. Harris said.'"

★

When a new senator arrives in Washington, he invariably blurts out something to the press that gets him in trouble. Senator-elect Paul H. Douglas made an offhand remark during his first term to the effect that more work could be done on Capitol Hill if fellow senators forgot about late afternoon cocktail parties. When the scent of cordite and the hail of debris had faded, Senator Douglas claimed that he had learned his lesson. "Now," he said, "if a reporter asks me what day it is, my instinctive reply is: 'No comment.'"

★

"You are doing your job as a politician," said a wise old congressman to a young newcomer, "when half your constituents are following you and half are leading you."

★

Many young congressmen headed for Speaker Joe Martin's office when they arrived in Washington. They wanted to find out from a real old pro how to stay out of trouble in the big league. Joe's favorite bit of advice was as simple as it was straightforward: "Just remember," he would tell his visitor, "a closed mouth gathers no feet."

*

A new congressman on the Washington scene, no matter how smart he is back home, is a babe-in-the-woods in the maze of Capitol Hill goings-on. One bewildered newcomer put it this way: "You feel like the young Eastern potentate whose father presented him with a hundred concubines on his coming of age. 'It's not that I don't know what to do,' he said. 'The question is where to begin.'"

*

Campaign-hardened members of Congress often give advice to new young colleagues who will take it. Representative Bob Steele of Connecticut was told by a member many years his senior, "Son, the job of a first-term congressman is not to worry about the welfare of the United States, but to get yourself re-elected."

*

A young man woke up the day after election and found himself a congressman. He went off to Washington with plenty of advice from his father, who was an old political pro. In a few weeks the father was disturbed to hear that his son was voting far left. He dispatched a telegram which read: "GET IN THE MIDDLE OF THE ROAD, SON." The reply came back: "I WOULD, DAD, IF I COULD FIND THE DAMN ROAD."

*

A House fixture known for his willingness to give advice to freshmen congressmen, said to a good young prospect who was anxious to get in some debating time: "I'll tell you, son," he said, "if you have the facts on your side, hammer them into your colleagues. If you don't have the facts on your side, hammer the hell out of the desk."

"And I'll tell you this," said a hoary veteran of congressional wars as he took a new congressman aside, "be careful of what you say around here and the words you use. Keep them soft, sweet, and tasteful, for you will never know from day to day which ones you might have to eat."

★

When they arrive in Washington, new young congressmen are so anxious to get into print that they become fair game for veteran reporters. "It's a good thing," said a wily chairman, "that these newcomers don't possess some of the nation's secrets, for half of them would spill the beans for a couple of paragraphs in the New York *Times*."

The same congressman always advised the new crop: "Be sure your brain is engaged before you put your mouth in gear."

★

"Never speak when you are angry," said an old lawmaker when a freshman asked him for some advice. "If you do, you'll make the best speech you'll ever regret."

★

When asked what formula he used to keep him in Congress for forty years, an incumbent said: "Well, you see, many, many years ago, I set up a four-point platform for my political career. At that time I spoke favorably of the Bible, the Constitution, the American flag, and prosperity. Nobody could assail me on that platform and survive."

★

A certain pompous senator remained aloof from his colleagues. One day a young senator approached him and inquired how he was going to vote on a particular measure. Rising to his full height, the vain veteran responded: "That's none of your damn business and I wouldn't tell you that much if you weren't a member of my party."

It was the congressman's first week in Washington. Like many others who had come from a farm state, he was goggle-eyed. Seated in his office with his wife, he was informed that he had a lady caller.

When the lady entered the congressman's office, he started to rise and the lady held up her hand, saying: "Don't get up, Mr. Congressman."

The wife immediately interrupted with: "Let him alone. He's just learnin'."

★

When he was in the House, William P. Hepburn of Iowa was the best all-round debater on the Republican side. Hepburn was deadly accurate with his verbal missiles and few Democrats were willing to engage him in debate.

One day a new young Democrat took up the challenge and opposed Hepburn on a certain measure. Not having much material, he laced his arguments with long passages in Latin, presuming to impress Hepburn.

When the young Democrat had finished, Hepburn rose and said: "Mr. Speaker, the presentation of my colleague across the chamber reminds me of the old Wisconsin lawyer who did not know any Latin, and who met a youthful antagonist from the city, who made an argument, jammed with Latin quotations.

"When the old man stood up to reply, he said, 'You know, I too understand Latin. I have roamed with old Romulus. I have ripped with Euripides and I have socked with Socrates. But what the hell has all that got to do with the statutes of Wisconsin?' "

★

Senator Alben W. Barkley was approached by a pushy young senator who brazenly asked the veteran for a vote on a specific bill.

"I'm sorry," said Barkley, "but I have already promised to vote against the measure."

"Look, Senator," said the freshman, "you know how it is in politics. Promising and voting are two different things."

"In that case," said Barkley affably, "I will be happy to give you my promise."

★

Talking is big business in Washington. In no time flat many newly elected congressmen can develop into steam-blowing orators. In commenting on the situation, a D.C. newspaperman stated: "There is quite a difference between a citizen and a political orator. You walk up to an average guy on the street and ask him how much is two and two, and he'd say four.

"Now if you were to ask a political orator how much is two and two, he'd say: 'When in the course of human events, it becomes necessary to take the numeral of the second denomination and add it to the figure two, I say unto you and I say it without fear of successful contradiction, that the result of this splendid piece of arithmetic will invariably be four.'"

★

Any man who has been through the legislative wars in Congress is well acquainted with the price of fame. To any young House or Senate member he will say: "I'm going to tell you what the mama whale said to the baby whale: 'Remember, my young one, it's only when you get to the top and start to blow off steam that you get harpoons thrown at you.'"

★

Senator Stephen M. Young of Ohio was a senatorial artilleryman. He would blaze away at anyone who crossed his path. When a pair of Ohio congressmen suggested that the senator's sharp criticism of the Vietnam conflict was giving aid and comfort to the enemy, Young took the floor of the Senate to inquire:

"Would it be a violation of the rules of the Senate were I to assert in this chamber at this time that Representative Hays of Ohio and one-term Representative Sweeney of Ohio are guilty of falsely, viciously, and maliciously making stupid, lying statements?"

He was told it would be a violation.

Following the ruling, Young said: "I, of course, will abide by the ruling of the chair. If, however, on some future occasion a similar contemptible attack is made on me with lying allegations by either or both of these publicity seekers, I shall surely embalm and imbed them in the amber liquid of my remarks."

★

A ninety-five-year-old retired Congressman was interviewed on his birthday and asked for some comments on his long legislative career.

"Well, I'll tell you," he said, "I was eighty-three years old and suffering from hardening of the arteries when we voted for Prohibition. If I'd a knowed that God Almighty was going to give me another dozen years I'd never a voted the country dry."

★

One of the all-time congressional put-downs took place in the well of the House when a brash young member approached a grizzled veteran. With a hint of sarcasm in his voice he said: "I understand you gave quite a speech at the Democratic dinner last night. Tell me, who wrote it for you?"

"My dear boy," was the devastating response, "I am delighted that you heard about my speech. Now tell me, who read it to you?"

★

"A man should always vote his conscience," advised Speaker Joe Martin. "The trouble is," he added, "that two thirds of the House didn't bring one with them when they arrived."

★

A veteran congressman was showing a new young solon from his state the ins and outs of Washington. "And now, take the press," he said. "Be careful what you say to the newspapermen. If you don't, someday they'll dig up something you said in the past, compare it with something you just said, then claim you're a liar."

"Well," said the freshman, "have they ever claimed that on you?"

"Hell, no," was the reply, "they proved it."

★

Senator Claude Swanson of Virginia had strong views on the evolution of a United States senator. "Immediately after election," said Senator Swanson, "they roar like lions. They are as free and independent as the Czar of Russia. They bow their heads to nobody. Their conscience is their only guide.

"In two years' time, they begin to listen to suggestions that come from home, although they are very much irritated when these suggestions are not in accord with their own views. Still they remain independent.

"At the end of four years, they are yearning to know what the people back home have to say, and are quite convinced that the man in the street really knows more about legislation than the man who is occupying a seat in the United States Senate.

"With only a year to go before election, they humbly submit to questioning from the audience, and more often than not agree that the questioner is right. They tell them what they want to hear, for after all, the name of the game now is to warm those Senate seats for the next six years."

★

"The average congressman," according to former minority leader Charlie Halleck, "can tell about all he knows on any given subject in five minutes. But over in the Senate they have unlimited debate and it takes them that long to prove that they know as much as we do."

★

Congressmen size each other up pretty well, and it doesn't take long for a man to be catalogued as a liberal, moderate, or conservative. In commenting on a certain colleague, a Midwestern House member said: "Harry is so conservative he doesn't even burn the candle at one end."

When a certain egotistical senator arrived in Washington for his first term, the story went the rounds that he advised his office staff as follows: "We've got a big job to do here in the nation's capital. I want everybody on this staff to speak up. I don't want any yes-men around me. I want all of you to speak up, even though it costs you your job."

★

Senator Carter Glass once engaged a new young member in debate. When Glass had finished with him, the new senator was totally embarrassed.

The next day the young senator sought out Glass and said: "I am afraid I made a fool of myself in debate yesterday."

Glass patted him on the shoulder and in a low voice said: "Son, I assure you I observed nothing unusual."

★

Many years ago a wet-eared young congressman, who was also rather voluble, approached a battle-scarred veteran of House debates. "Do you think," he said, "I might improve my speech as did Demosthenes, by putting pebbles in my mouth?"

"Yes indeed," was the response, "but don't use pebbles. Use Portland cement instead."

★

A vinegary House member was sipping his soup in the House cafeteria when a new congressman approached him and asked: "I understand you've got to keep your ear to the ground in Washington so you can really find out what is going on."

"I can give you some advice on that, son," said the veteran. "When you've got your ear to the ground, be careful lest somebody take advantage of your peculiar posture and gives you a good swift kick in the pants."

★

Sooner or later most congressional tyros search out old codgers for advice and counsel. Most of what they hear in return will help them out when the going gets sticky, as it often does.

Years ago, a newcomer asked Representative Luther Patrick of Alabama how he should handle trouble and accusation if they ever came his way.

"Well, son," said Patrick. "The first rule is: Don't get caught at whatever it is."

Then Patrick went on: "The second rule is: If you get caught, don't admit a thing.

"If they press you," said Patrick, "point at something else. Plead innocence. That's the third rule.

"The fourth rule," said Patrick, grinning at his uneasy colleague, "is one you use in sheer desperation: Deny everything, wrap yourself in the American flag, tell them you have a sick mother, get yourself a good lawyer, and start looking for another job."

★

Venerable Senator George Aiken of Vermont retired from Congress in his eighty-second year and made some observations about the flood of newcomers in Washington. Said Aiken: "I have a growing sense of futility. The job has become more complicated and the new member coming here hires a press agent as his first appointment. The agent then gets out daily stories to the folks back home telling them what a wonderful job the new congressman is doing before he's even started to work."

★

Complaints by veterans about the inroads made by freshmen congressmen make little impression on the newcomers. "Don't these old chieftains know," said a hard-driving first-termer, "that Adam was the only indispensable man?"

★

Interviewed by a reporter on the changing scene over forty years in Congress, a veteran House member observed: "Well, I've seen them come and go. First they come here with a swelled head. Then they are going to remake the world. Then they are going to bust up the seniority system. Then they get White House fever. The world pays no attention to them. The seniority system swallows them up, the White House fever cures itself, and all they have left is the swelled head."

★

Many people say that there is no truth in Washington, but Senator Henry L. Myers of Montana disproved this tenet to a degree when he declared: "At the end of my second term I retired voluntarily. I did so for two reasons, each sufficient of itself, i.e., I did not desire another term and I believed that I could not get re-elected, had I desired to."

★

"Well, I'll tell you," said a three-term congressman to a reporter, "a guy has to be some kind of a nut and an oddball to want this damn job as congressman—but please don't quote me on that. As you know, I'm running for re-election."

7

Under the Capitol Dome

Legislative life under any capitol dome is not made up of run-of-the-mill happenings. Wherever there is a legislative assembly, be it Parliament, Congress, a state legislature, or the common garden variety of local government, there is always plenty of action.

These deliberative bodies are composed of individuals with diverse interests. They are arenas where the stormy passions of the people are presented, debated, maneuvered, and put into law or shunted aside.

All shades of human weakness, strength, conscience, skills, literacy, illiteracy, wit, wisdom, seriousness, foolishness, fun and laughter pass through the portals of legislative halls. Some members, like Halley's comet, blaze briefly across the sky, contribute nothing or something, then disappear. Others stay on in the arena, often for decades. Each day they face the stifling heat of legislative conflict. They meet the adversary in open forum, no hiding or slinking allowed. It is hard work.

Despite its frustrations, endless hours, problems of re-election, baby-kissing, etc. scarcely a man or woman voluntarily gives up legislative office—unless, of course, he or she sees the deadly handwriting on the wall.

"It may tax your pocketbook to the limit," said a congressman about his service in the House, "and it can wear down your brain, and get you home every night at midnight, lose you lots of friends, and what not—but it does have its compensations: after all it's an inside job, there's no heavy lifting, and the roof don't leak."

★

Senator Alben Barkley was at one time explaining to a group of young newsmen the complications of legislative activities. "We have," he said, "the House Foreign Affairs Committee and the Senate Foreign Relations Committee. The difference is that the senators are too old to have affairs—they only have relations."

★

Representative Henry Cabot Lodge had this to say about service in the so-called Upper Branch in Washington: "The Senate is a nice, quiet sort of place, where good representatives go when they die."

★

In a crowded, stuffy room just off the House floor at the State House in Austin, Texas, a controversial hearing had been raging for several hours.

The issue involved livestock registration controls, and tempers were growing shorter by the minute. Into the witness chair stepped a courtly old gentleman with a neatly trimmed white mustache and goatee. An auctioneer by trade, he looked for all the world like the living embodiment of a Kentucky colonel. Over the years he had, in fact, acquired the affectionate title of "Colonel."

A brash young lawmaker knew this and decided to use it to discredit the old man's testimony. "Tell me," he sneered, "were you a colonel in World War I or World War II?"

The old gentleman smiled softly. "Well, no," he explained. "I guess the 'Colonel' in front of my name is just like the 'Honorable' in front of yours. It doesn't mean a damn thing."

Senator Hiram Johnson was standing outside the Senate chamber one day chatting with a visitor from California. The curious visitor asked Johnson: "Every time I visit the Senate gallery, I note that Senator G—— is on the floor giving a speech. What does he talk about all the time?"

"He doesn't say," replied Johnson, shaking his head.

★

Conversation in the Senate cloakroom generally centers on the abilities of fellow senators. One lawmaker had this to say about a colleague: "He's got a lot of depth on the surface, but deep down he's shallow." Another cloakroom sage referred to a colleague this way: "His ignorance on the subject of tariffs is inexhaustible."

★

The House of Representatives in Washington made no impression on Alexis de Tocqueville, who wrote about a visit there more than a century ago: "One is struck by the vulgar demeanor of that great assembly. Often there is not a distinguished man in the whole number. Its members are almost all obscure individuals, village lawyers, men in trade and even persons belonging to the lower classes of society . . ."

★

"What has passed in the Senate?" a visitor asked one of the doorkeepers. Looking down at the near-empty chamber, the doorkeeper sighed: "Seven weeks."

★

A foreign diplomat revisited Congress after an absence from Washington of many years. He asked one of the attachés about a certain senator he had known.

"He's dead, sir," the attaché said.

"Poor fellow," reflected the diplomat. "Joined the great majority of his colleagues, eh?"

"I wouldn't say that, sir," said the attaché. "He was an honest man as far as I know."

Senator Tom Corwin had this to say about a colleague: "I won't say he is a liar, but he always keeps a respectful distance from the truth."

★

Two salty senators became involved in an argument over government problems. Finally, one of them shouted: "You talk about the Constitution. Why, man, I'll bet you twenty-five dollars you can't recite the first words of the preamble to the Constitution."

"Is that so?" replied the other. "It's a bet."

With that he started: "I pledge allegiance . . ."

He got no further when his fellow senator interrupted with: "Here's your twenty-five dollars. I didn't think you knew it."

★

A leather-lunged United States senator was pounding away on the floor for an interminable length of time. A colleague declared to a neighbor: "Let's get out of here. The way G—— is going, this place will be out of oxygen in ten minutes."

★

Senator Allen J. Ellender of Louisiana was once asked if there was any such thing as keeping a secret in Washington. This was Ellender's response: "You can't mumble something to a mirror in this town without it getting around in a few hours."

★

Speaker Sam Rayburn did not believe in long press conferences. When a group of reporters visited his office for some news, Rayburn asked: "You know how things were yesterday?"

"Yes, Mr. Speaker," the reporters chorused.

"Well," said Sam, "they're the same today."

★

Commenting on Washington attitudes, James Forrestal once said: "If you tell a congressman too much, he panics. If you don't tell him enough, he goes fishing."

A noted senatorial grump was the topic of some heavy discussion in the cloakroom one day. A colleague came up with this observation: "Harry is such a sourpuss that every time they publish his picture on the front page, it puckers the paper."

★

There is a humorous story in every area of Washington life. Even the tour guides have their smiles. Just as one guide was dismissing a group of tourists, a little old lady asked: "You have shown us the House and the Senate, now where does Congress meet?"

★

The late Senator Carl Hayden of Arizona was one of the best newspaper dodgers in Washington. The longtime senator admitted that he gave a wide berth to newsmen because "If you don't see them, you don't have to talk to them."

★

Congress is a magnet for every type of character. Some of them become unbearable pests to House and Senate members.

One such individual bothered several senators so much that he became a nuisance. Every morning he would visit the Senate offices and force himself on each senator, asking wide-ranging questions and giving opinions on every imaginable subject. The senators gathered in the cloakroom and decided to do something about the situation.

The next morning the man showed up as usual in the office of the first senator. He was greeted with these words from the senator: "Gracious, man, what happened to you? You look sick."

"Never felt better in my life," the man replied.

But the senator continued to talk about how badly the man looked, and finally the man departed to visit another senator. There he got the same treatment. He had not visited more than five senators when he went home sick, as each gave him the "you look sick" treatment.

"You can't beat the power of suggestion," said the first senator.

"One of the principal problems with congressmen," a tired observer of their actions commented, "is that their brains often are not synchronized with their tongues."

★

During a House lull, a congressman confided to a colleague that one of the members was having nightmares and was on the verge of a nervous breakdown.

"Hmpf," sneered an opposition party member, who overheard the comment, "he must be dreaming that all the money he is spending is his own."

★

When Tom Reed presided over the House of Representatives, he wielded the gavel with such telling effect that a member commented: "Tom works that gavel faster than an auctioneer with a rainstorm approaching."

★

Asked to comment on a colleague's two-hour Senate speech, a dry old veteran said: "The best I can say for J——'s offering this afternoon was that he engaged in a two-hour losing battle with the English language."

★

A certain senator who had been involved in many difficult issues was finally defeated for re-election when a resentful electorate went for a new face. Fishing around for a job, he was finally hired by the Department of the Interior to work on the national rat-extermination campaign.

A friend ran into the senator one day and remarked how well he looked. Then he asked him what he was doing for a living.

"I never felt better in my life," said the former senator, with a satisfied grin. "This job is just wonderful. I'm working on the rat-extermination program, and *everybody's* against rats."

When Alaska was fighting for statehood, one of the opponents commented: "Statehood for Alaska will raise hell with the flag. Can you imagine forty-eight stars and a snowball?"

★

One of the best of all Washington jokes came out of a school in the District of Columbia where a teacher was discussing with her class the War of 1812. "When the British forces approached Washington," she said, "the members of Congress left the city, but of course they came back again when the danger was over."

"Well, if they did," said one small boy, wise to the ways of politicians, "they probably collected mileage both ways."

★

Just like athletes, politicians are very adept at hiding their ages, but they often find it difficult to fool their colleagues on the subject. When a Western senator of ancient vintage remarked that he was born in 1898, a cloakroom wag said: "If he was, he was four years old at the time."

★

Senator Alben Barkley was asked his opinion of a well-known soft-back colleague. "Well, I'll tell you about him," said Barkley, "once he makes up his mind, he's full of indecision."

★

"Do you think a politician has a chance to get into heaven?" a congressman asked a visiting minister. The cleric thought a moment and then replied: "I think so, just so long as he gives his name and doesn't say another word."

★

The chaplain of the House of Representatives had just offered a flowery opening prayer. As he stepped from the rostrum someone asked: "Do you think that opening the sessions with a prayer will help the country?

Looking out over the House, the chaplain sighed and whispered: "It never has yet."

Once when Thad Stevens was pursuing a very careful course during a House debate, Representative Whaley of West Virginia interrupted several times with: "Will the gentleman yield?" Finally, the exasperated Stevens shot him dead with: "Yes, Mr. Speaker, I will yield to the gentleman from West Virginia for a few feeble remarks."

★

The talk in Washington these days is that everything is relative: The dollar is worth so much, the population balances expenditures, and on it goes. When a Democrat reminded a Republican that, after all, things were relative, the weary G.O.P. lawmaker said: "Yes, that's right. You Democrats have a relative in this job, a relative in that job, and a few more waiting outside."

★

No tougher or sharper individual ever sat in the Speaker's chair in the National House than Tom Reed of Maine. When an angry Democrat stormed up to the rostrum demanding: "What becomes of the rights of the minority?" Reed squelched him with: "The right of the minority is to draw its salaries and its function is to make a quorum."

★

Upon his arrival in Washington young Senator Henry Cabot Lodge of Massachusetts was greeted by Vice-President John Garner, who said: "You know, suh, everybody goes round saying I hate Yankees from the North. But it isn't so. The fact is, I like to see you here." Then he paused and added: "That is, so long as there aren't too many of you."

★

When debate drones on in the House of Representatives, it often becomes difficult for members to stay awake.

Following one particularly boring debate, a newsman approached one of the debaters and asked him if he was annoyed that a colleague sitting next to him had fallen asleep.

"I didn't mind his falling asleep," was the response, "but it hurt me when he didn't say good night."

★

A cynical observer of the Washington scene had this comment on Congress: "If Congress were on the *Titanic* and the order came to abandon ship, they would take a week out for Lincoln Day speeches, another for Jackson Day and ten days for Easter. Then they would look around for the lifeboats."

★

Like it or not, the most powerful force in American politics is the lobby which operates in the corridors of every state house and the national Capitol as well. The lobby is the true constituency of many legislators on all levels.

The power of the lobby was demonstrated by a California operator who boasted: "Give me a case of scotch, a case of gin, one blonde, and one brunette and I can take any liberal."

★

George Clark, a Boston newsman, once said: "Sure I am in favor of giving Congress a raise in pay. If we can get those congressmen into a higher tax bracket, they may take more interest in cutting them."

★

Two congressmen were discussing a third member of the House. "I wouldn't trust his veracity," said one.

"What do you mean, 'veracity'?" said the other. "Did you ever catch him in a lie?"

"No, I never exactly caught him in a lie, but more than once I have caught him jumping from one lie to another."

★

In one of the Western legislatures, a newly elected House member, appalled at the obvious corruption abounding in the State House, said: "It's damn hard to play a clean game up here when all the players are holding dirty cards."

A New England governor who was elected without much political experience asked his predecessor just what he might expect when he took over the governor's chair.

"Well, I'll tell you," said the outgoing governor, "you'll sit in that big chair behind the desk, and you'll say, 'Do this! Do that!' You'll push a lot of buttons, make a lot of telephone calls, order a lot of people around—and absolutely nothing will happen!"

★

Discussing the problems of men in public office, a friend said of onetime Governor Roger D. Branigan of Ohio: "I know how Roger feels. He's had his back to the political wall so long the handwriting's on him."

★

The telephone at the State House in Boston rang early one afternoon. A voice at the other end asked: "Is this the gas company?"

"Why, no," said the operator, "this is the State House."

There was a moment of silence, then the cutting voice on the other end of the line remarked: "Well, I didn't miss it by much, did I?"

★

One of the good jokes around Washington was about the congressman who went to Walter Reed Army Hospital for a physical examination. When the doctor had completed the examination he said: "There you are, sir, you're as sound as a dollar."

"Holy mackerel," cried the lawmaker, "am I that sick?"

★

During their period of service in the House, William R. Morrison and William M. Springer came to dislike each other intensely.

One day Representative Morrison fell ill. Several House members dropped off at the Willard Hotel to cheer him up. Morrison said: "I get the feeling I am in a bad way. Therefore, I want to say something to you. If I die, you will move resolutions and have a few words to say about me on the floor. That is all right.

Anything that Sunset Cox might say would please me very much. What Bill Holman would say would delight me, and if Bill Breckinridge speaks well of me it will be eloquent and sincere. His words will fall about me like fresh flowers.

"But," said Morrison, gritting his teeth, "if that SOB Springer rises to speak, one of you call for the previous question."

★

Long hair and beards are back in style in Washington as well as elsewhere. One House member said to a colleague: "I can't understand why my beard should turn gray so much quicker than the hair on my head."

"Very simple," was the response. "You have been working much more with your jaws than with your brains."

★

Lyndon Johnson, as Senate Majority Leader, was a master at working out arrangements for Senate debates. Almost everything with Johnson was compromise, and his formula for getting things done was simple and direct. Said LBJ: "You've got to work things out in the cloakroom and the committee room. When you've got them all worked out, you can debate a little before you vote."

★

Two senators were discussing a colleague. One proclaimed: "Brown is his own worst enemy."

"Not while I'm alive," said the other bitterly.

★

Attendance in the United States Senate in the mid-1800s had become so poor that it was a topic of national dismay. Hard-working senators, who had to carry the burden, were angered that so many of their colleagues were neglecting their floor responsibilities. In some cases, senators failed to show up in their seats for weeks on end.

One day, a pompous and long-absent member showed up in his seat. He gained the floor and hammered everything in sight for more than an hour, demanding better government, more action in the Senate, etc., etc.

Finally, a conscientious old senator rose and buried the offending senator by asking a parliamentary inquiry. "Is it not true, Mr. President," he said, "that visitors to this Senate are required to sit in the galleries?"

The obnoxious senator got the message from the hail of laughter that greeted the inquiry.

★

Lifelong bitterness and hatred can develop under any capitol dome, national or otherwise. A particularly vicious ten-year feud between two congressmen ended only with the death of one of the adversaries. When the news reached the House lobby, his old enemy said: "Well, Slater, where he has gone, won't find much difference in the climate or the company than what is here."

★

Every legislature has its share of tall and short members. Texas is no exception. The tallest member of the Texas House was a giant from the southwest, scaling six feet six inches and weighing well over 260 pounds. The smallest member was from Houston and was but five feet tall and weighed about 100 pounds.

One day the two members engaged in a blistering debate which became extremely personal. Finally the big member made a vicious reference to the short member. It was too much for the speaker and he called for a recess to cool things down. A moment later, the big member felt a great tugging and pulling on his coat. Looking down, he saw his opponent wildly gesticulating and dancing all around.

"What the hell are you trying to do, Buxton?" he asked.

"By Gawd, suh," screamed the short member, "I'm fightin', suh!"

★

A leg-weary House doorman was preparing to retire after more than forty years of service in the national Capitol. Fishing around for a story, a reporter asked the old gentleman: "With all these tourists and visitors coming up to you day after day, wanting to know about government, what question was asked of you the most often?"

"Where's the men's room?" replied the old-timer.

★

When the Teapot Dome investigations were rocking Capitol Hill in Washington, dozens of congressmen and senators became jittery as the taint of scandal spread through both chambers. Outside the Senate chamber, a Midwestern lawmaker was introduced to a lady tourist who gushed innocently: "I have heard a great deal about you, Senator."

Thrown off guard, the Senator quickly responded: "I've got six witnesses, lady, to prove it is not so."

★

Newspaper writers apply various names to the national Congress. Here are some of them: "The House of Misrepresentatives," "Malfunction Junction," "The Cave of the Winds," and "Dodge City." The writers also say that Congress is the only institution in the country which is run by the inmates.

★

The Wyoming Legislature for years had been dominated by the Republicans. One year, however, Thurman Arnold was elected as the only Democrat in the House. Naturally he was appointed minority leader without opposition. When the time came to elect a House speaker, Arnold stood up and nominated himself, stating: "I have known this young man all his life. I would trust him as far as I would trust myself."

Arnold then sat down briefly, then popped up again to second the nomination. As laughter echoed through the chamber, Arnold then said: "Mr. Speaker, I withdraw my name for Speaker of the House. Some misguided enthusiast, some impulsive admirer of mine, has placed my name before this body."

The selection of legislative attachés in an Eastern state legislature was based strictly on political favoritism. Educational requirements meant nothing. The result was that a number of pages and court officers could barely read and write. This exasperated senators and representatives, particularly when names were spelled wrong and telephone numbers written inaccurately along with all manner of other problems.

One day, an important note for a certain senator was badly fouled up. The angry legislator sought out the guilty court officer and yelled: "For C—— sake, what the hell is your IQ, anyway?"

"20-20," was the proud response.

★

Shortly after the Civil War, Congressman Ben Butler had the reputation of being the most quarrelsome member of the House. He debated anybody and everybody on every subject imaginable.

One of Butler's Massachusetts colleagues, George F. Hoar, then a freshman representative and much impressed with Butler's oratory, commented to a friend: "Don't you think Butler will be the next President of the United States?"

"Never," replied the friend.

"But the papers are filled with him every day," said Hoar. "People seem to be reading about nobody else. Wherever he goes he gets big crowds. Nobody else gets such applause, not even General Grant."

"Mr. Hoar," said the other member, "when I came to the House this morning, there was a fight between two monkeys on Pennsylvania Avenue. There was an enormous crowd, shouting and cheering. They paid little attention to me or any other House member. But when they come to elect a President of the United States, they won't elect either monkey. And Butler is in the class of those monkeys."

★

When Congressman J. D. Walker took his seat at the conclusion of a House speech, Representative Thomas B. Reed of Maine rose with an introductory statement: "I cannot expect to equal the volume of the voice of the gentleman from New York, that is equaled in this world only by the volume of things with which he is not acquainted."

★

Former Representative Clarence Clifton Young of Nevada, commenting on a quick-tempered member of the Cabinet, said: "The trouble with him is that he picks a quarrel before it is ripe."

★

Many years ago, card-playing was the big pastime among United States senators. The little inns around Washington were hideaways for the Senate gamblers. One night Senator Tom Corwin became engaged in a high-stake poker game, when he inadvertently dropped a ten-dollar bill under the table. Old Tom did not discover his loss until he had reached his room.

He went back to the table where he had been playing cards and noted that his Senate friends had left. The waiter came forward and said: "I know what you want, sir; you have lost something."

"Yes," responded Corwin, "I have lost a ten-dollar bill."

"Well, sir," said the waiter, "I have found it, and here it is."

"Thanks, son," sighed Corwin, "and here is a dollar for you."

"No, sir, I want no reward for being honest," said the waiter, smiling and with a knowing look, "but wasn't it lucky for you that none of the other senators found it?"

★

A vacillating congressman once asked his aide: "About that charge that I am indecisive—do you think I should answer it, or let it go, or answer it in part, or what?"

The aide just shook his head.

★

Members of Congress might be imposing figures in the eyes of the public and the press, but sometimes among the employees of the House and Senate they are less than heroes.

When Chauncey Depew was riding high as a United States sen-

ator from New York, a constituent visited the Capitol to look
him up.

Walking along the corridor, the visitor stopped a page who was
hurrying along to his station.

"Sonny," said the visitor, "can you tell me where I can find
Chauncey Depew?"

"Has he got anything to do with the pages?" inquired the boy.

★

During an emotional debate on the death penalty in the Massachusetts Senate, Kevin B. Harrington, president of that body, received a call from a disturbed constituent, demanding that the
death penalty bill be passed.

Harrington told the constituent that the bill was probably un-
constitutional. There was a pause on the phone and then the constituent cried: "To hell with the Constitution. It's up to you to
uphold the law."

★

A caustic debate had raged on for several hours, when a
member asked for a recess "so that I can go back to my office and
do some thinking about this bill."

"Thinking," snorted a colleague to a neighbor, "boy, will that
be unfamiliar territory for him!"

★

Thomas C. Platt of New York was a solid United States Senator, not given to boasting or bragging. He had little use for colleagues of long service in the Senate who spent most of their time
bemoaning the degeneracy of the times and looking back on "the
good old days" in the Senate.

Said Senator Platt: "If I ever become reminiscent, please go to
the nearest drugstore and get an ounce of cyanide of potassium
and I'll swallow it in one gulp."

★

Massachusetts Senator Charles Summer demanded to be right
on all occasions. A huge man, he bridled at anyone who disagreed

with him. During a discussion with a fellow senator, Sumner glared as his colleague said: "Yes, Senator, but you forget the other side of the issue."

Slamming his clenched fist on the table, Sumner roared: "There is no other side."

★

Every state legislature has its share of windbags. Once, in the Massachusetts legislature, a run-off-at-the-mouth senator was admonished by a colleague with the following story:

Said the senator: "A young man was walking across Boston Common, eating a baloney sandwich. A piece of the baloney fell from the sandwich and was immediately pounced upon by a robin. It was early morning and the robin was pleased that it had become filled with food so early and would not need to scrounge the rest of the day.

"So the robin started to sing with joy. This brought a neighboring cat upon the scene, who pounced upon the singing bird and ate it.

"That's the end of the story," said the senator as he looked across the chamber at the windbag, "except for the moral, which is: never open your mouth when you are full of baloney."

★

Hard-boiled lobbyists, either in Washington or around state capitol buildings, have a common feeling for legislators, which goes like this: "Dine them, wine them, love them, but never trust the SOB's around the corner."

★

During a harsh debate in the Massachusetts House, a stuffy old-line Yankee shouted across the chamber: ". . . and furthermore, I want my colleague to know my ancestors came over on the *Mayflower*."

It was a beautiful opening for his adversary, who then said softly: "I didn't know there were any steerage passengers on the *Mayflower*."

★

A news reporter intercepted a tired-looking congressman shuffling along a House corridor. After a few introductory questions, the newsman asked: "And what would you like to do most as a legislator?"

"I'd like to tell a lot of people to go to hell," was the sharp response, "only I don't dare to do it."

★

Confronting Sam Rayburn, a reporter asked: "I'm going to ask you a very candid question, Mr. Speaker: "Are you going to run for President?"

"And I'm going to give you a very candid answer," said Sam.

"Yes?" was the expectant response.

"No comment," said Old Sam, smiling as he moved along to the House chamber.

Be It Enacted . . .

Representative Nicholas Longworth of Ohio was one of the great Speakers of the national House. In an interview after his election to the speakership of the Sixty-ninth Congress, Longworth had this to say about the frustrating troubles of serving in Congress:

"I have been a member of the House of Representatives ten terms. That is twenty years. During the whole of that time we have been attacked, denounced, despised, hunted, harried, blamed, looked down upon, excoriated, and flayed.

"I refuse to take it personally. I have looked into history. I find that we did not start being unpopular when I became a congressman. We were unpopular before that time. We were unpopular even when Lincoln was a congressman. We were unpopular even when John Quincy Adams was a congressman. We were unpopular even when Henry Clay was a congressman. We have always been unpopular.

"From the beginning of the Republic it has been the duty of every voter to look down upon us, and the duty of every humorist to make jokes at us.

"Always there is something—and, in fact, almost always there is almost everything—wrong with us. We simply cannot be right.

"Let me illustrate. Suppose we pass a lot of laws. Do we get praised? Certainly not. We then get denounced by everybody for being a 'Meddlesome Congress' and a 'Busybody Congress.' Is it not so?

"But suppose we take warning from that experience. Suppose that in our succeeding session we pass only a few laws. Are we any better off? Certainly not. Then everybody, instead of denouncing us for being a 'Meddlesome Congress' and a 'Busybody Congress,' denounces us for being an 'Incompetent Congress' and a 'Do-Nothing Congress.'

"We have no escape—absolutely none.

"Suppose, for instance, that we follow the President. Suppose we obey him. Suppose we heed his vetoes. What do we get called? We get called a 'flock of sheep.' We get called 'echoes of the master's voice,' a 'machine.'

"Suppose, then, we turn around and get very brave and defy the President and override his vetoes. What, then, do we get called? We get called 'factionists.' We get called 'disloyalists.' We get called 'disruptors of the party.' We get called 'demagogues.'

"We have no chance—absolutely no chance. The only way for a congressman to be happy is to realize he has no chance."

★

Crusty legislative veterans are usually survivors of many hard and bitter campaigns and stormy House or Senate debates. Years of serving fretful and demanding constituencies imbue many congressmen with a cynicism about statutes, petitions, bills, resolutions, and issues. When a newspaper reporter asked a thirty-year House member from a knock-down, drag-out district what he thought was a good bill, he got this response: "A good bill, my son," said he, "is one that helps my friends and raises hell with my enemies."

★

Legislation is something that new members of legislative bodies often have difficulty figuring out. Bills are written in complicated language which can puzzle a new member. One lawmaker summed up a difficult bill in this manner: "I can identify the words, but I cannot understand the sentences."

Two loud-voiced senators slugged it out on the floor over a certain national issue. The debate was torrid and personal. When it had ended, a senate newcomer turned to a colleague and said: "Wow, that was some debate."

The colleague, who had heard the two senators go at each other over a period of years, heaved a sigh and responded: "Son, that was no debate. That was a confrontation of egos."

★

Former Congresswoman Bella Abzug of New York was considered to be one of the most colorful individuals in Washington. As outspoken as an auctioneer, Bella had a reputation for toughness unmatched on Capitol Hill.

When a Great Dane was brought to the House office building by Congressman Andy Jacobs, a Massachusetts colleague, Representative James Burke, said to Ms. Abzug: "Bella, couldn't you use a dog like that?"

"I don't need a dog like that," snapped the witty New Yorker. "I have my own bite."

★

One of the national Capitol guides was asked how he came to lose the index finger of his right hand. "Well, I'll tell you," said the guide. "I've been a guide here for more than twenty years. I simply wore off the finger pointing out senators, representatives, and statues to thousands of tourists."

★

"My quarrel with Congress," said an observer, "is not so much the acts passed, but rather the acts committed."

★

The Ways and Means Committee of a Midwestern state legislature was discussing a series of bills for increased appropriations. A member asked: "These bills are fine, but where will we get the money?"

A newcomer perked his ears and remarked: "Oh, are we going to get some money?"

Congressmen are forever pressing their colleagues for votes on favorite bills. It makes no difference to some eager House members that certain votes would do harm to a fellow member. They press anyway, always hoping.

Many years ago, a pushy member moved in on Congressman Charles F. Joy of Missouri, asking for a vote that would have put Joy on the spot with his constituents.

Joy handled the situation with the following story: "A hen and a pig were going down the road and they came to a sign which read: 'Ham and Eggs.'

" 'See,' said the hen, 'we are partners.'

"Mournfully the pig said, 'Yes, for you it is only a day's work, but for me it is a real sacrifice.' "

Joy moved along the corridor, leaving his colleague to ponder the response.

★

When he was majority leader of the United States Senate, Lyndon B. Johnson was a hard-driving politician. When he wanted a bill enacted, he hounded everybody in sight to get it through.

Once when Johnson was riding herd on a committee chairman to get a bill to the floor, the chairman complained to a colleague, stating: "For C—— sake, Rome wasn't built in a day."

"It would have been," said the colleague, "if Lyndon Johnson had been the architect."

★

"Every man in this body," said a veteran member, "talks about looking to the horizon. The trouble is that to him the horizon seldom exists beyond the last town in his congressional district."

★

Senator Hoar of Massachusetts was one day delivering a long speech against a certain bill for which Senator Roscoe Conkling stood as the sponsor. As he outlined his points against the bill, Senator Hoar kept first his right hand and then his left hand in his trouser pockets.

Senator Conkling, who was noted for his wit, rose to remark:

"The Senator from Massachusetts seems to be leaving no stone unturned to prevent passage of this bill."

★

A honey-tongued Southern congressman once rose in the House and proceeded to speak on the merits of a favorite bill. In every other sentence he inserted the expression "This bill has merit and should be passed."

Finally, a colleague rose and asked: "What are the facts? The people have a right to know the facts on this bill."

"Facts have nothing to do with it," roared the Southerner. "This bill has merit, and so far as I'm concerned that's enough."

★

Guilt feelings are as prevalent in Washington as elsewhere. One senator put it this way: "I'd hate to go out and make a living under some of the laws we have passed this session."

★

When a tough bill came up in the New Hampshire legislature a representative first called for its defeat, then asked postponement of the measure over the weekend "so I can discuss the matter with my constituents."

On Monday, the doubter spoke out strongly in favor of the bill. A puzzled colleague asked: "Did you see the light over the weekend?"

"No," said the representative, "I didn't see the light. I felt the heat."

★

During debate on a bill in the New York Assembly, an assemblyman shouted at a colleague: "I don't know why you're against this measure. I'll wager 80 per cent of the people in your district are in favor of it."

"That's not so," was the angry reply. "There ain't that many people in my district."

Advised that his vote on a bill would benefit posterity, a not so literate but grasping member of the old Illinois House commented: "I'll vote for it, but you tell posterity he'd better do something for us."

★

Huey Long was filibustering for all he was worth one day in the Senate. A fellow senator leaned over as Huey was gasping for his fourth or fifth wind. "Look, Huey," he said, "don't you think you have been talking long enough? You must be tired."

"Hell, no," replied the Kingfish, "I never get tired of talking. It's the listening that bores the hell out of me."

★

"There was a time," lamented a House member, "when we sat in Congress and passed laws. Now we wave at them as they go by."

★

During a lengthy House debate on an agricultural bill, Wilmer D. "Vinegar Bend" Mizell of North Carolina, a onetime pitcher for the Pittsburgh Pirates, was recognized for a five-minute speech.

He commenced by saying that he would not need all of the time. His announcement was met with loud applause. Mizell waited for the chamber to quiet down, and then said: "I think the last time I got that much applause was when I was knocked out of the box in Cincinnati."

★

Senator Everett Dirksen was an unmatched orator. One colleague described the craggy Dirksen "as a man who would never use a single word where four or five would do." Once when Old Ev was interrupted during a Senate speech, he turned to the lawmaker who had caused the interruption and said: "Sir, could you wait until I have finished and then honor us with your proposal? You are interrupting my favorite speaker."

Very often when a politician involves himself in a debate on the floor of the assembly he opens with: "I really don't know much about this bill, but . . ." etc. One Maine state senator who commenced his speech with that remark, and then went on for twenty minutes, was rebutted by a colleague with the following: "The senator from Bangor, across the chamber, admitted that he started this debate ignorant of the subject. He has talked for twenty minutes and has lost ground all the way."

★

Speaker Sam Rayburn had a favorite expression whenever a colleague started ripping a bill apart. Said Sam: "Any jackass can kick a barn down, but it takes a good carpenter to build one."

★

During the joint legislative struggle to reduce the size of the Massachusetts House membership, a senator rose and asked for recognition. He had previously voted to cut the House and now approached the rostrum to change his vote. He had long service in both the House and Senate and was also well known as an individual who admired a pretty girl.

In stentorian tones he told the hushed chamber: "I have been lying awake nights wrestling with my conscience . . ."

He got no further when a voice from the rear of the chamber broke up the place with: "What was her name?"

★

Stinging retorts during senatorial debate are not as brutal today as they were in the Washington of the 1800s. Once during a rousing debate a senator shouted at a colleague: "I simply cannot bear fools."

"Why not?" was the response. "Your mother could."

★

For ten years the New Jersey Assembly had tried to solve reapportionment and assessment problems. When asked to comment on why these problems had not been solved, a veteran assemblyman stated: "Of course they haven't been solved, but that's the American way."

★

A Louisville reporter sent this message back to his newspaper: "The Kentucky Legislature is settin' and settin' and doing nothin', like a hen on a porcelain egg."

★

Senator Edmund Muskie of Maine put together some guidelines for addressing a colleague during debate: "If you and he are in agreement, you address him merely as 'The Senator from such and such a state.'

"If you are not too sure he agrees with you, you should refer to him as 'The able Senator from . . .'

"But if you know there is violent disagreement on an issue, then the only way to address him is: 'The able and distinguished Senator, my dear friend from . . .'"

★

Senator Everett Dirksen was a master of the corny touch. Once he surprised his colleagues by announcing: "I am going to treat you to something very special today. I shall depart from my usual custom and talk about the bill that is before us for discussion today."

★

Samuel Foote was one of the sharpest of all English politicians. He was a tough man in debate and impossible to pin down. One of his parliamentary opponents said of him: "Foote is the most incomprehensible fellow that I know. When you have driven him into a corner and think you are sure you have him, he runs between your legs, or jumps over your head and makes his escape."

★

During debate on a Civil Service bill, a Massachusetts House member complained that some of the questions asked in Civil Service examinations were ridiculous. "Why should an applicant for sewer work need to know how close the sun is to the earth?" he cried. "The job don't call for sunbathing."

★

Arguing for a bill to send food to foreign markets, a Western house member told his colleagues: "We can't eat all we raise. We must have a foreign market. If we are compelled to consume all our grain, beef and pork, we will be called upon to eat a barrel of pork at every meal, two cows a week, ten loaves of bread a day and go from three to six meals a day."

★

Two congressmen, one from Kentucky and the other from Tennessee, became involved in a roaring and personal debate over boundary lines between the two states. The Tennessee member was trying to prevent passage of a bill which would have benefited Kentucky.

As the debate raged on, the Kentucky member finally shouted at his adversary: "Why is the Tennessee member barking so furiously?"

"Because," responded the Tennessee congressman, "I think I hear a thief."

★

Knowing the futility of it, very few congressmen take the floor of the House. They do their work in committees and back at the office and leave the oratory to the few eagles who entertain the tourists every afternoon.

Former Congressman Alvin O'Konski was one of those House members who spoke infrequently on the floor. Once, however, O'Konski concluded a rare floor speech early in the session with these words: "This is the first time this year that I have taken time to speak on any bill. I probably will not take the floor again this session, so before I close, I want to wish you all a Merry Christmas and a Happy New Year!"

★

Speaking before a college group one day, Hubert H. Humphrey was taken to task for his "liberalism." The question asked was why Humphrey, a four-alarm liberal, could oppose a bill to allow the coloring of oleomargarine.

"Very simple," said Humphrey with a smile. "I counted the dairy farmers in Minnesota and then I counted the oleo manufacturers in Minnesota. I discovered there were more dairy farmers. Does that answer your question?"

★

According to one cynical Congress-watcher: "There are two enemies to every bill proposed in Congress—the fools who favor it and the lunatics who oppose it."

★

Early legislative sessions were generally riotous, rum-soaked affairs, with little or no decorum. During one such boisterous afternoon in the California Assembly, the speaker pounded his gavel and shouted: "This chamber will be in order. We have already passed six bills without being able to hear a word that was in them."

★

When an inflammatory senator had completed a two-hour tirade on an irrigation bill, a colleague rose and drowned his argument with: "Mr. President, we have just been treated to a Niagara of words and a drought of reason."

★

Many years ago, Illinois had as its House speaker a tough, uncompromising representative. He had a reputation for getting through any bill he wanted, notwithstanding its merit or lack of it. Woe unto any legislator who crossed him.

Once during a committee caucus, a House member refused to sign a report on a bill. His reticence locked the matter up in a tie vote. No amount of pleading by the committee chairman could change the maverick's mind. The report languished for more than a week. One afternoon the reluctant committee member approached the committee chairman and declared meekly: "I've decided to sign the report."

"That's great," said the chairman, "but what finally persuaded you to change your mind on this bill?"

"Well, I'll tell you," explained the holdout. "This morning the Speaker called me into his office. He no sooner shut the door than he grabbed me by the throat and put his nose close to mine, shouting all the while: 'If you haven't signed that bill by four o'clock this afternoon, I'll knock your teeth down your throat, after I have broken both your arms and legs.'"

Then, reaching for a pen to sign the report, the member added: "You see, Mr. Chairman, nobody ever bothered to explain the bill to me so clearly before."

★

"What is the caliber of the members of the Senate?" a visiting Englishman asked a veteran columnist as they walked through the Capitol.

The response was quick and to the point: "Large bores and small bores," was the way he put it.

★

The passing of time makes many changes in the attitude of most individuals. Illinois Senator Paul Douglas was no exception. In his later years as a senator, Douglas became interested in the Indiana Dunes National Lakeshore on Lake Michigan. In response to a question on this interest Douglas said: "Until I was thirty, I wanted to save the world. Between the ages of thirty and sixty, I wanted to save the country. But since I turned sixty, I've wanted to save the dunes."

★

A popular story about the Massachusetts legislature centers on a laundry bill that was sent to the House of Representatives by mistake. When the manager of the laundry company noted the error, he immediately called the clerk of the House and informed him that his billing department had forwarded a laundry bill to the Massachusetts House by mistake and would they please return it.

"It's too late," said the clerk. "They have already passed it."

Henry Clay was a master of the barbed phrase. When an obnoxious colleague who had offended Clay stopped by to see him on a certain matter, Clay listened for a few minutes, then ushered his visitor to the door. As the man left, Clay said: "Thanks for dropping in, my friend. Come and see me again when you have a little less time to spare."

★

Congressional battles over farm subsidies cause some of the most powerful debates in the nation's Capitol. Shortly after a compromise farm bill was approved, an Eastern congressman announced: "Hell, man, if we didn't tighten up the farm belt, we'd lose our pants at the next election."

★

Speaker Joe Cannon once referred to some weak members as "chocolate soldiers." A reporter asked him what he meant by the reference. Laughed the Speaker: "They melt in the heat."

★

When six-foot four-inch Christian Herter was Speaker of the Massachusetts House, a diminutive Democrat was a thorn in his side. All through any given afternoon, the little man kept interrupting the decorum of the chamber with parliamentary questions and other nuisances.

One day, the representative in question wanted to make a point and screamed for recognition. Herter looked down from the high rostrum and said coldly: "When a member wishes to speak, he must stand and address the chair. The chair will not recognize any member who is sitting."

"Mr. Speaker, I *am* standing," cried the troublesome member. "I have been on my feet for ten minutes."

"I didn't know that," said Herter, smiling as the House roared at the perfect squelch.

★

Senator "Pat" Harrison of Mississippi was a powerful debater, one who could be dangerous to any colleague who crossed him.

Once a fellow senator became entangled in an attempt to explain an appropriations bill. Pat pounced on him, stating: "The position of my friend reminds me of the man standing in a pasture, holding a rope in his hands, and saying to himself: 'I don't know if I have lost a horse or found a rope.'"

★

Exasperated at the way things were going during a long debate in which the Republican majority was showing its muscle, Representative Jack Beall exploded: "The Republicans are expert mathematicians. They can add, subtract, multiply, and divide all in one operation. They can add to the wealth of the rich, subtract from the substance of the poor, multiply millionaires, and divide themselves—all in one bill."

★

Many years ago a bill came out of the House Committee on Rivers and Harbors. It called for improvements in a number of rivers with such names as the Skagit, Stillaguamish, Nooksack, Snohomish, and Snoqualmie rivers in the Washington Territory.

After the bill was read, Representative Byron M. Cutcheon of Michigan rose and offered an amendment, stating: "Mr. Speaker, I move an amendment in the nature of a proviso that at least one thousand dollars of the money hereby appropriated shall be used to straighten out the names of said rivers."

★

Although he appeared to be a fearless politician, Huey Long had his ear to the ground more often than an Indian scout. An expert at changing direction, Senator Long was always tuned in on his constituents.

During the course of a rugged debate on a traction bill, one of Long's henchmen reported: "A lot of your constituents, Huey, don't see eye to eye with you on this bill."

"Stay right on the ball, Jim," advised Long, "and if ever enough of them oppose it to become a majority, I'll come out against it myself."

There was a time in the old Texas legislature when some members would grab anything that smelled of cash. To prove it was so, one of the honest members jokingly placed a notice on the washroom door, stating he had found a ten-dollar bill in the House chamber and the owner could have it back.

"Would you believe it?" the honest member told some friends. "I got nine calls from colleagues proclaiming they had lost the money and demanding I return it."

★

During an interview with a tough-minded congressman of many years, a reporter asked: "What do you think of Congressman G——'s track record on the hill?"

"Very spotty," snickered the veteran. "Like all race track liberals, he comes in first in appropriations and last in taxes."

★

Almost nothing can deter a legislative orator once he has gotten going. This was proved in the Connecticut legislature when a persistent debater on the Republican side was in full flight. His upper false teeth popped out of his mouth and bounded off his chest. However, this did not faze the determined Republican, who caught the teeth on the first bounce and clapped them back in his mouth without missing a single word.

★

The League of Women Voters has become a powerful influence in legislative assemblies. Many legislators are wary of their efforts, calling them "The League of Women Vultures," the "Plague of Women Voters," and other uncomplimentary names, despite the League's excellent record of supporting needed legislation in many fields.

When the president of the League of Women Voters in Connecticut visited a veteran House member, she assured him that the League was nonpartisan.

"So you say," replied the skeptical veteran, "but what are you nonpartisan against?"

"One thing about B——," said a House member about a wishy-washy colleague. "He always takes a firm neutral stand on every issue."

★

A long-winded senator was going on and on during debate on a rivers and harbors bill. His points were so weak that a fellow senator turned to a colleague and remarked: "G—— reminds me of a young lad in my state who, passing through a graveyard, stopped to read an inscription on a tombstone. The inscription read: 'Not dead, but sleeping.'

"The kid scratched his head and observed: 'He sho' ain't foolin' nobody but hisself.'"

★

The issue before the Commerce and Labor Committee of the Massachusetts legislature was unemployment benefits and the hearing was noisy and hostile. After about four hours of testimony, Chairman Allan R. McKinnon rose to leave the hearing room while a militant witness was speaking.

"Look at him," shouted the speaker, "he's bored listening to us."

Some of the listeners in the audience yelled: "Yah, where are you going?" and "Come on back and listen. Who do you think you are?"

McKinnon kept on going and was back in a few minutes. Taking his seat, he interrupted the speaker and announced: "I went to the men's room. Do I have to raise my hand?"

9
Roll Call

"This would be the greatest job in the world," said a harried congressman as the bell sounded for a roll call, "if you didn't have to vote on the damn bills." Another House member observed: "The trouble with service in this chamber is that, unless you take a walk, you must vote 'Yes' or 'No' on every controversial bill. Wouldn't it be beautiful if you could just vote 'Maybe'?"

The roll call is the record of a politician's votes on legislation before the assembly, and it follows him to his grave. In every legislative chamber, the calling of the roll for a vote on a measure immediately separates the men from the boys and the women from the girls. A public servant talks bravely on a particular subject. The debate ends and the roll-call bell sounds. It is amazing how the rattle of the bell quickens the pulse and changes the hearts and minds of so many legislative members.

Roll-call time is the moment of truth. It is the period when the palms of the hands get wet and the hangdog expression takes over as worried legislators scurry toward the chamber. A member's thoughts are usually focused on his options: "Shall I vote to help the next generation, or shall I concern myself with the next election?" More often than not, the next election will carry the day.

When an important and controversial bill is up for a vote, a legislator may find himself stopped in the corridor by a group of constituents who demand: "We hope you have the guts to vote

'No' on this bill." A little further on he meets another group who crowd around him and press their point by saying: "We hope you have the guts to vote 'Yes' on this measure."

"Whichever way you vote," says the harassed legislator, "you're going to be a coward to somebody."

The period after the roll-call bell rings is one of the most interesting in any legislative chamber. It is at this time that every lame and weak excuse known to legislators is bandied around the chamber in order to explain a voting decision. It is also a time when men stand against the storm and are secretly admired by other members, who often say: "Did you see how Harry voted? He's right, but he's crazy."

Legislators do not always say what they mean, particularly when justifying their votes. The following are some of the more frequently heard expressions . . . and their interpretations.

★

"What's my vote?" (A common expression among legislators and congressmen who don't know or care what's going on.)

"I voted against the bill because I received some last-minute information." (The lobbyist twisted his arm.)

"The Speaker says this is a good bill." (He better vote right or there goes the committee assignment.)

"I'm voting with Harry Brown on this because I like him." (Harry is chairman of the congressional campaign fund committee and is watching closely.)

"I'm changing my vote on this because of mail from my constituents." (One letter from a little old lady in tennis sneakers.)

"I was well off selling insurance and didn't know it." (He's in trouble back home no matter which way he votes.)

"Why the hell did they roll call this bill anyway?" (His opposition is keeping a check on every vote and this one can hurt.)

"I voted my conscience on this one." (The League of Women Voters pestered him into the ground. He yearned one way and voted the other.)

"It's about time we showed some concern for the taxpayers." (He couldn't care less, but there's a tough campaign coming up.)

"Those labor fakirs aren't telling me how to vote. It's a good bill, that's why I supported it." (The labor boys had him against the wall and he responded satisfactorily.)

"Business wants you to vote with them on every bill." (They'd drop dead if he gave them one vote.)

"I was against this bill, but the President called and I switched. After all, you've got to help him once in a while." (If not, there go two postmasterships.)

"I voted that way because it will save the taxpayers some money." (Enough for toothpicks and ice water and he knows it.)

"This budget is too damn high, but I'm voting for it anyway, for we've got to end the session." (It's loaded with pork for his district and he isn't kidding anyone.)

"I'm voting against more jobs for the Commerce Department. It's a patronage haven already." (Retaliation because they left his brother-in-law off the list for a job.)

"How are you voting on this bill, Charlie?" (He's scared to death and is looking for comfort.)

"I didn't hear my name called." (He did, but wants to wait to the end of the roll call to see which way the tide is running.)

"I know I voted wrong on this bill, but hell, fellers, I want to come back." (The most honest statement of the day.)

"I call them as I see them, and that's how I vote." (There are a few in every legislative branch. They mean it and do it and they have a tough job staying on.)

★

"When that bell rings," said a cagey roll-call dodger, "there is no more independence on the floor of this chamber than there is in jail. Everybody is under some kind of pressure on a tough bill. Your views may be one thing, but very often your vote had better be something else, or the fires of political hell will be waiting.

"Roll call boils down to a game of Truth *and* Consequences," continued the member. "The Truth comes when that little bell rings or the red and green lights start to flicker on the tally board. It is now for real. It is for the record. No complaints of misquoting, out of context, or omission. How do you misquote a 'Yes' or 'No', anyway? When that bell stops or those lights stop flickering, the big black roll-call books then take over. They are indelible, permanent, and often devastating as they lie there waiting to ambush you some night out on the campaign trail. That is when you get hit with the Consequences."

★

Following a murderous House debate, Congressman Henry L. Pierce of Massachusetts was listed as having changed his vote. A colleague rushed over to Pierce and cried angrily: "How come, Pierce? You voted the other way when this bill was up last year."

"I know I did," replied the Bay State congressman, "but my conscience finally broke loose."

★

A representative with a bad hangover lifted his head slowly during a roll call in the Massachusetts House, and when his name was called he muttered: "Not guilty."

★

Senator Tom Connally of Texas had a story for every occasion. Once, following a close Senate roll call, Connally and several fellow senators were concerned that they had voted wrong. "No matter which way we voted," said one of them, "we are in trouble."

Connally agreed and then proceeded to illustrate the point with a story of a semiliterate Texas judge who presided in a little town through which ran the Texas-Arkansas border. The justice tried always to preserve an impartial frame of mind.

"Well," said Connally, "up before this judge came a man charged with stealing a mule and killing a man in the bargain. The judge reminded him that he had the choice of two laws, Texas law or Arkansas law. 'Which do you want to be tried under?'

"The prisoner thought a moment and then decided on Arkansas law. 'Then I discharge you for stealin' the mule, an' hang you for killin' the man.'

"'Hold on a minute,' said the prisoner. 'Better make that Texas law.'

"'All right, then,' said the judge as he banged the gavel. 'I fine you for killin' the man, and hang you for stealin' the mule.'"

One of Senator Norris Cotton's favorite roll-call stories had to do with a little old lady seated in the Senate gallery one day when the buzzer sounded for the quorum call. She turned to another elderly lady tourist and asked why the bells were ringing so frantically.

"I'm not so sure," was the worried response, "but it could be that one of them has escaped."

★

Arm twisting is a big thing in all legislative chambers. Whenever the pressure is on to pass or kill a measure, the administration sends its minions to the hill to twist a few arms, one way or the other. During the SST debate, the Nixon pressure was so great that House member Silvio Conte commented: "The arm twisting was so powerful that I doubt if many Republicans will be able to lift a cocktail glass for several days."

★

At an eighteenth-century assembly in France where a number of members were talking loudly the presiding officer said: "If the gentlemen who are talking would make no more noise than the gentlemen who are sleeping, it would be of great help to the gentlemen who are listening."

★

A certain Massachusetts state senator of long service had a reputation of waiting on every roll call to see which way the tide was running before he voted. An exasperated colleague commented: "G—— wants to come up smelling like a rose on every issue—and dammit, he does."

★

An emotional debate was drawing to a close in the United States Senate. Hiram Johnson of California was listening to the proceedings when an Eastern senator leaned over and said to him: "I'm counting my votes on this issue. Can I get a definite 'Yes' or 'No' from you?"

Peering over his glasses at the upstart senator, Johnson replied: "The best I can do for you is a definite 'Maybe.'"

★

As Senate Majority Leader, Lyndon B. Johnson was a salty character. Whenever he wanted to make a caucus point or berate a recalcitrant senator, LBJ could dredge up some real riverboat language.

One day Johnson was not in the Senate when a roll-call vote was taken on an important issue. The Republicans won the roll call because a Democrat had switched his vote.

Later in the day, the switch senator sought out a colleague and asked him what Johnson had said about his vote. "Do you want me to leave out the swearwords?" he was asked.

"Yes, of course."

"Then he didn't say anything."

★

When the legendary Proctor Knott went to Washington from Kentucky, he found the going difficult. Unused to the daily routine of interruptions during speeches, with calls to order and to yield the floor for a question, Knott finally exploded: "I believe," he shouted, "that if some members had been present at the Sermon on the Mount, they would have asked their Saviour to yield for a question."

★

A Midwestern senator, pitching for an irrigation project for his state, bolstered his floor argument as follows: "Mr. President, we need that water for our farming and our cattle. Why, right now, our cows are so skinny that it takes three or four of them just to cast a shadow."

★

Wearied from hours of listening to debate, a Senator rose late one night and proposed that a surgeon be brought into the chamber to split the tongues of the orators in order that some work might be accomplished.

"Heavens," a colleague retorted, "that would only double the gabble."

*

During raging House debates over hog prices, a Midwestern congressman roared at a colleague: "You can't tell me anything about hogs. I know more about hogs than you ever dreamed of. I was brought up among hogs."

He melted like lard before the laughter.

*

Majority Leader John McCormack was once taunted by Republican Clare Hoffman during a scrappy House debate. McCormack, in his comeback against Hoffman's charges, stated: "I have always held my colleague in high regard. However, it is a minimum high regard."

*

Two congressmen were discussing a pair of their colleagues, and one commented: "There's a mutual feeling between Brown and Hopkins."

"That's nice," said the other.

"No, it ain't," said the first. "They hate each other."

*

A couple of long-winded senators were slashing each other during an appropriations debate when one of them shouted: "I assume my colleague across the chamber knows all about economics?"

"Of course, of course," parried the other senator, "but assume for a few minutes that I do not understand the principles of economics; I woud then like my friend across the chamber to explain them to me."

That ended the debate.

*

Two senators were cutting each other to ribbons in a brutal demonstration of character assassination. Finally a colleague turned to another senator and said: "This is just awful. Can anything be done to stop this terrible vilification?"

"I'm afraid not," was the response.

"Why don't they get together and go out and have a drink?"

"They did," said the first senator. "That's how the whole damn thing started."

★

Senator Charles Sumner of Massachusetts was a supreme egotist. But he was punctured once during a rough debate when Senator Matthew Carpenter said: ". . . He identifies himself so completely with the universe that he is not at all certain whether he is part of the universe or the universe is part of him. He is a reviser of the decalogue. You will soon see the Sermon on the Mount revised, corrected, and greatly enlarged and improved by Senator Sumner."

★

John J. Ingalls represented Kansas in the Senate for many years during a period when that state was the butt of many Capitol Hill jokes. One day a Delaware senator made a typical derogatory remark about Kansas. Ingalls was on his feet in an instant and flashed back: "Mr. President, the senator who has just spoken represents a state which has two counties when the tide is up— and three counties when it is down."

★

The deadly Pitt made an attack on a colleague and denounced him, among other vicious accusations, as a fraudulent contractor. When Pitt's invective had run out and quiet prevailed in the House of Commons, the colleague rose and said: "The honorable gentleman is a great orator and has made a long and serious charge against me. I am no orator, and therefore I shall answer him in two words— Prove it!"

That was enough for Pitt and he folded amid a House full of snickers.

A man never knows in congressional debate when he will be stung badly by the opposition. He is always afraid that his "record" will be laid open in the fierce give-and-take that is part of many hot debates.

Once during an exchange on additional horses for the Army, a House member shouted at a colleague: "You cannot assail *my* record."

He was crushed when his opponent calmly replied: "I never go into such small matters."

★

The 1962 congressional session was rough and tough. It was an election year and many of the legislators were itching to get out of Washington and back to the home territory. A newsman approached Majority Leader Mike Mansfield and noted that a number of congressmen were praying for adjournment. "That's right," said Mansfield. "I'm one of them and if I pray any more I'm going to have housemaid's knee."

★

Senator Tom Corwin could cut a man in half with his tongue. A colleague found that out when he made some humorous though skin-piercing remarks about Corwin during a rough Senate debate.

Corwin's retort was deadly: "The senator thinks himself quite a wit," said Tom. "I'll just go far enough in reply to say he is half right."

★

The House of Representatives in New Hampshire, the largest legislative body in the United States, is jam-packed with members. One member whose seat was crowded near a window cried out during a debate: "If I'm not telling the truth on this bill, I hope lightning strikes me dead here and now."

"Better pull the shade," a wag cried from the other side of the chamber.

Debate over an appropriation for the Grand River in Michigan caused quite a stir on the floor of the Senate. William A. Smith, a Michigan senator, favored the appropriation, while Senator Theodore Burton of Ohio opposed the bill.

The debate became very heated as Burton insisted that there was no need for the appropriation. Finally Senator Smith said: "Well, you are the man for whom, when you were in the House of Representatives, we gave a dinner in Grand Rapids and you came back to Washington and introduced the first appropriation bill for the river."

"Yes," said Burton, "I know that is so. You gave me a dinner there and after the dinner, I saw water where there was no water; but I'm sober now. I have reformed, and I am against this appropriation."

★

One senator's observation of his colleagues goes like this: "Those who know but little of government finances talk a great deal. Those who know a great deal talk but little, and those who know all about it do not talk at all."

★

It was filibuster season on Capitol Hill and a Southern Democrat was holding sway over the Senate. When someone tried to stop him, the senator bellowed indignantly: "According to the Constitution, I've got a right to talk."

"I know it," was the weary response, "but the United States has a constitution that can stand it—mine can't."

★

When James Buchanan was a member of the U. S. Senate, many years before his rise to the presidency, he often tangled with Henry Clay. One day the debate centered on Buchanan's alleged disloyalty during the War of 1812. To prove his loyalty, Buchanan stated that he had entered a company of volunteers at the time of the Battle of North Point and marched to Baltimore. "True," he said, "I was not in any engagement, as the British had retreated before my company got there."

"You marched to Baltimore, though?" Clay asked.

"Yes, sir, I did," Buchanan shot back.

"Armed and equipped?" Clay continued.

"Yes," said Buchanan, "armed and equipped."

"But the British had retreated when you arrived?"

"Yes."

"Will you be good enough to inform this Senate," demanded Clay, "whether the British retreated in consequence to your valiantly marching to the relief of Baltimore, or whether you marched to the relief of Baltimore in consequence of the British having already retreated?"

That was too much for Buchanan and he was quiet for the remainder of the session.

★

Two angry senators were dealing rapid-fire insults at each other during the debate on Kansas lands. Finally, in exasperation, one senator shouted: "I see the villain in your face on this measure."

It was a perfect setup for his adversary to reply: "It must be the personal reflection of my colleague."

★

Two senators were talking about a contrary colleague. "He's a mean SOB," said one of them. "He sure is," was the response. "If he goes to heaven when he dies, he won't even like God."

★

An Irish orator gave a volcanic speech before Parliament. It was a passionate, fervid performance which went on for four hours and drew from the Irishman every ounce of his physical strength as he bombed and blasted, cried and laughed, and went into every known physical exercise to make his points.

After the speech someone asked Lord Palmerston for a comment, and the old fellow commented: "It was a speech long to be remembered by all who *saw* it."

★

Daniel O'Connell, the great Irish liberator, was a brilliant and devastating debater. Once during a debate in the British Parliament he engaged Benjamin Disraeli (no slouch himself) in a war of words. Firing all guns, O'Connell said that Disraeli was not fit to wheel dung from a dunghill.

The presiding officer called O'Connell to order and told him to apologize for the unfortunate remark. O'Connell stuck his hand in his breast and with a calm exterior said: "I certainly owe the honorable member an apology. I said he was *not* fit to wheel dung from a dunghill. I apologize. He *is* fit."

The House of Commons was convulsed with laughter and the apology was allowed to stand.

Sir Stafford Cripps, the British Laborite, was a haughty, pontifical man and often a thorn in Winston Churchill's side. Once as Cripps passed him in Parliament, Churchill said to a friend: "There but for the grace of God goes God."

A tedious senator had appeared before the Senate Foreign Relations Committee with a long, complicated, and foggy speech about America's foreign policy. Following the tiring dissertation, one of the committee members was asked about the effectiveness of the speech. "I'll tell you this," said the tired senator. "He would have made a hell of a lot better impression if he had read it backwards."

During debate on the swollen national budget, a member of the House Ways and Means Committee, wearied from floor amendments offered by pork-barrel senators, commented: "There is only one part of government finance the members of this Senate understand—disbursement."

Whenever a legislator is controlled by a lobbyist or has given his word on a vote to the governor, business, or labor interests, a favorite Massachusetts State House expression is that "He's in the tank."

A wishy-washy House member was forever telling his colleagues at the Republican caucus that he couldn't go along on every bill that came up, for he had promised his vote. The situation got so bad a colleague said: "G—— has been in the tank so often he's growing duck feathers."

*

Tom Reed of Maine was one of the wittiest of all congressmen. When a colleague had used up twenty minutes in useless oratory, Reed commented: "My friend across the chamber does not understand the theory of a five-minute debate. The object is to convey to the House, in a space of five minutes, either information or misinformation. You have consumed several periods of five minutes this afternoon without doing either."

*

Winston Churchill and Lady Astor became embroiled in a debate over farming. As the issue dragged on, Churchill, anxious to move to another matter, said: "I venture to say that my Right Honorable friend, so redolent of other knowledge, knows nothing about farming. I'll even make a bet that she doesn't know how many toes a pig has!"

"Oh yes, I do," quipped the irrepressible Lady Astor. "Take off your little shoesies and have a look!"

That finished Churchill for the day.

*

The chairman of a House committee had occasion on one day during a hearing to reprimand a witness for continually veering off the subject and finding fault with the conduct of the hearing. "Are you the chairman of this committee?" demanded the House member.

"No, sir; of course not," answered the witness.

"Well, then," thundered the congressman, "don't talk like a fool."

The eighth Duke of Devonshire once told some friends: "The other night I dreamed that I was addressing the House of Lords. Then I woke up and, by God, I was!"

*

Louisiana Senator Huey Long rose one day in the Senate and asked the chair: "How should a senator who is half in favor of the bill and half against it cast his vote?"

That was too much for Vice-President John Nance Garner, who was presiding and had become fed up with Long's tactics. He stopped Huey cold by stating: "Get a saw and saw yourself in two. That's what you ought to do anyhow."

*

When Winston Churchill first went to the House of Commons, he brushed against Lord Charles Beresford, a doughty former Navy man who could hold his own in any debate. Lord Charles commented, during a set-to with Churchill on a Navy question, that he was commanding one of His Majesty's ships when Churchill was doing his best at the business end of a feeding bottle.

A while later, during another encounter on an important issue, Churchill retaliated with the following: "When my right honorable friend Lord Charles rose to his feet, he had not the least idea what he was going to say. Moreover, he did not know what he was saying when he was speaking. And when he sat down, he was doubtless unable to remember what he had said."

*

For better or worse, congressmen try to abide by the Ten Commandments. However, there is a sort of Eleventh Commandment, which all understand and many try to live by. Where it came from is not known, but it directs that "Thou shalt not demagogue with thy colleagues."

*

Lyndon Johnson had a mile-high ego. One day while he was riding high as Senate Majority Leader, several disgruntled aides were leaving his office just after he had dressed them down. One of the aides said: "You know, sometimes I wish Johnson was the Pope instead of the Majority Leader."

"But why?" asked one of the group.

"Because," came the reply, "then we'd only have to kiss his ring."

★

A corridor joke had a visitor asking Lyndon Johnson if he had been born in a log cabin?

"No, you're thinking of Lincoln," LBJ was supposed to have said. "*He* was born in a log cabin. I was born in a manger."

★

On another occasion when Majority Leader Johnson was limping around the office with a sore toe, an aide passed along this gem: "LBJ went for a walk last night and was hit by a motorboat."

★

"Some people," said an observant newsman, "run for a seat in the House, and when they get there never sit in their seats."

★

A booming orator waddled into the House cloakroom late one afternoon and remarked to a colleague: "Did you notice how my voice filled the House chamber this afternoon?"

"Most certainly," responded his colleague, "and did you notice how a lot of the members left the chamber to make room for it?"

★

Tired of listening to personal-puff statements about the physical and mental strain congressmen say they are subjected to, a weary newsman stated: "The only pressure on these birds is on their consciences."

10

No Mutiny on
the Public Bounty

Any President, governor, or mayor will admit that office-seekers give them more trouble than any state or local problem. A persistent individual, determined to get himself an office, can all but shatter the nerves of the strongest man who ever lived. If there were a single prayer permitted a chief executive, it would be simply this: "Please, God, deliver me from the office-seekers."

Stooped and bent by the awful disasters of the Civil War, President Lincoln nevertheless was compelled to spend a great deal of his valuable time listening to aspirants for all sorts of government jobs. Honest Abe cried out for relief from this terrible burden, declaring: "This struggle and scramble for office, for a way to live without work, will finally test the strength of our institutions."

The best story of Lincoln's headaches with office-seekers concerned a friend who met him one day and expressed anxiety about the President's obvious depression. "What is wrong, Mr. President," he asked, "has something gone wrong at the front?"

"No," responded Lincoln wearily, "it isn't the war; it's the post office in Brownsville, Pennsylvania."

Charges of nepotism flared up shortly after President Kennedy appointed his brother-in-law, Sargent Shriver, as the first head of the Peace Corps in 1961. In explaining the appointment Shriver said that the President had been warned by everyone that the project would be a resounding flop. "That being the case," said Shriver, "it would be easier to fire a relative than a friend."

*

After a few terms in public office, the elected official becomes pretty cynical about the favors he does for his constituents. He understands that, with some exceptions, nothing he does is ever enough.

Senator Alben W. Barkley loved to tell the story about a man he had helped on a number of occasions. Every time Barkley returned to his home state office, the man was sitting waiting for him with another request for a favor. Finally Barkley said: "You're here again for another favor. For heaven's sake, I've done dozens of favors for you already."

"I know," said the constituent, "but, Senator, you haven't done anything for me lately."

Another politician summed up favor-doing with this comment: "I don't know why Jones is mad at me. I've never done him a favor."

Still another gem of cynicism was this from a harassed office-holder: "When you do a man a favor, he really never forgives you."

*

A weary congressman made this observation of his obligations to relatives: "In politics, if a man has relatives, he can be certain they will never ask him for favors—they ask him for miracles."

*

Mark Twain once said: "Of course President Grant will remember me. I was the person who *did not* ask him for an office."

In every language in every country, the theme is always the same: Politics is politics. Public appointments are often made without regard to ability or qualifications.

Many years ago a British Prime Minister wanted to give a close friend named Casey an appointment which was supposed to be filled by a lawyer. Casey was not a lawyer, but by a little string-pulling, the Prime Minister got another friend appointed as a special examiner to quiz Casey on his knowledge of the law.

"Now, Mr. Casey," said the examiner, "what do you know about the law?"

"To tell you the truth, sir," replied Casey, "I do not know a single thing about the law."

The examiner reported to the Prime Minister that he had duly examined Mr. Casey, "as to his knowledge of the law, and to the best of my knowledge and belief he answered correctly the question put to him."

Mr. Casey got the position.

*

A bitter struggle for a school superintendency ended in a Rhode Island city with one of the candidates receiving five votes and the job. With only nine votes on the committee it was a tight squeeze.

A supporter of the loser approached the chairman of the school committee and demanded to know what qualifications the winner had that entitled him to the job. "He had the best qualifications in the world," said the chairman with finality, "five votes!"

*

A local Massachusetts judge had passed away, and support was generated for a certain lawyer to replace the deceased. When inquiries were made by the governor's office as to the character of the applicant, a townsman offered this recommendation:

"For twelve years we have been holding cockfights behind Sam Crosby's barn. Lawyer Blake has judged every one of these cockfights. His impartiality and fairness have been such that we feel that if he can do a good honest job judging cockfights, he ought to be able to judge human fights, which ain't nearly so complicated."

Needless to say, Lawyer Blake was not appointed.

★

A freshman congressman moved into a seat beside a colleague and said: "I am sorry to read that the *Post* editor is giving you such a hard time over that appointment the President is scheduled to give you. If I were you I'd throw the book at him."

"Well, I'll tell you, son," responded the veteran, "I learned a lesson long ago about throwing books. One night I was on my way home and I mistook a skunk for a rabbit and threw a book at him. I received in return a copious charge of unmistakable character and I had to bury my clothes, my shoes, and the book in order to make myself presentable.

"Right then and there I made up my mind never to throw a book at another skunk."

★

For all his outgoing ways, President Theodore Roosevelt started to chafe under the burdens put upon him by persistent office-seekers. Once at a ship launching, a friend remarked to the President: "You don't get much time for hunting now, do you, Mr. President?"

"No," said Roosevelt. "The fact is, I am sort of a gamekeeper now, watching the Government preserves while hordes of poachers are trying to break in and bag the offices."

★

A certain Rhode Island state senator was forever pressing his governor for patronage appointments for his constituents. It exasperated the chief executive to the point that he would quickly shift the senator off to a department head or whoever was in charge. His ongoing expression was: "Talk to Bill Jones. He's a sharp guy." The next time he would tell the senator: "Talk to Sam Gross. He's a very sharp guy," and on it would go.

One day the senator visited the governor with his usual request for a patronage job for a friend. The governor gave him the same old treatment: "Why don't you go down and see Charlie Powers? He's a very sharp guy."

As he reached the door, the senator looked back at the governor and responded: "Damn it, Governor, I'm sick of seeing these sharp guys. When are you going to send me to see somebody I can overwhelm?"

★

Following his election as mayor of New York, Fiorello La Guardia promptly disposed of office-seekers. He called his entire campaign force together and said in a very few sentences that a cause and not a man had been elected.

"My first qualification for this office," said the Little Flower as he wound up his speech, "is my monumental ingratitude."

★

A woman once approached President Lincoln, demanding a colonel's commission for her son. When the President hesitated, she insisted. "Sir," she said, "I demand it, not as a favor, but as a right. Sir, my grandfather fought at Lexington. Sir, my uncle was the only man who did not run away at Bladensburg. Sir, my father fought at New Orleans and my husband was killed at Monterey."

"I guess, madam," answered Mr. Lincoln dryly, "your family has done enough for the country. It is time to give somebody else a chance."

★

A small-town politician had been pressing President Theodore Roosevelt for an appointment as Receiver of Customs. A friend met him and asked how he had made out with the Chief Executive.

"Well, I can't really say," said the appointment-seeker. "I could get no satisfaction from him. One minute he would make me think everything was all right, and the next minute he would say something that would crush my hopes. It was like plunging from a hot bath into a cold one, and since the interview I've contracted an optimistic appetite and a pessimistic digestion."

Disraeli disposed of a persistent applicant for a baronetcy in the following manner: "You know, sir, I cannot for many reasons give you a baronetcy." Then, putting his arm around the title-seeker, Disraeli smiled and said: "But you can tell your friends I offered you a baronetcy and that you refused it. That will be far better."

★

There is an old saying in politics that nobody ever gets rid of anything that can vote. Once a person is put in a patronage job, regardless of any condition, that job is seldom abolished. Proof of this was contained in the story of an attendant who had been standing at the foot of the stairs in the House of Commons for twenty years and nobody seemed to know why he was there. Finally someone checked into the matter and found out that the job had been in the man's family for three generations. It had originated forty-five years earlier, when the stairs had been newly painted and the man's grandfather had been assigned to warn the people not to step on the wet paint.

★

The governor of an Eastern state had been discussing some names for certain appointments he was to make. The conversation got around to a political pro who was pressuring for one of the jobs. "I wouldn't appoint him," warned one of the governor's advisers. "That guy takes money."

"I know he'll take money," interrupted the governor, "but what I'd rather know about him, is he honest?"

★

When Al Smith was serving as president of the New York City Board of Aldermen, a former schoolmate cornered him for a job as elevator starter in City Hall.

"That job is covered by Civil Service," said Smith, "and there's a tough examination involved."

"Examinations in what?"

"Hydraulics, for one thing, and a lot of other things you probably don't know anything about."

"Now look here, Al," was the hurt response, "save that baloney for the Italians and the Poles. Remember, I went to school with *you*."

★

An English public servant came to America to study the system of military pensions in this country. When he noted how liberal it was compared to that of Great Britain, he said: "If England had a system of military pensions like yours, all that would be left of the Noble 600 would be six thousand pensioners."

★

When advised that the governor had appointed a longtime political enemy of his, a senator commented dryly: "Well, I see the governor shook the plum tree again, and out dropped another lemon."

★

When George Romney was governor of Michigan, the news was getting around that he would be a good candidate for the presidency. In laughing it off Romney said: "Each of my Mormon grandfathers had four wives and therefore I have 231 cousins. I couldn't possibly find jobs in Washington for all of them."

★

During his first term President Grover Cleveland held off appointing a certain politico as a postmaster. When Cleveland was re-elected, the job-seeking politician sent a flowery telegram of congratulations. President Cleveland replied: "Your application for the postmastership has been duly filed."

★

Boston Democrats are known far and wide as get-even politicians. "We never get mad," said one of them. "We just get even." This was proved when a voter sought out a tough old officeholder and asked for his support for a job. He had opposed the veteran in the previous election but now needed him.

"Will you help me get this appointment?" he asked the politician.

"You're my second choice," was the curt response.

"And who is your first choice?" asked the voter.

"Anybody else," was the devastating reply.

*

"The Democrats," said a crusty Republican, "are great believers in public relations. In fact, they have most of their relations working for the public."

*

The governor of a Northern state was pestered to the point of exhaustion by a certain individual seeking a patronage job. No matter where the governor went, the man popped up, pressing his request.

One day as the governor was leaving his State House office, he was nailed again by the office-seeker, pleading his cause. The exasperated chief executive tried to brush by him, saying: "Come back later."

Immediately the patronage hound responded: "When?"

"In about ten years," said the governor desperately.

"Morning or afternoon?" was the eager question.

*

A bitter legislative battle raged at the State House in Boston over who was to control the new state lottery. Republican Governor Frank Sargent fought to place the state lottery in the executive department. Treasurer Robert Crane, a Democrat, battled to place the lottery under his control. Crane won out on the override of the governor's veto, and all the patronage fell into Democratic hands.

As the lottery was set up, rumors spread that no Republicans would be considered for jobs. A Republican state senator regaled an audience of G.O.P. stalwarts with his story of trying to get a lottery job for a constituent. He told it like this:

"I went to the Democratic-controlled lottery commission office and asked the man at the desk for a job application. He treated me cordially, even rising from his desk and pointing down the hallway to a door marked 'Applications.' I opened the door and entered a large room on the other side of which were two doors, one marked 'male' and the other 'female.' Inasmuch as I wanted the job for a male constituent, I opened the door marked 'male' and found myself in another room. On the other side of the room were two more doors. One was marked 'Democrat' and the other 'Republican.'

"Feeling that the rumor that there were no jobs for Republicans was a lot of propaganda, I hurried happily across the room and opened the door marked 'Republican.' You know something, I found myself out on the street again."

★

President Lincoln had many responses for the hordes of office-seekers who pestered him at every turn. Old Abe told an associate: "I have discovered a good way of providing offices for this government: put all the names of applicants into one pepper box and all the offices in another, and then shake the two, and make appointments just as the names and the offices happen to drop out together."

★

"There are no dusty roads in the vicinity of Washington," observed Senator Tom Corwin, "for the reason they are kept wet down by the tears of the disappointed office-seekers who come and go by the thousands."

★

Years ago when lobbyists were crawling over the Texas State House like ants, a newly elected legislator visited a battle-worn veteran and inquired: "Every day some lobbyist comes tempting me with money. What shall I do?"

"Be firm, resist them," warned the veteran, "and you'll get your reward in heaven."

A few weeks later the same young legislator complained to his colleague again: "I don't know what to do," he wailed. "These lobbyists are persistent. They say they will offer me anything if I support their bills."

The old-timer patted the worried youngster and replied: "All I can tell you, son, is to resist them, and you'll get your reward in heaven."

"I know," pleaded the young House member, "you told me that before, but I don't know how long I can resist. And by the way, sir, if I do resist, what do you think my reward will be in heaven?"

Looking the young man straight in the eye, the other growled: "A bale of hay, you jackass."

★

A partisan state senator approached his governor pressing for a patronage appointment for a constituent. When the governor heard the name, he hissed: "Why, that guy is a no good ornery son-of-a-bitch."

"I know," responded the senator, "but, Governor, he's one of our own."

★

There was a time in an Eastern state legislature when it seemed that there was a price tag on every piece of legislation of any importance. One day a lobbyist visited the House leader and declared that he would like to see his favorite bill enacted into law, adding that if money were needed, he'd take care of it.

"Now look here," snapped the seemingly indignant leader. "We're going to look that bill over carefully to see if it has any merit. And I want you to know that the last thing we think of in here is money." Then after a short pause he added: "That is until just before we make a decision on whether or not to report the bill favorably."

★

As the Democrats grabbed additional seats in the national House and the liberals among them started pushing for more and more social programs costing millions of dollars, a reporter asked Minority Leader Joe Martin why the Democrats were gaining so many congressional seats.

Old Joe grunted a simple response: "How the hell are you going to beat Santa Claus?"

★

Following his appointment as Secretary of Agriculture in the Roosevelt administration, Henry Wallace was at his desk before eight o'clock in the morning.

On the third day as he began working, a scrubwoman, unaware of his presence, came in with her bucket and engaged herself in the process of mopping the floor.

Presently, Wallace coughed and the woman looked up.

"Who are you?" she asked.

"I'm the new Secretary of Agriculture," said Wallace.

"Well, I'll be . . ." sighed the scrubwoman. "I've been working in this office for twenty years and this is the first time any Secretary of Agriculture ever got in here early enough for me to see him."

★

President Benjamin Harrison had been very kind to his relatives and had appointed a great many of them to public positions. This had disturbed a Westerner who visited the White House and wanted to talk to the President about it.

"I want to see the President," the Westerner demanded of the secretary.

"You can't," said the secretary.

"Why not?" puffed the Westerner.

"He's tied up for a couple of hours with the Committee on Foreign Relations."

"Good God!" exclaimed the Westerner. "Has he got foreign relations too?"

11

The Constituents
Always Write

Sooner or later every congressman gets his come-uppance from one of his constituents. It happened to Representative Keith Sebelius, whose office sent out several blank sheets of paper instead of his monthly news letter. A lady constituent wrote back: "This was the only newsletter I have received from you that I really understood."

*

A man wrote his congressman that he'd like to be an inventor but didn't want to waste his time on things already invented. "Will you please go down to the patent office," the letter read, "and get me a list of things that haven't been invented. Get me the answers by return mail as I am anxious to get to work."

*

When he was United States senator from New York, Bobby Kennedy received scores of letters about his family. One which he always mentioned was from a lady who observed: "I think it is terrific that you have nine kids and you still smile."

Vice-President Spiro Agnew received his share of correspondence praising and condemning him. Agnew's efforts on the sports scene brought this humorous letter from a youngster: "Dear Mr. Vice President, I saw pictures of you playing tennis. I think you ought to try bowling."

★

Pleased with his voting record in Congress, a new lawmaker sent out a proud announcement to his constituents declaring that he had a record of perfect attendance and had voted on all matters before the House.

A few days later he received a letter from a disgruntled voter who apparently didn't appreciate the effort. The letter read: "So you didn't miss a session or a vote in Congress. Well, I have looked over your record and how you voted and I wouldn't have cared if you *had* missed a few."

★

Whenever a legislative body raises its pay, all hell breaks loose among the taxpayers, with the flames generally fed by the newspapers. During the Forty-second Congress the members raised their pay. A storm broke across the country, and it became so bad that many members turned back the extra money.

Ben Butler, the controversial congressman from Massachusetts, took his share of the storm of protest. When a letter came from a constituent raging at Butler for voting a pay raise, Old Ben replied in kind. He told the voter that he had figured out that the pay increase would amount to about two cents a man, and if the constituent would write him a letter enclosing four cents postage, he would return to him his share of the so-called salary grab.

★

Congressman Clem Zablocki told of a colleague who wrote to a critic: "Dear Sir: This is to warn you that some crackpot is writing idiotic letters and signing your name."

Back from a speechmaking tour, the lawmaker got a letter from the same critic: "Dear Sir: This is to advise you that some crackpot was here in my town giving idiotic speeches and using your name."

★

Senator George Vest was one of the best platform speakers of his time. He was also a controversial figure who was often obliged to defend his votes and actions on the campaign trail. Entering a hall one night to speak to a hostile audience, Vest was approached by a man who slipped him a note. When the senator opened it, he found written a single word: "Fool."

When it was his turn to speak, Vest held up the note explaining how he had gotten it and that it contained a single word: "Fool."

"I have known instances of a man writing a note and failing to sign his name," said Vest with a sly wink, "but this is the first time I have ever known of a man signing a note and failing to write down what is bothering him."

★

Congressman Joe Martin had a favorite story concerning a letter written by a young lady to her lover. It read:

"Dear John: Words cannot express how much I regret having broken off our engagement. Will you please come back to me? Your absence leaves a space no one can fill. Please forgive me and let us start all over again. I cannot live without you. I do not sleep. I love you, I love you, I love you. (Signed) Yours eternally, Jane.

P.S. By the way, congratulations on your winning the Irish Sweepstakes."

★

Replying to rough letters is always a harrowing task in any congressman's office. However, one Pennsylvania legislator came up with this answer to a crackpot letter:

"Sir, my stenographer, being a lady, cannot type what I think of you. I, being a gentleman, cannot say it. You, being neither, will understand what I mean."

One of Congressman Joe Martin's "letters to Washington stories" involved the Fish and Wildlife Service. This agency banded birds with metal strips inscribed "Notify Fish and Wildlife Service, Washington, D.C." The bands formerly read, "Notify Washington Biological Survey," abbreviated to "Wash. Biol. Surv."

"Well," said Joe, "they changed the whole thing when a farmer shot a crow and then in disgust wrote to the Government the following letter:

" 'Dear Sirs: I shot one of your pet crows the other day and followed instructions attached to it. I washed it and boiled it and surved it. It was turrible. You should stop trying to fool the people with things like that . . .' "

★

One of the best responses to a nasty letter ever recorded was devised by Senator Henry Ashurst of Arizona several years ago. This was the letter to Ashurst:

> Dear Senator:
> I think you are an ass.

Replied Ashurst in the next mail:

> You may be right.
> Fraternally yours,
> Senator Ashurst

★

President Harry Truman announced that he was getting rid of several government bureaus. This prompted a lady to write to the President, stating that she was building a new house and needed some new furniture and would be thankful for a few of the discarded bureaus. In a quick response Truman told the lady that he had disposed of the bureaus, but that if she was interested, he had a secondhand, no-damned-good cabinet he'd like to get rid of.

★

Senator Everett Dirksen smiled and laughed his way through many rough days in the political arena. One of his prize letters concerned the presidential race in 1952, when he was considered a dark horse for the presidency. The letter was as follows:

"Dear Senator Dirksen: Why do they call you a dark horse? I saw your picture and you're not dark at all and you don't even look like a horse."

★

A Far Western congressman, who had neglected his home district for some time because of social activities in Washington, started to get worried about how the people felt. He wrote to his campaign manager and asked him to take a poll of the district to find out if he was still the fair-haired boy.

A letter came back from the manager: "Dear Bill, We have been taking the poll as instructed. I will personally state that 98% of the voters are still with you—but it's a strange thing, our pollsters keeping running into the other 2%."

★

Abraham Lincoln once received a letter asking for a "sentiment" and his autograph. He replied: "Dear Madam, When you ask a stranger for that which is of interest only to yourself, always enclose a stamp."

★

Representative Charles L. Weltner of Georgia received a letter from an irate businessman in which the gentleman proceeded to berate Weltner's ability, comprehension, and intelligence, among other things. He was against everything Weltner had ever voted for, and concluded with a vow to "devote all my time during the remainder of your term in Congress to making sure it's your last in public office."

The businessman then signed his name, and as usual to the left were his initials and his secretary's. Typed in at the bottom, however, were these words: "I have to type this stuff, but I don't have to believe it. I think you're great!"

The secretary's initials followed.

During some trouble at a New Jersey state mental hospital, one of the state senators received a letter from an inmate which read: "Please get me out of this damn place. They're driving me nuts."

★

A Massachusetts state senator received the following letter from a lady in his district: "Dear Senator, I am to be the speaker at my club next Thursday and I am going to talk on government. I know the highest officer we have is the governor. Then comes the lieutenant governor, the attorney general, the treasurer, the auditor and the secretary of state. Next on down are the senators. But right here I am stuck. So will you kindly let me know by return mail, is there anything *lower* than a senator?"

★

Former Senator Leverett Saltonstall was governor of Massachusetts during World War II. Because of wartime restrictions there was little that could be done to repair roads, many of which were in bad shape. One day the governor received a letter from an irate constituent condemning the road situation in this manner: "Dear Governor, the roads are so bad that you ought to be thrown out of office. My wife boarded a bus for Pittsfield. Before the bus had gone six miles it slammed into a huge pot hole in the road, throwing my wife against the front of the bus with such force that she gave premature birth to an eight-pound male child, for which I hold *you* personally responsible."

★

As Vice-President, Richard Nixon became deeply involved in foreign policy and foreign affairs. He once received a letter from a worried constituent who said: "I read in the papers every day that you are involved in foreign affairs. A man in your position should know better and it is surprising that Mrs. Nixon has not divorced you."

★

Congressman Frank Becker once received a letter from a lady constituent asking: "Dear Congressman, Am I entitled to a military pension. I ain't a veteran, but I lived with a couple of soldiers during the war."

★

Governor Foster Furcolo of Massachusetts received a check in the mail from a conscience-stricken taxpayer, and with it a letter which read: "I can't sleep nights, so I am sending a check for five hundred dollars for taxes I have owed the state since 1953."

There was a postscript to the letter: "And if I still can't sleep nights, I'll send you the balance."

★

The Department of Internal Revenue received a typed income tax return from a bachelor who listed one dependent son. The examiner returned the blank with a penciled notation: "This must be a stenographic error."

The blank came back in the next mail with this notation: "You're telling me!"

★

Every so often a member of Congress rises in his place in the House chamber and blasts away at government extravagance. One afternoon a House member severely criticized the Department of Agriculture for its free and easy way with the taxpayers' money, pointing out that hundreds of pamphlets were being printed in which the public had not the slightest interest.

During his tirade he held aloft several pamphlets such as "The Recreational Resources of the Denison Dam," "The Wolves of Mount McKinley," "The Ecology of the Coyote," and "The Habits of Woodchucks." "Why, Mr. Speaker," he shouted, "they print everything about nature but the love life of the frog."

The newspapers dutifully reported the congressman's speech. Shortly thereafter the Department of Agriculture was surprised to find in the mail five or six letters from congressmen asking for copies of "The Love Life of the Frog." Similar orders kept coming in so regularly that the department was forced to state in a circular. "We do NOT print 'The Love Life of the Frog.'" After the public announcement was made, requests for "The Love Life" were trebled. It got to be such a headache that the department finally issued a press release stating that it had never printed a pamphlet about the love life of the frog and wanted to hear no more about the matter.

When the news item was published, requests began to climb into the hundreds. By now the matter had got out of hand and the Secretary of Agriculture himself was called in. Determined to stop the foolishness once and for all, he took time during an address on the air to deny vehemently that the department had ever prepared any pamphlet concerning the love life of the frog, that to his knowledge there never was such a pamphlet, and even if there had been the department wouldn't have printed it.

After the broadcast there were more than a thousand requests in the mail for the pamphlet "The Love Life of the Frog."

★

An Illinois state senator received a strong letter from a constituent complaining that the local school department had given her son a test and had classified him as "illiterate." The letter read: "Dear Senator: I am terribly annoyed that the school department has branded my son as illiterate. That is a damn lie as I was married a week before he was born."

★

With the mobility of present-day Americans and the ease with which a husband or wife can disappear, a new type of letter shows up in congressional offices, the so-called missing person letter. Congressmen who represent urban communities get lots of "find my husband" or "find my wife" letters.

One letter received by a New York City congressman read: "Please find out for certain if my husband is dead. The guy I am now living with can't eat, sleep or do anything until he knows."

★

For a number of years Congressman Thomas C. Abernethy of Mississippi sent "Infant Care" booklets to constituents from lists compiled by the State Bureau of Vital Statistics.

In response to one of his mailings, Abernethy received a letter stating: "Dear Congressman: I received your letter and also the book about me having a baby. There was a woman down the street here what had a baby. They are trying to pin it on my husband, John. He say it ain't so. But I don't know. Now the news is all the way to Washington."

★

The cynicism that permeates politics was never more evident than in a story about a politician who obtained a job for a constituent. In a few months the officeholder received a letter from the constituent requesting a promotion. Promptly the politician obtained the promotion.

Not content, the constituent then bugged the politician for a transfer to a better-paying job. This was also done. Then came another letter requesting an upgrading. This too was accomplished, although the politician was becoming a bit weary.

A few months later a letter arrived at the politician's office in which the same pesty constituent reminded the pol that the department head was retiring and he would like the job. After lots of maneuvering the job was secured.

When the politician notified the constituent that the big job was his, all he got in reply was a simple: "Thanks, Joe."

"For God's sake," cried the exasperated politician into the phone, "I've been through hell for you for four years, getting you promotions, transfers, upgradings, and what not, and now the department head's job. Is that all you can say, 'Thanks, Joe'?"

There was an ominous silence on the other end of the phone, and then the constituent responded: "Well, Joe, thanks a lot."

★

The chairman of the Social Welfare Committee of the Massachusetts legislature wrote a speech on the evils of public welfare and how it was contributing to creating broken homes. The legislator delivered his speech at many women's clubs, and one day he received a letter from a constituent which read:

"Sir, my wife was all ready to divorce me. Now she tells me she listened to your talk about the evils of broken homes. She tells me also that no matter what, she is going to stick with me through thick and thin. You convinced her. And so let me tell you something, mister. You'll never get my vote again."

★

Officeholders never know what the mail will bring. Senator Dennis Chavez once opened a letter which said simply: "Dear Senator Chavez, In how many states is Sex illegal?"

★

Congressman Dan E. Garrett of Texas had received fifteen applications for pea seeds from one of his constituents. He complied with each request, but when the sixteenth application came in, he sent the package of seeds along with the following letter:

"I am sending you the seeds, but what in Heaven's name are you doing with so much seed? Are you planting the whole State of Texas with peas?"

"No," came the answer. "We are not planting them at all. We are using them for soup."

★

Over the years the heavy use of the automobile has jeopardized public transit systems. This, combined with incompetence, political interference, union demands, and antiquated equipment, often results in rocky and uncertain public transportation.

A disgusted citizen wrote to the Massachusetts Bay Transportation Authority in Boston, complaining that the service was getting worse each day, "even worse," he wrote, "than that enjoyed by the people 2000 years ago."

The letter reached the general manager, who in a moment of pique wrote the commuter reminding him that he was confused in his history, that the only transportation available two thousand years before was by foot.

In due time, the manager was stopped in his tracks by a second letter, which read: "You are the ones confused in your history. If you read the Bible, you will find in the Book of David, 9th verse: 'Aaron rode into town on his ass.' That, gentlemen, is something I have been unable to do on your damn trains with any certainty for the last six or seven months."

12

The Care and Feeding of Politicians

Every politician has four after-dinner speeches. First is the speech he prepares in advance. That one is pretty good. Second is the speech he really makes. Third is the speech he delivers to his wife on the way home, which is a beauty and best of all. Fourth is the speech the newspapers next morning say he delivered, which bears no resemblance to any of the others.

For forty years Congressman Joe Martin of Massachusetts battled the rubber-chicken and bullet-bean circuit, up and down and across the United States. Homespun Joe had seen and heard it all. Often he humorously described a political dinner as, "an array of cold mashed potatoes, withered peas, wrinkled olives, stringy celery and rubber chicken, completely surrounded by stale speakers and moldy jokes." Joe also had a few words for the rostrum riders. "I never did mind," said Martin, "when a fellow said he was not much of a speechmaker. What bothered me was the damn time he spent proving it."

In the southeastern Massachusetts district that Joe Martin represented in Congress, summer clambakes were the weekly fare of almost every fraternal, ethnic, political, veteran, and church organization. Politicians were expected to attend these clambakes and join in the gorging of enormous quantities of corn, potatoes, sausage, brown bread, onions, watermelon, fish, lobster, and clams. When the bake was over, the tables looked like huge garbage pails, with their stacks of clamshells, lobster claws, corn cobs, watermelon rind, and other leftovers.

"With the clambakers waddling about," said Martin, "rubbing their stomachs and burping in gastronomic satisfaction, it was expected that the politicians then earn their free tickets with a flight or two of oratory.

"It was damned hard going," continued Joe, "trying to convince those overfed citizens in front of you that all was not well with America. Well-fed voters are not mad at anybody, and no calamity-howler who ever lived could rouse a clambake crowd to be for anything but a grassy knoll under a shady tree to sleep it off."

Every politician wants to spice his after-dinner speeches with humor, whether or not he has an ounce of wit in his system. No speech is worth its salt unless it contains a few choice witticisms or humorous barbs. "It's all well and good," said an expensive presidential speech-writer, "until we find ourselves in the ridiculous position of spending more time digging up after-dinner jokes than in digging up facts about the state of the nation."

"After-dinner speaking is not an easy task," said a veteran of the circuit. "You turn a speech over in your mind before dinner and when you stand up, the damn thing turns over in the pit of your stomach."

Winston Churchill offered advice on about everything including banquet speakers. "Say what you have to say, and the first time you come to a sentence with a grammatical ending, sit down," was the way he put it.

Chauncey Depew put it another way when he advised rising young banquet speakers: "When you finish speaking it is a good idea to stop talking." When a pompous congressman asked a Chicago toastmaster how long he should speak, he was told: "There is no limit upon the time you may speak, but may I tell you that nobody in this hall will believe you can say a damn thing that will save this country after the first ten minutes."

Like all public figures, Abraham Lincoln became weary of the continuous round of Washington dinners and social functions. He laughingly referred to banquet orators as "persons who stand at the rostrum, fill their chests, throw back their heads, glaze their eyes, open their mouths and leave the rest to God."

At the height of his fame as an inventor, Thomas A. Edison bored to death as the long-range orators poured out the verbiage, complimenting the genius for his invention of the talking machine. One night, as a particularly long-winded politician praised Edison almost beyond human endurance, old Tom turned to a table companion and whispered: "Well, at least I am glad I invented a talking machine that can be shut off."

When Calvin Coolidge was governor of Massachusetts, he received an invitation to speak at the annual dinner of a well-known Vermont organization. This was Coolidge's reply: "Dear Newt: Won't go. Don't care to make speeches. Nobody cares to hear them."

An Illinois minister was asked to give the invocation at a huge political dinner in Chicago. The clergyman looked up and down the head table and noted the several fat politicians readying their throats for the verbal onslaught.

The minister's prayer had covered about everything, when he intoned: "O Lord, be with the first speaker and give him the power to move this audience. And be with the second speaker and inspire him with thy spirit. And Lord have mercy on the last speaker!"

Congressman David Patterson Dyer of St. Louis was a tough foe of the Democrats and he passed up no chance to rock them with verbal insults.

Once, by a quirk, Dyer found himself assigned as toastmaster at a civic banquet where a long list of Democratic politicians was scheduled to speak.

Dyer began his introduction with: "Ladies and gentlemen, it is the duty of the toastmaster to be so stupidly dull that the main speakers will appear brilliant by contrast."

As the ripple of laughter from the speakers died down, Dyer shook his head and continued: "But, I have looked up and down

the head table at these Democratic officeholders, and I don't
think I can do it."

★

A nervous congressman asked a banquet-hardened veteran how
he managed to control the butterflies in his stomach when he got
up to speak.

"I take an aspirin," advised the senior congressman, "and the
butterflies go away."

"But," groaned the young legislator, "I tried that before my last
speech, and all during my talk, the damn butterflies were playing
Ping-Pong with the aspirin tablet."

★

It was a noisy hall and the politician was having a tough time
making himself heard. His jokes, right off the chestnut tree, were
not making much of an impression either. Suddenly from somewhere to the left a voice rose above the crowd: "Louder
. . . louder . . ."

"And funnier . . ." was the response from the rear.

★

Politicians become bleary-eyed attempting to follow the cocktail circuit. The hostess at a Washington cocktail party came
upon a congressman looking thoughtfully through his notebook.
"Ah," she said, "I bet you're checking on where you must go
next?"

"Not at all, madam," the tired congressman replied, "I'm just
trying to find out where I am now."

★

General Carlos Romulo, when he was a United Nations delegate, was asked one day what sort of a speech he intended to
deliver to a dinner that evening. "Well," said Romulo, "I have
two types. My Mother Hubbard speech is like an old woman's
garment—it covers everything and touches nothing. Then there's
my French bathing suit speech—it covers only the essential
points."

Will Rogers was to be the speaker at a huge Democratic dinner in California at which he was scheduled to be introduced by the governor of the state. The chief executive could not appear because of illness and sent the lieutenant governor as a substitute.

The lieutenant governor tried to poke some fun at Rogers and said that he would not try to make jokes, since the biggest joke in California was scheduled to follow him. He thought it would get a laugh but it failed. Then he continued: "Like all conceited actors, I see him whispering to his table companion now, instead of listening to me and trying to learn something."

Rogers mounted the rostrum and said: "First of all, ladies and gentlemen, I want to apologize. It is quite true that I was whispering to the lady next to me and I feel very bad about it. I am sorry. The reason it made such a disturbance was that I asked her a question. I asked her: 'Who is that man talking?' and she said she did not know. Then she turned to the lady next to her and asked her who he was, and—well, it had to go all the way down the aisle to the door. When they found out, it had to travel all the way back: 'Why, it's the lieutenant governor.'

"That sounds pretty big and when she told me: 'Oh, it's the lieutenant governor,' I said: 'What does he do?' Then the lady said: 'Oh, he don't do anything.' Then I said: 'He don't do anything? Don't he even get up in the morning?'

"'Oh yes,' she said, 'he gets up every morning and inquires whether the governor's any worse.'"

From that point on it was said that every time the lieutenant governor introduced a speaker, he confined it practically to name, rank, and serial number. He wanted no more embarrassing responses.

★

Governor Christian Herter of Massachusetts loved to tell the story of a call he received from the program chairman of a political club, asking him to speak at an upcoming dinner. "We are looking for a topnotch speaker," said the program chairman smoothly, "and we have decided on you."

"If I'm that good," said the governor jokingly, "I should charge you a fee for the speaking engagement."

There was a slight pause on the other end of the line. Then the chairman responded seriously: "Gee, Governor, we can't do that. We're giving you a free ticket, ain't we?"

★

Many years ago, the national Congress was a real hayseed outfit. Most of the members were from rural districts, uneducated, uninformed, and forever on the prowl for something free to eat and drink.

A large banquet at a Washington hotel drew a sizable crowd of farmer/congressmen. The tables were dazzling, but at several of them there were no decorations.

"Hey, you," said a congressman to the headwaiter, "why don't you put them things on our tables too?" pointing to the beautiful palm plants on the other tables.

The headwaiter did not know that the complainer was a congressman. "We can't do it, mister," he whispered confidentially. "They is mostly congressmen at these tables, and if we put palm plants on the tables they will take them for celery and eat them all up. They sure would, sir. We know them."

★

A friend stopped by Calvin Coolidge's office during his tenure as governor of Massachusetts. He told Cal that he had a short speech to deliver at an advertising club dinner and wanted Cal to look it over.

The governor glanced at the material and then said: "It's three pages too long."

Taken aback, the visitor pleaded: "But, the speech covers only three pages."

"That's what I said," replied Coolidge, looking at the clock.

★

Theodore E. Burton, for many years chairman of the Congressional Committee on Rivers and Harbors, often stated that the most effective way to get legislation through was not the committee meeting. He pointed out that the complimentary dinner at a swank hotel, attended by committee members, had a greater effect on legislation.

Said Congressman Burton: "I have myself attended dinners given by certain local interests, when at nine o'clock there was some doubt in the minds of the legislators as to whether a certain harbor should be widened and deepened at all.

"At ten o'clock, as the wine flowed, they had decided that a channel ten feet wide might reasonably be provided for. At eleven o'clock they had deepened it to twenty feet. When it got along to the hour of midnight they concluded that the channel should be forty feet deep and it was so decreed."

★

Senator Leverett Saltonstall of Massachusetts was a conservative Yankee. One night at a buffet supper in Washington, a careless waiter spilled something on the senator's knee. As he moved to rub the trouser leg, his supper partner commented: "That's good material; it won't spot badly."

"It should be good material," confided Saltonstall. "These pants belonged to my father."

★

An enemy is an enemy. When a politician stood up at a New York dinner and merely said: "Thank you," after being given an award, a dedicated enemy in the audience turned to a table companion and said: "I wonder who wrote that for him?"

★

When a veteran congressman had reached the forty-year mark as a member of the House of Representatives, his colleagues honored him with a dinner. A long array of speakers extolled and praised the white-haired lawmaker "as a public servant with a multitude of friends and not a single enemy."

After the dinner, a newspaperman went up to the congressman and said: "I fully agree that you have a multitude of friends, but I can't believe that anyone who has been as active as you in public life can't have a single enemy."

The old war-horse knitted his shaggy brow and said: "My friend, I have outlived all those SOB's."

★

Tennessee has sent some great characters to Washington to serve in Congress. Stories always came back of the activities of these unusual individuals. One of the great anecdotes concerned a real hillbilly who made it to the national capital. In no time flat he was invited to state dinners and other functions available to congressmen.

A bystander told the story of the Tennessean's adventures at one such affair: "The first course at a state dinner was consommé. The Hillbilly looked puzzled but consumed it. Someone passed him a bunch of hearts of celery. He ate it. Then the waiter put a choice broiled lobster in front of him. The Hillbilly pushed back from the table with a snort, shouting over his shoulder as he headed for the exit, 'I drank the dishwater, and I et the bouquet, but I'll be durned if I'm going to eat that dang bug.' "

★

Senator Robert Kennedy was one of the speakers at a luncheon for Jewish philanthropies. He was scheduled to speak after the eloquent lawyer Louis Nizer. Describing how he felt on the occasion, Kennedy told this story by way of analogy:

"A man bored everyone he met by relating his experiences during the Johnstown flood. . . . Finally he died and went to heaven. There he asked St. Peter to gather an audience so that he could tell them the story of the Johnstown flood. St. Peter agreed but warned him: 'Remember, my friend, Noah will be in the audience.' "

★

When Calvin Coolidge was lieutenant governor of Massachusetts and not so widely known as in later years, he was seated beside a woman at a Boston dinner. The lady apparently did not know who Coolidge was, for she asked:

"And what do you do, sir?"

"I'm lieutenant governor," said Silent Cal.

"Oh, how exciting," she beamed, "tell me all about it."

"I just did," replied Cal.

★

A diplomat at a Washington luncheon was asked what he thought about a certain international problem. "Don't bother me," said the diplomat. "I must talk at this luncheon and this is no time for thinking."

★

A wily veteran of the political wars was asked to speak at a big Washington dinner. He was at his best, and when his speech was ended he found himself surrounded by several colleagues extending congratulations for a marvelous effort.

"Brother," said the spokesman for the group, "you really laid it on the line. You made it crystal clear how you stood on every controversial issue."

"Good God!" groaned the congressman. "I did?"

★

A well-known politician was unable to say "Thank you" before an audience without putting on his glasses and reading the two words from prepared notes. One day he was delivering a speech at a barbecue held in honor of the anniversary of a Revolutionary War battle. "Let us not forget," he proclaimed, glancing down at his notes, "those brave men who—" another quick glance at the notes "—shed their blood for us on this hallowed ground back in—" again he looked down at the notes, and then went on "—back in one-seven-seven-six."

That was too much for a listener in the rear of the crowd who yelled: "Yes, and if a man answers, hang up."

★

A veteran congressman handed a speech on federal taxes to a friend for review before delivering it at a taxpayers' dinner. The friend returned the speech with the comment that he did not believe the congressman's constituents would be able to understand a word of it.

"Good," was the reply, "it took me seven hours to write it that way."

★

A politician's wife arrived home from a campaign trip and was regaling her children with a description of her various experiences, the big dinners, luncheons, and assorted buffets. One youngster asked her: "Mommy, what did you eat?"

"Chicken, mashed potatoes, and 6,792 peas," she replied.

"Aw, come on, Mommy," protested the youngster, "how do you know how many peas?"

"My child," said the politician's wife wearily, "what do you think I do when Daddy is speaking?"

★

A visiting minister was scheduled to deliver an address at the Congregational church in Northampton, Massachusetts, and was invited to the home of President Coolidge. In anticipation of his visit, Mrs. Coolidge prepared a special dinner, but the missionary declined to eat anything, explaining that a meal would spoil his delivery.

Mrs. Coolidge was annoyed, so she stayed home and the President escorted the missionary alone to the church. When he came home, Mrs. Coolidge asked: "How did it go?"

Coolidge's reply was simply: "He might as well have et."

★

Winston Churchill was an extremely frank politician. On one occasion he was forced to cancel a dinner engagement in London because of an invitation to spend a weekend with some dear friends in the country. He wired the chairman of the London event: "Sorry. Can't come. Lying excuse follows."

★

Governor Christian Herter of Massachusetts, a fine Yankee gentleman, had been out on the campaign trail since early morning. He arrived at a church barbecue late in the afternoon, famished. Moving through the line, he held out his plate for the waitress to place on it a piece of chicken. "Do you mind if I have another piece of chicken?" the hungry governor asked the waitress. She refused, saying that her orders were for one piece of chicken to all who came through the line.

"But," said Herter, "I'm starved."

"I'm sorry, mister," said the waitress.

Then Herter, who was a humble man, thought he would turn on the power. "Do you know who I am?" he said. "I'm Governor Herter."

"Do you know who I am?" replied the unrattled waitress. "I'm the lady in charge of the chicken. Move on, mister."

Herter often told the story later, adding that, no matter how mighty a man thought he was, among the electorate there are those who can humble you quickly.

★

When a newsman called a certain congressman's office for a copy of a speech to be delivered at a Washington dinner, he was floored with this comment: "I am sorry, but I am unable to give you a copy of the congressman's speech. I just talked to the man who is writing it and he said the congressman is going to talk off the cuff."

★

All kinds of stories float around Washington, and one concerns a well-known but long-winded politician who commanded good fees as an after-dinner speaker.

It seems that the politician visited a psychiatrist and was asked: "Do you, sir, talk in your sleep?"

To which the politician was reported to have said: "No, doctor, I talk in other people's sleep. Aren't you aware that I am a politician?"

★

An extremely popular congressman was asked to explain his success. "Short speeches," was the reply, "and a silent prayer before I rise. It goes like this: 'Dear Lord, fill my mouth with worthwhile stuff, and nudge me when I've said enough.'"

"And," said the congressman with a smile, "the Lord must hate long speeches also, because in twenty years he has never let me go beyond five minutes."

★

With the increased role of the big lobbies and various pressure groups in America, officeholders find it more and more difficult to speak in public without offending someone. "There was a time," said a veteran of the chicken circuit, "when you could go down the middle of the road, but now there are more people there who are mad at everything than there are in the right rut or the left rut."

In any event, a storm-battered old politician, sly as a fox to boot, was invited to speak at a dinner where there was a mixed group. Sitting at the head table, he asked the toastmaster if he knew what type of an audience was present at the dinner. "Well, I'll tell you," said the M.C., "you've got to be careful. Over there is a big group of industrialists. Next to them are the labor people. On the left there are some people representing the Temperance League and behind them are the liquor people.

"Up front," he continued, "there's a group from the NAACP and the next table is filled with Dixiecrats. The farm block is near the exit and the federal employees have five tables in the center."

"I see," said the alert congressman. Then for three quarters of an hour he proceeded to knock hell out of the railroads.

★

Senator Tom Connally loved his native Texas and never passed up an opportunity to extol at length the virtues of the Lone Star State. When invited to deliver a dinner speech to a New York advertising club, Tom was asked by the toastmaster what his subject would be. Replied Tom: "Why I Am Glad to Be a Texan in 25,000 Words or More."

★

Adlai Stevenson once addressed a completely dead audience. He was disappointed not only at the turnout, but at the response as well.

The committee chairman remarked as he walked out of the banquet hall with Stevenson: "Never mind, Mr. Stevenson. The audience was not representative of the people of this town. There was nothing but the ragtail and bobtail at the dinner. Everybody with any sense stayed home."

★

Senator Paul J. Fannin of Arizona was present at a cocktail party where he was introduced to a young lady who said: "I have heard so much about you. Now I would like to give you a chance to tell your side."

★

Commenting on his wife's visit to India, President Kennedy told a Democratic fund-raising dinner: "I know my Republican friends were glad to see my wife feeding an elephant in India. She gave it sugar and nuts. But, of course, the elephant wasn't satisfied."

★

In a speech before some Republicans in York, Pennsylvania, Mrs. Clare B. Williams of the Republican National Committee had this to say about the Kennedy administration: "As of now, this broad-A administration seems to consist mostly of wall-to-wall carpeting, wall-to-wall government and back-to-wall financing."

★

A congressman returned to his hotel after giving a speech at a political dinner. He met a friend in the lobby who asked him how the speech went. "Why, they congratulated me heartily," said the congressman. "In fact one of the guests came to me after my speech and told me that when I sat down he said to himself it was the best thing I had ever done."

★

At a Lincoln Day dinner in Chicago, a verbose old senator withered his audience for nearly two hours, stopping only occasionally for a glass of water to keep going.

Finally, as he roared into his peroration and a look of relief started to show on the faces of his listeners, a head-table guest leaned over to the toastmaster and said: "He would have become more famous if he had dropped dead in the middle of his speech."

★

"The best after-dinner speech I ever heard," said Adlai Stevenson, "is 'Waiter, I'll take the check.'"

★

Former Ambassador to Italy John A. Volpe was once governor of Massachusetts and a hard-working campaigner to boot. One of his favorite after-dinner stories concerned a certain government official who was pacing up and down in a room at a well-known Boston hotel.

A lady entered the room and, recognizing the official, asked him what he was doing there. "I'm going to deliver a speech at a luncheon upstairs," he said.

"Do you ever get nervous or upset before addressing a large audience?" asked the lady.

"Nervous?" replied the official. "Not me. I've been delivering speeches for twenty years and it never bothers me a bit."

"In that case," demanded the lady, "what are you doing in the ladies' room?"

★

Onetime Georgia governor Eugene Talmadge used to tell a story about a runaway couple who arrived in a small south Georgia town and immediately headed for the justice of peace. The justice demanded ten dollars to perform the wedding ceremony.

"How is this?" said the bridegroom. "I know a friend of mine you married last month and he told me you only charged him six dollars."

"True," said the old justice, "but there is a great deal of difference between you and him. I have married him five times. He's a good customer. And who knows, you I may never see again."

The din in the banquet room was overwhelming as the congressman opened his speech. It would not die down, and finally the toastmaster rose angrily and shouted: "I wish you people in the back of the room would quiet down and pay a little attention to the speaker."

A voice came ripping through the smoke: "We're paying as little attention as possible, mister."

★

Former Governor George Romney of Michigan tells the story about a guest of honor at a banquet who discovered at the last moment that his upper plate had cracked. "You'll have to cancel my speech," he told the toastmaster. "Nonsense," said the latter, "here's a spare upper I have in my pocket."

The guest of honor inserted the plate in his mouth and essayed a few words with disastrous results. "No good," he cried, pulling out the plate. "It just doesn't fit."

Like a magician pulling rabbits out of a hat, the toastmaster produced a second plate, which didn't fit either. Then he came up with a third plate, which fit perfectly.

The guest of honor made a great speech, received a fine ovation, then turned gratefully to the toastmaster. "It's lucky for me," he said, "that you happen to be a dentist."

"Dentist nothing," laughed the toastmaster, "I'm an undertaker."

★

When Secretary of State Henry Kissinger was leaving office, he was a guest at a number of cocktail parties in his honor. Finally, after about fifteen farewell receptions, a weary Kissinger said: "Did you ever see a lame duck receive so many swan songs?"

★

A newsman met a senator in the Willard Hotel lobby in Washington and started talking with him about the problems of the nation. "You know, Bill," said the senator, "this country has gone to hell."

"That's a strange remark for you to make," said the reporter.

"Last night at the Democratic dinner you spoke for more than an hour about how wonderful everything was in America and all the prosperity the people are enjoying."

"Yeah, I know," said the senator, "but last night I was talking. This morning I'm thinking."

★

Prince Bismarck was once pressed by a certain American politician to recommend his son for a diplomatic post. "He is a very remarkable fellow," said the proud father; "he speaks seven languages."

"Indeed!" said Bismarck, who did not hold a very high opinion of linguistic achievements. "What a wonderful headwaiter he would make."

★

During the War of 1812, a dinner was given in Canada at which both American and British officers were present. One of the latter offered the toast: "To President Madison, dead or alive!"

An American offered the response: "To the Prince Regent, drunk or sober!"

★

Fred Allen, the famed radio and vaudeville comedian, was attending a political dinner in New York. It was an uneasy night, and a politician cranked on and on with tired clichés and fluffy phrases. After more than an hour of saying practically nothing, the speaker said: "Well, to make a long story short . . ."

"It's too late now," stage-whispered Allen, much to the delight of the audience.

★

When Winston Churchill finished a dinner speech during a visit to America, a woman rushed up to him and said: "Doesn't it thrill you, Mr. Churchill to know that every time you make a speech, the hall is packed to overflowing?"

"It is quite flattering," replied Churchill, "but whenever I feel this way, I always remember that if instead of making a political speech I was being hanged, the crowd would be twice as large."

★

William M. Evarts, former Secretary of State and U.S. senator, had a rare sense of humor. Once at a dinner in Omaha, he was complimenting the West for many things. He went on to say: "I like the West; I like her self-made men; and the more I travel west, the more I meet with her public men, and the more I am satisfied of the truthfulness of the biblical passage that states: 'The Wise men came from the East.'"

★

Theodore Francis Green, the oldest member ever to serve in the United States Senate, always talked about a valuable lesson he learned after delivering an after-dinner speech. A woman complimented him on the speech, and Green said modestly, "Oh, madam, you couldn't mean that. The talk wasn't all that good."

"Of course I mean it," she retorted. "Your speech wasn't good at all. You must learn when you receive a compliment, to accept it in the spirit in which it is given."

★

Senator Alben W. Barkley was one of the most popular after-dinner speakers in Washington. Whenever fellow senators had a home-state banquet, they considered it a great catch if they could induce Old Alben to be the main speaker.

Whenever Barkley was called upon at a dinner to praise one of his colleagues, he would say: "I'm here tonight because there is nothing in the world I wouldn't do for Senator W——. On the other hand there's nothing in the world he wouldn't do for me. That's the way it has been during our twenty years together in the Senate. I haven't done anything for him and he hasn't done anything for me."

★

"The Democrats," once said Will Rogers, "are the only race of people that give a dinner and then won't decide who will be toastmaster till they all get to the dinner and fight over it. No job is ever too small for them to split over."

★

Lord Rosebery once described after-dinner speaking as "a prolonged harangue, uttered by a man who does not want to say anything, and addressed to people who do not want to hear him."

★

Vice-President Hubert Humphrey was asked to limit a commencement speech to twelve minutes. He responded: "The last time I spoke for only twelve minutes was when I said hello to my mother."

★

Mayor Jimmy Walker of New York attended a father-son banquet one evening and gave a great speech on the problems of youth. When he had finished he asked if there were any questions.

"I have a question," said a bright-eyed thirteen-year-old.

"Why is it that you're always getting into trouble?" was the knockdown question.

★

State Senator John M. Quinlan of Massachusetts was delivering a commencement address at a small down-state high school. Quinlan was getting to the crux of his speech when a stray cat strolled through the open door of the auditorium at the rear of the platform and started to purr around Quinlan's legs.

The senator interrupted his speech, observing: "I think I have some competition." He then picked up the cat, displayed it to the crowd, and handed it over to a nearby person who escorted the animal out.

As the cat was dropped outside the door, Quinlan resumed his speech by commenting: "Can you imagine a politician putting someone out of a hall who is willing to listen to his speech?"

At a Republican fund-raising dinner, a well-known but verbose United States senator had spoken for almost an hour and looked like he was going on for another forty-five minutes.

One of the guests turned to a woman nearby and remarked: "I wish something could be done to shut this guy up."

"Well," responded the woman, "I'm his wife, and frankly I've been trying to do it for twenty-two years."

★

"I've never missed one of Congressman Smith's speeches," remarked an elderly men's club member. When someone asked him why that was so, he answered: "Just a streak of bad luck, I guess."

★

Once in a while there is a politician honest enough to tell the truth. This happened in the Midwest where a speech was handed a state senator just before he approached the rostrum.

As the senator proceeded to read the speech, he began to wipe his brow. After about five pages he paused, looked out at the audience, and commented: "My God, this stuff is boring."

★

The committee for a political banquet was discussing politicians they were considering for the annual banquet. "What we need," volunteered one committeeman, "is a man who can give it to us in very few words—somebody like Senator Brown."

"He'll never do," warned the chairman. "He may be a man of few words but he keeps using them over and over again."

★

Service clubs such as the Rotary, Kiwanis, Lions have a hard-and-fast rule about closing their luncheon meetings at one-thirty. Said onetime Massachusetts senator Leverett Saltonstall: "I like speaking at service club luncheons, because you know damn well when you've got to stop talking."

Many years ago speakers memorized their talks, no matter what their length. As time went on, however, this oratorical rule was broken, and rarely does a modern politician talk off-the-cuff.

Some years ago, just as the changeover from off-the-cuff to read speeches was taking place, a United States senator delivered a speech from a manuscript at a ladies' club dinner.

· When he had completed his offering, he noticed an old lady at the head table who said rather indignantly: "How do you expect us to remember your speech when you can't remember it yourself?"

★

A young liberal entering politics for the first time accepted an invitation to speak at a hard-nosed conservative club dinner. Like most liberal political aspirants, the youngster promised cradle-to-grave legislation if he were elected.

When he arrived home, his wife asked how he had made out with his speech. "I knocked 'em in the aisles," said the youngster. "Why, do you know, Mary, that when I finished my talk, they said they were going to invite me back to speak again next winter?"

"How was that?" asked the wife.

"Well," was the completely naïve response, "when I stepped down from the stage, the chairman of the event came up to me and said: 'Smith, it will be a damn cold night when we invite you back again.'"

★

A well-known political egotist had been invited to speak at a local Republican dinner. When he arrived he discovered there would be only a small gathering. Annoyed at the supposed slight, the politician asked caustically: "Don't the people in this damn town know who I am?"

"I'm not sure," answered the beleaguered chairman. "It might have leaked out."

★

Senator Edward O. Wolcott, a Republican from Colorado, was sent to a Southern state to advocate Republicanism. He was advised that because of Southern hatred for Republicans he would be introduced with as few words as possible.

According to Senator Wolcott: "My introduction by the bitter Democratic toastmaster came out this way: He merely stood at the rostrum, pointed at the audience, then turned, pointed at me, and sat down."

★

The Spartans of old despised people who talked too much. They themselves expressed their views in as few words as possible and expected everybody else to do so also, as is evident in the following story.

A famine struck a neighboring island in the Aegean Sea and the population sent an envoy to Sparta to ask for help.

The envoy made a long speech describing the distress of the islanders, but the Spartans sent him back empty-handed and told him: "We have forgotten the beginning of your speech and we understood nothing at the finish."

The famine-stricken population sent another envoy to Sparta urging him to be as concise as possible in his request. He took a lot of empty flour bags with him and opening one for the Assembly of Sparta, he said: "It's empty. Please fill it."

The chairman of the Spartan Assembly immediately ordered the bags filled. Then he drew the envoy aside and told him: "You need not have pointed out to us that your bags were empty. We would have seen it, anyway. It was not necessary to ask us to fill them. We would have done so, anyway. Remember, if you come another time, do not talk so much."

13

"What I Meant to Say Was . . ."

There is a well-known expression that when a man rises to speak very often only he and God know what he is going to say. When he commences his oration, his mind slips into low gear and from that point on only God knows what he is going to say.

Another version is that when a man stands up to speak, his mind sits down. Nothing plays more tricks on public officials than the failure of the brain to mesh properly with the tongue. The outcome is usually a mixed metaphor, a garbled phrase, or a bad choice of words, followed by the high laugh of ridicule from the audience.

While these slips of the tongue cause embarrassment to the speaker, they nevertheless provide newsmen with choice bits of humor and the general public with an insight into the fallibility of public officials.

One veteran of the platform circuit expressed it well when he said: "One minute you're a proud oratorical eagle, soaring on high, with wings spread in beautiful flight. Then you blow a phrase, and before you know it you're a wounded goose."

As was the case of a matchless orator of the old school who had spent an hour mesmerizing his audience. They were in the palm of his hand as the time came to end his speech with a burst of flowery oratory.

". . . and tomorrow, fellow citizens," he spouted, "the American people will be called upon to give their verdict at the polls, and I believe you, as American freemen, will give that verdict against slavery [applause]. Yes, tomorrow we will take freedom's ballot in our hands, trampling slavery's shackles under our feet, and while the Archangel of Liberty looks down approvingly upon us from the throne of Omnipotence, we will consign Stephen A. Douglas to the *pittomless bot!*"

★

Soon after Al Smith was elected governor of New York, he visited Sing Sing prison. After being shown the buildings by the warden, the governor was asked to speak to the inmates. He was embarrassed, never having spoken to the inmates of a prison before, and he did not know quite how to begin. Finally, he said: "My fellow citizens." Then he remembered that when one goes to prison, one is no longer a citizen. So the governor, now even more embarrassed said: "My fellow convicts." That brought a roar from the inmates. Al broke up the place by finally blurting: "Well, anyhow, I'm glad to see so many of you here."

It was one of Al Smith's worst days, and he suffered the repercussions for years.

★

Al Smith was not the only governor to tangle himself in a laugh-provoking situation. A New England chief executive, speaking at a political dinner, blurted: "There are three subjects which now agitate our Commonwealth. The first is pollution. The second is our airport problem, and the third is the state prison. I shall pass over the first two briefly, as my sentiments are well known, and move to the state prison, where I shall dwell for some time."

He had a tough time recovering from the laughter.

★

Mayor Richard Daley of Chicago was one of the master word mixers in politics. At a dinner Daley once said: "We must restore to Chicago all the good things it never had." He followed that by introducing Carl Sandburg as the poet "lariat" of Chicago. Still another Daleyism had the mayor opening his speech with: "Ladies and gentlemen of the League of Women Voters."

★

The speaker at a dinner honoring a Midwest governor who had just won an unprecedented third term meant to say that one day the governor would be canonized. The words did not come out that way and he said: "When Governor G—— leaves the State House, after this term, he undoubtedly will be cannonaded."

★

While state legislatures and city councils generally are great sources of upside-down-and-backwards humor, Congress receives the most recognition for its verbal blundering. Many red-faced congressmen have had their day ruined by a fractured sentence.

Shortly before America's involvement in World War II, a Southern congressman shouted during debate: "The best way to avoid war is to meet it head on." Another cried: "The United States is at peace with all the world and maintains friendly relations with the rest of mankind." With finger on high, a House member shouted: "There is not a man in this House who has arrived at the age of fifty but has felt the truth thundering through his mind for centuries."

When debate on a tax bill became extremely bitter, a House member shouted: "What have we here, a golden cow that wants its cake and eats it as well?" Another frenzied debater yelled: "I don't like to be backbitten to my face." A fast-talking congressman brought down the House when he proclaimed: "I want to bring this bill within gunshot of the Constitution." A blistering personal exchange between two Senate enemies ended in laughter when one of them charged: "I've got more brains in my head than my colleague has in his little finger." Still another legislator cried out: "We need this bill like a horse needs a fifth wheel."

The *Congressional Record* carries none of these blunders. Vain congressmen make certain their bloopers never get into print. Garbage speeches on the floor show up in the *Record* reading like the best of Cicero's orations, for the reason that all remarks are carefully steam-cleaned and proofread before the *Record* is published. "After all," said one cagey congressman, "we've got to let the people back home think we know what we are talking about—even though half the time we don't."

★

Legislative debate on the subject of capital punishment has produced more bulls and blunders than almost any other subject. The emotional steam generated by "death penalty" debate has injected much humor into an otherwise serious matter.

Benjamin Disraeli once cried out in the House of Commons: "Life imprisonment is too short a term to be a deterrent." Another English House member rocked the chamber when he shouted: "Crockett ought to be hanged, so it will be a warning to him." Debating the death penalty, a Michigan Senate member yelled: "I believe in capital punishment, so long as it ain't too severe." Fighting to retain the death penalty, a Massachusetts House member shouted: "A murderer in my district once *emasculated* a poor old lady." A suicide wave in Ireland compelled a native legislator to insist: "The only way to stop this suicide wave is to make it a capital offense, punishable by death."

★

Sir Boyle Roche was an Irish politician more famous for his mixed metaphors than for anything else. No man who ever served in public life could mangle the language like Sir Boyle. Among his more famous blunders were the following: "I smell a rat; I see it floating in the air; but mark me, sir, I will nip it in the bud." And on another occasion: "Single misfortunes never come alone, and the greatest of all possible misfortunes is generally followed by much greater."

Fearing the progress of revolutionary opinions, Sir Boyle drew a frightful picture of the future, remarking that the House of Commons might be invaded by ruffians who, said he, "would cut us to mince meat and throw our bleeding heads on that table to stare us in the face." When arguing for the habeas corpus suspension bill in Ireland, Sir Boyle said: "It would surely be better, Mr. Speaker, to give up not only a part, but if necessary, even the whole of the constitution, to preserve the remainder!"

Sir Boyle hit the brass ring for blunders when he wrote the following resolution for a new jail in Dublin: "Resolved that the new prison shall be built on the site and with the materials of the old one, and that the prisoners shall continue to reside in the old prison until the new one is completed."

★

William Gladstone, the usually precise English statesman, often let his tongue gallop ahead of his brain with such gems as: "My Honorable opponent is shaking his head in the teeth of his own words." On another occasion he declared: "All along the untrodden paths of the past we see the footsteps of an unseen hand."

★

Out on the campaign trail, the deadly blunder follows a politician like a poor relative, popping up when he least expects it. Roaring into his peroration, a Senate candidate blurted: ". . . and that's my platform, ladies and gentlemen. It won't cost anybody anything unless they are taxpayers."

A New York legislative candidate told his constituents: "The contract labor system is a vital cobra that is swamping the lives of the workingman." A Civil War veteran, running for a House seat and pleading for pension rights for G.A.R. members, cried: "Is it possible that we have died in vain?"

One of the best of all campaign blunders was uttered in New Hampshire, where a tremendous debate developed over pasteurized milk. A candidate, in a blaze of indignation, shouted: "What this state needs is clean, fresh pasteurized milk and if elected, I'm going to the State House and demand that we take the bull by the horns and get it." This was matched by a Southwestern congressional aspirant who said: "My opponent deserves to be kicked to death by a jackass, and I'd like to be the one to do it!"

★

The banquet circuit has provided such bloopers as: "I am happy to introduce our Chief Executioner, Governor John Dempsey." Introducing a distinguished politician, a toastmaster declared: "For the last fifteen years, Senator Blatz has been a lifelong resident of our state."

One unfortunate master of ceremonies wrecked an evening by saying: "And Congressman Smith is a public servant who is equal to few and superior to none." A ladies' club chairlady stated: "We had intended to increase the dues this year, but now we won't have to, for we have been able to arrange for several cheap speakers, starting with Representative Rogers."

An old lawmaker came out with: "I am not going to talk to you tonight in generalities. I am going to speak to you at random." During a moment of oratorical inspiration, a Lincoln Day speaker declared: ". . . and it is fitting to pay tribute to Abraham Lincoln, who was born in a log cabin that he built with his own hands." Another M.C. chopped down a politician by announcing: ". . . and now we'll hear the latest dope from Washington, so here's Senator Crosby."

A stuffy British Prime Minister offered this gem: "The British lion, whether it is roaming the deserts of India or climbing the forests of Canada, will not draw in its horns or retire into its shell." This was matched by a United States senator who observed: "What I am going to tell you is more truth than poultry. The United States has got to rise to greater and greater platitudes of achievement." During a budget battle a House member exclaimed: "I want to make it perfectly clear that the exact figures I am using are only approximations."

One particularly memorable blunder was made by a young man who was to be awarded a trophy by the mayor of his city. Shaking with fright, the youngster approached the head table. The mayor handed him the trophy and extended his congratulations. The nervous youngster responded: "From the heart of my bottom I thank you."

*

Sitting at banquet tables, politicians hope for the best from toastmasters but often get the worst. "Our next speaker," said a lady toastmaster, "will be Governor John Chaffee of Rhode Island. Now please no one leave the room because when he is finished we'll have a drawing for door prizes. So please stick around, folks

—for the prizes are good. It's a pleasure to introduce Governor Chaffee."

★

The late Governor Harold Hoffman of New Jersey always got a laugh out of a story about a Republican toastmaster who tried to gild the lily when introducing Hoffman. This is how he put it: "I am happy to introduce to you our distinguished Chief Executive, who during his term in office has tried to do *everybody* for something." "He collapsed in the laughter," said Hoffman, "and I almost went down with him."

★

In the old frontier days of legislative government, House members were generally a roughhewn lot. The Arkansas House had such an individual, right off the farm. He was made chairman of the Committee on Education, despite the fact that he had probably never gotten beyond the fourth grade.

At the first hearing, he opposed a bill with this comment: "In the first place it ain't wrote right. And in the second place, it ought to incarcerate some provision giving recognition to those in the more obscene walks of life."

★

The American Legion commander was explaining the program for Memorial Day services at the town cemetery. This is how he put it: "We will march from the Legion hall to the soldiers' monument. There we will start our services with a prayer by the chaplain. Then there will be a selection from the band. A high school student will recite the Gettysburg Address. Then there will be a speech by Congressman Smith, followed by the firing squad."

★

Mayor Jimmy Walker of New York once sent a communication to the Board of Aldermen calling for a sizable appropriation to purchase a hundred gondolas for Central Park. A Brooklyn alderman rose angrily and protested that the amount was excessive.

"I move," he shouted, "that we buy one male gondola and one female gondola and let nature takes its course."

★

During a heated budget debate in the City Council of an Eastern city, an item asking nine thousand dollars for a dumbwaiter for the city-owned hospital was questioned. One councilman rose and inquired: "I don't remember any request coming to this council for a Civil Service examination to fill this job, and anyway, nine thousand dollars is a lot of money to start a man on a new job."

★

A new representative had been invited to speak to a Parent-Teacher Association. He was a little nervous as he started his speech with: "My friends, the schoolwork is the bulhouse of civilization."

A ripple of laughter went through the room as he tried it again: "The bulhouse is the schoolwork of . . ."

The laughter spread as he began once more: "The workhouse is the bulschool of . . ."

His embarrassment was becoming painful, but still he made another attempt: "The schoolhouse, my friends . . ."

A sigh of relief went up. The representative gazed around and the light of confidence started to shine as he made another effort: "The schoolhouse, my friends, is the woodbark . . ."

Then he lost consciousness.

★

"Sir Henry is a man of unquestioned honor," said a Dublin toastmaster at a dinner for Sir Henry Irving. "He is not only an artist of the first rank, the first in his profession to be honored with a knighthood, but is also a man of utmost integrity. It would not be too much to say that his has been a life of unbroken blemish."

★

In the years following the Civil War, special pension bills were filed by the thousands on behalf of Union soldiers. One day a

Connecticut congressman was blazing away in support of a pension bill. He gave it everything he had and wound up his speech by crying: ". . . and, Mr. Speaker, there stood Lieutenant Brown, facing Pickett's charge, with a sword in each hand and a pistol in the other . . ."

He was lucky; the bill was approved.

★

"Uncle Joe" Cannon was one of the giants of the House of Representatives. He spoke his mind, come hell or high water. On one occasion an inexperienced congressman was making a speech at a banquet at which the House Speaker was also present.

"Gentlemen," commenced the young fellow. "My opinion is that the generality of mankind in general is disposed to take advantage of the generality of . . ."

"Sit down, son," interrupted Cannon. "You are coming out of the same hole you went in at."

★

An upstate New York congressional district had been represented by a slow-moving, do-nothing individual for more than twenty years. Finally, he just went to sleep and died.

At the funeral, a small-town preacher was called upon to deliver the oration. Somehow his subconscious thoughts about the congressman came to the fore as he said: ". . . and the corpse has represented this district in Congress for twenty years."

★

A member of Parliament named Stanley was an excruciating speaker. Nervous and embarrassed, he never failed to mess up his floor speeches. One day he rose with a large sheet of paper in his hand. He fumbled around to find out what he had written for notes and then proceeded: "I think, sir," he said, "I think that is, I would venture to say."

Then came a long pause and more fumbling with the notes, after which Stanley continued: "Now this question is one which a colonel at the front, or, I may say, a major, or was it a captain? in point of fact—that is, I think, issued an order to his regiment, or was it his company . . . ?"

After another long pause and continued fumbling of the notes, Stanley, his knees buckling, declared: "The major, I mean the captain, or was it the colonel? issued . . ."

At this point Stanley was falling apart but he managed to blurt out: "And what should I do now?"

A fife-like voice from across the chamber cried shrilly: "Sound retreat!"

★

A blustery old senator had just completed his address when an elderly lady approached the head table, extended her hand, and said: "I thoroughly enjoyed your speech, Senator. I don't know why it is, but whenever I make a speech I seem so nervous, but when you speak, you seem so unconscious."

★

Sir Colin Campbell was responsible for one of the most talked-of "bulls" in British history. When he was an officer with the British Army and stationed in India, he was asked to report to the British War Department on why there was so much grumbling among the soldiers about the climate.

Campbell's report, which was a classic on the records of the War Department for years, read: "A lot of young fellows come here and they drink and eat and die. Then they write home and tell their families the climate killed them."

★

During the course of a women's Republican club meeting in a small Connecticut town, the president announced that one of the members would be celebrating her hundredth birthday.

"I will take suggestions," said the president, "as to what we can do at the next meeting to honor our oldest member."

"I think it would be a wonderful idea," said a lady in the front row, with all sincerity, "to give her a life membership."

★

A lobbyist for a taxpayer group approached a Texas legislator of minimal educational attainments and asked him to oppose budget increases for the state university.

"Do you realize," he said, "that the boys and girls use the same curriculum and on top of that they even matriculate together? To make matters worse, a young lady student can be forced to show a male professor her thesis?"

"Why, those unholy educators," yelled the lawmaker. "I won't vote them a damn cent!"

★

Senator Hattie Caraway of Arkansas was a shy little lady and could melt into any crowd. Yet, in Washington, she did her job well and was loved by her constituents.

One day before a home audience, she was being honored for her efforts. A talkative chairman became very enthusiastic about Hattie's record and reviewed her career in glowing terms. He was shouting when he reached the climax: "Ladies and gentlemen, we will now hear from the most notorious woman in Arkansas."

★

A wealthy conservative from a Southern state had been swept out of office by a self-educated politician. The old conservative took the defeat rather hard. Visiting the Senate chamber one day, he slipped into a seat in the lobby and meditated on the degeneracy of the times which permitted a person of humble beginnings to hold a seat in that body.

It just so happened that his opponent of the previous election was at that time debating a certain bill. In the course of his remarks, he used a quotation from the 137th Psalm: "Let my right hand wither away . . ."

The old senator could contain himself no longer and, turning to a friend, said: "Isn't it disgusting to hear such an ignoramus attempting to quote Shakespeare?"

★

Every legislator sooner or later delivers his so-called "maiden speech." Very often he thinks the eyes of the world are upon him as he rises in his place for the first time to say: "Mr. Speaker . . ." Generally he is mistaken, for few men have ever caught the ear of the House or the country with a "maiden speech."

One Massachusetts House member, however, broke into print on his first visit to the House microphone. Unfamiliar with the timeworn expression "maiden speech," the member proudly stood before the House, addressed the speaker, and announced that he was about to deliver his "virgin speech."

★

An old Dutchman who some years ago was elected a member of the Pennsylvania legislature said in his broken English style: "Ven I vent to the lechislatur, I tought I vould find dem all Solomons dere, but I soon found out dere vas some as pig fools dere as I vas."

★

When Syngman Rhee, then President of Korea, visited the national House of Representatives, Speaker Joe Martin was in the chair. Apparently Joe had not been briefed completely on who his visitor was, for he announced: "It is a distinct honor to present the President of India."

There was a murmer throughout the House at the obvious gaff. Martin tried it again: "I mean the President of Indiana."

★

In the middle of a hot debate, a senator called over a pageboy to deliver a verbal message back to his office. A little while later, he called the boy to his desk and said: "Why didn't you deliver that message as I gave it to you?"

"I did the best I could," was the boy's response.

"You did the best you could?" yelled the senator angrily, "Why, you fouled up the whole thing. If I thought I was sending a jackass, I would have gone myself."

★

When President McKinley died, Theodore Roosevelt succeeded him as the nation's Chief Executive. A New York editor thought it would be clever to contrast the event with a recent coronation in Europe. But—the compositor, coming to the word "oath" in the manuscript, struck a wrong key and the sentence appeared:

"For sheer democratic dignity, nothing could exceed the moment when, surrounded by the cabinet, Mr. Roosevelt took a simple bath as President of the United States."

★

A leading politician had just finished delivering a rock-'em-sock-'em speech, when a little old lady approached the head table. "Do you think they will publish your speech, Senator?" she asked.

"Oh, they may, posthumously," he laughed.

"That's good," said the old lady innocently, "and I hope it's soon."

★

A Texas oil man announced that he was going to throw the biggest victory party for Thomas E. Dewey ever held in the Lone Star State. "It'll be a two hundred and fifty thousand dollar complimentary banquet in honor of Dewey's election as President of the United States," he boasted.

"That's great," said a friend, "but what do you do if Dewey don't win the election?"

"In that case," said the Texan without a ruffle, "we'll have a complimentary banquet in honor of his defeat."

★

Every politician has a favorite religious story. Senator George Vest of Missouri squeezed out many a laugh with this anecdote about a new young preacher who on his first pulpit assignment announced nervously:

"I will take for my text the words, 'And they fed five men with five thousand loaves of bread and two thousand fishes.'"

At this misquotation, an old parishioner in the corner said audibly: "That's no miracle—I could do that myself."

The young preacher let the incident pass, but the next Sunday he announced the same text again. This time he got it right: "And they fed five thousand men on five loaves of bread and two fishes."

The minister waited a moment, and then, leaning over the pulpit, he looked at the old parishioner who had questioned him the previous Sunday, and said: "And could you do that, Mr. Smith?"

"Of course I could," Smith replied.

"And how would you do it?" asked the preacher.

"With what was left over from last Sunday," replied the parishioner.

★

It was the custom among the clergy in England to include in their prayers a word to the Almighty about the mentally ill. Once when a clergyman was asked to give the opening prayer at the Edinburgh Town Council, he offered this: "Lord have mercy on all fools and idiots, and particularly on the Town Council of Edinburgh."

★

One day a secretary informed President Coolidge that an imposing delegation was at the White House insisting that the President had promised to address their annual convention.

"What did you tell them?" asked the President.

"I told them there must be a mistake—that there is no such entry in your engagement book."

Chuckled the President: "That's right. You stick to it. And I'll amplify your statement by saying nothing."

★

The mayor-elect of a small Iowa city was quite a showman. For his inaugural ceremonies, he planned an elaborate parade filled with small-town pomp and ceremony. Above all else, the mayor-elect wanted favorable weather and a good crowd. Two days before the inauguration he caused to be placed in the local newspaper the following notice:

"On the occasion of the inauguration ceremonies and parade honoring our new mayor, they will be held in the afternoon, should it rain in the morning, and in the morning should it rain in the afternoon."

The Civil War general William T. Sherman, who was rather deaf, was attending a reception at the White House as the guest of the President, when he noticed a man who looked familiar to him.

"Who are you?" asked the general.

"I made your shirts, sir," replied the man.

"Of course, of course!" exclaimed Sherman, and then, turning to some congressmen nearby, he said: "Gentlemen, allow me to present Major Shurtz."

★

A candidate for the California Senate was addressing a G.O.P. meeting of nonincumbent candidates for public office when he made the following statement: "What are the qualifications for public office? Well, first of all a man has to recognize he's a public serpent."

Laughter filled the room as the red-faced senator tried to correct himself, but the damage had been done.

★

A member of the Nebraska Legislature was debating with all pistons pumping when he exclaimed: "In the words of the great Daniel Webster, who wrote the dictionary, 'Give me Liberty or give me death!' "

One of his colleagues pulled his coat and whispered hurriedly: "Daniel Webster didn't write the dictionary; it was Noah."

"Noah, nothing," replied the speaker. "Noah built the ark!"

★

While campaigning for George McGovern, Rhode Island Governor Frank Licht came up with the top gaffe of the 1972 election when he cried: "Nixon has been sitting in the White House while George McGovern has been exposing himself to the people of the United States."

★

A not so knowledgeable toastmaster was performing at the rostrum in a not so capable fashion, when he brought down the house by announcing: "And now, ladies and gentlemen, I will ask Senator Crosby to come to the rectum."

★

The Governor of the Virgin Islands was a guest in Washington. The toastmaster, in the introductory remarks, said the usual things and ended with: "It's a great pleasure to present the Virgin of Governor's Island."

★

When Vice-President Spiro Agnew proposed that his case be tried by the House of Representatives rather than the courts, Representative Charles Vanik of Ohio became incensed. "He's trying," cried Vanik with feeling, "to take the decision out of the hands of 12 honest men and give it to 435 congressmen."

★

The petite chairlady opened her remarks with this gem: "We did not have to pay anything to get Senator Crossman here tonight, and after he speaks I am sure we will all agree he was worth every penny of it."

★

Whenever a man is sworn into office, the usual expression is: "I hope you have a successful administration." It didn't come out that way for an ancient city clerk in Massachusetts, who had just administered the oath to the new mayor.

Just as the city clerk was about to extend congratulations, his teeth slipped and instead of wishing the mayor a successful administration, he blurted: "And now, Mr. Mayor, I wish you a very sexual administration."

★

A congressman was about to deliver his speech at a big banquet when a man rushed up to the platform waving a screwdriver. Then followed a hasty conversation with the chairlady, who moved up to the rostrum, pushed the congressman aside, and announced: "I am sorry to say there will be a slight delay. Word has just been received that there is a screw loose in our speaker."

★

Defending a colleague during a torrid debate in the Massachusetts House, a member cried out: "I will defend to the last drop of your blood . . . er, er, I mean *my* blood . . . your right to express an opinion."

★

A nervous House speaker was introducing a newly elected governor during inaugural ceremonies. This is how he put it: "The ship of state is embarking on a new voyage and I am pleased to introduce the Shiptain of the Cap."

Then quickly recovering himself, he blurted: "I mean the Shaptain of the Kip." Again, in an instant he cried: "I should have said the Kiptain of the Shap."

The governor moved in to save the ship from sinking completely.

★

Fed up with the caliber of candidates elected to the state legislature, an Alabama citizen requested that a bill be filed making it mandatory for all candidates to take an intelligence test before running for public office.

When the news spread around the State House that such a bill had been filed, an unlettered legislator commented: "What the hell are they trying to do, destroy representative government?"

14
Presidential Humor

Scores of United States senators, congressmen, and governors have been noted for their sharp wit and splendid humor, and these qualities have served many of them well. And yet only a handful of the thirty-eight men who have served as Presidents of the United States could tell a joke or come out with a witty remark.

Of these, Abraham Lincoln is the acknowledged master. Surprisingly, he is followed by Calvin Coolidge, who was an accidental humorist. The others are William Howard Taft, Andrew Jackson, and John F. Kennedy.

For the most part, the remaining Presidents were sedate men, seldom stirred by the breezy incidents that whirled around them. Small exceptions can be made for John Quincy Adams, Woodrow Wilson, Franklin Delano Roosevelt, and perhaps a couple of others.

"Most of our chief executives," observed one President-watcher, "were incarnate serenities." What he meant was that many of our Presidents were on the stuffed shirt side and left the wit and humor to others.

Not so with Jackson, Lincoln, Taft, Coolidge, and Kennedy. Intentionally or otherwise, wit and humor bubbled from and around these men.

Once, during a tough election battle, Jackson was concluding his speech when one of his supporters leaned over and whispered: "Tip 'em a little Latin, General—they won't be satisfied without it."

Jackson thought quickly and in a voice of thunder wound up his speech, exclaiming, "*E pluribus unum! Sine qua non! Ne plus ultra! Multum in parvo!*

The effect of the Latin was electrifying, and the villagers' shouts could be heard for miles.

★

Jovial President William Howard Taft had great good humor, much of it directed at himself. Campaigning for U.S. senator in Ohio, Taft was in fine form one night when a cabbage arched out of the crowd, hit the platform, and rolled to a stop at Taft's feet. A roar of laughter greeted this event. Taft looked down at the smelly cabbage and won the night by saying: "Well, I see one of my hecklers has lost his head."

On another occasion, President Taft was asked to address a group of New Yorkers on the subject "The Christian in Politics." Looming large behind the rostrum, Taft spread all his 330 pounds and said: "I've done research on the topic given me and I've come to the conclusion there ain't no such thing as a Christian in politics." He then sat down.

★

Calvin Coolidge, our thirtieth President, said very little, but often his words were extremely humorous in a down-home sort of way. Coolidge's very makeup and his Vermont twang made him a natural subject for anecdotes, and more were told about him than about all other Presidents combined. Cal had no desire to be funny. It just so happened that many things he said came out that way.

Noted as a man who knew what both sides of a dollar bill looked like, Coolidge left the White House one day for a needed rest and checked into a swank hotel. When he got the bill, he was shocked. Having left a two-dollar room at the Adams House in Boston when he was governor of Massachusetts, Coolidge could not understand the twelve-dollar rate at the Washington hotel. Fuming, he paid the bill. He then noted that he needed some stamps to send off a few letters.

"How many two-cent stamps do you want?" the clerk asked.

"Depends," replied Coolidge suspiciously. "How much are you asking for them?"

A lady reporter was interviewing President Coolidge. "What is your hobby?" she asked. "Holding office," was Cal's quick reply. When someone asked the President how many people worked at the White House, he responded: "About half of them." Looking out the window of the White House, he saw nonconforming, irascible Senator William Borah riding a horse. "Must bother the senator," remarked Cal, "to be going in the same direction as the horse." Seated next to a talkative lady at a state dinner, Cal was minding his business until she said: "Mr. President, you must attend a great many dinners." Reaching for another olive, Coolidge muttered: "Well, lady, a man has to eat someplace."

Gluyas Williams told it all about Coolidge in a famous cartoon depicting the outgoing President, defiantly sitting on his suitcase in the White House lobby and refusing to leave until somebody found his other rubber.

★

President John F. Kennedy was blessed with natural wit and humor. Not particularly adept at telling long jokes, he nevertheless enlivened his campaigns, speeches, and press conferences with witty one-, two-, and three-liners. In fact, JFK gave the short, witty stab a new respectability. The press appreciated the Kennedy sense of humor and the people loved him for it. It was instinctive, penetrating, and thoroughly a part of the man.

During the presidential campaign of 1960, an enthusiastic crowd greeted JFK in Los Angeles. He won them over even further with his opening remarks: "I appreciate your wonderful welcome. As the cow said to the Maine farmer, 'Thank you for a warm hand on a cold morning.'" At a stop in Columbus, Ohio, he told a receptive crowd: "There is no city in the United States in which I get a warmer welcome and fewer votes than Columbus, Ohio."

Kennedy managed to kill off criticism of his brother's appointment as United States Attorney General, despite Bobby's obvious lack of legal training, by stating: "I see nothing wrong with giving Robert some legal experience as Attorney General before he goes out to practice law."

During World War II, Kennedy's PT boat had been sunk by the Japanese. A little boy, on a visit to the White House, asked him: "Mr. President, how did you become a war hero?" The President smiled and replied: "It was absolutely involuntary. They sank my boat."

Speaking at a Democratic fund-raising dinner at which the guests paid a hundred dollars per plate, President Kennedy said: "I am deeply touched—but not as deeply touched as you, who have come to this dinner." At his forty-fourth birthday dinner Kennedy brought down the House by stating: "When we got into office, the thing that surprised me most was to find that things were just as bad as we'd been saying they were."

★

Abraham Lincoln was an exquisite humorist, the best by far of any of the Presidents. He defied tradition and dignity to tell his little stories, and his humor was always spontaneous and fit for the occasion.

During the worst days of the Civil War, Lincoln once read to his cabinet some passages from a book by Artemus Ward. Old Abe laughed heartily as he read, but noted that not another cabinet member joined him. Laying down the book, Lincoln said:

"Gentlemen, why don't you laugh? With the fearful strain that is upon me night and day, if I do not laugh, I shall die and you need this medicine as much as I do."

Then he submitted to them for consideration a paper on a very important phase of the war. He had prepared himself for the awful strain of the decision to come with a few nerve-settling laughs from a book by an old friend and humorous writer.

While still a young frontier lawyer, Lincoln arrived at a country inn one bitterly cold night. He noted that the fire was surrounded by numerous fellow attorneys. When he remarked that it was colder than hell outside, one of the lawyers asked: "You been there, Abe?"

"Yes," replied Lincoln, "and it's just like here—all the lawyers are near the fire."

Concerning the clergy, Lincoln once said: "I don't like to hear cut-and-dried religious sermons. When I hear a clergyman preach, I like to see him act as if he were fighting bees." When a certain pompous politician died, Old Abe commented: "If George had known he was to have such a large funeral, he would have died years ago."

Numerous complaints reached Lincoln concerning General Grant's competency to lead troops. One of his advisers pleaded: "You better face it, Mr. Lincoln, Grant is drunk all the time." Turning to his visitor, the President responded: "Find out what brand of whiskey Grant is drinking and I'll send some to the rest of my generals."

Lincoln's wit and mirth gave him a passport to the thoughts and hearts of millions. This extraordinary man summed it up by observing: "They say I tell a great many stories; I reckon I do, but I have found in the course of a long experience that common people take them as they run, are more easily informed through the medium of a broad illustration than in any other way, and as to what the hypercritical few may think, I don't care."

★

When it comes to witty sayings, former President Gerald Ford is no Abraham Lincoln. While in the White House he realized that nothing could warm an audience better than a funny line or two before the heavy part of a speech. The word was always out to Ford's writers: "Doll the speech up with some laughs."

When the people heard President Ford, they knew that he was giving them canned humor. Unlike Lincoln, Kennedy, or Taft, President Ford was never very comfortable with after-dinner humor and, left on his own, could garble a joke or foul up what could have been a nifty one-liner. But out of the can Jerry did as well as could be expected.

A sample of President Ford's humor was included in a Chicago speech in the course of which he said: "The Chicago Police captured a kangaroo which had escaped from the zoo. The Chicago Bears wanted the kangaroo for their backfield, and of course, the Democrats wanted to register him to vote at least once."

He came on again at a Washington dinner with: "I am sorry that Henry Kissinger isn't here to speak. He's so calm and relaxed and is the only man I know who can hold a press conference and have his shoes shined at the same time."

Referring to his brief term as Vice-President, Ford stated: "It was like being the best man at a wedding. You never get a chance to prove it."

★

President Jimmy Carter has a million-dollar smile, but not much humor. Nevertheless, he once told some friends, "It's hard to make decisions. I avoided them all during the campaign. That's the good thing about campaigning. You can be fuzzy and get away with it."

This gave rise to one of the first Carter jokes according to which Jimmy's father asked his son one day: "Were you the one who chopped down the peanut plant?" Little Jimmy answered: "Father I cannot tell a lie. Maybe I did and maybe I didn't!"

★

When President Harrison died, Vice-President Tyler succeeded him in the White House. The new President's first act was to commission his coachman to purchase a carriage. In a few days the coachman returned and reported that he had searched Washington and had found a very handsome carriage for sale, but it had been used a few times.

"That will never do," said Tyler. "It would not be proper for the President of the United States to drive around in a second-hand carriage."

"And sure," responded the old coachman, "but what are you, sir, but a secondhand President?"

★

George Washington came as close to becoming King of the United States as any man could. He toyed with the idea of being called "High Mightiness" until some friends talked him out of it. He wanted the executive mansion to be called "The President's Palace," but that was discarded as too formal, so it became the

"President's House." Not to be denied, Old George, who loved his pomp and ceremony, had a presidential coach painted canary yellow and adorned with cupids holding garlands and flowers.

★

When President John Quincy Adams was criticized by a young politician about his mounting years, he replied: "Tell that young man that an ass is older at thirty than a man at eighty years."

★

President Martin Van Buren was a suave and smooth Chief Executive. He loved clothes and wore them in the highest style of the times. He was often referred to as the "dandy in the President's House."

One of Van Buren's enemies described him thus: "He struts and swaggers like a crow in a gutter, laced up in corsets, such as women in town wear, and if possible, tighter than the best of them."

★

President John Adams had no illusions about the presidency. He knew it was a "no win" job and he summed it up with the following observation: "Panegyrical romances will never be written, nor flattering orations spoken to transmit me to posterity in brilliant colors."

★

President Woodrow Wilson placed great value on education. He felt that honorary degrees from colleges belonged only to those who had attained great educational heights. One day the news reached the President that a certain half-educated politician had received his third honorary degree. An aide asked Wilson how this could be.

Wilson, who had more humor than people gave him credit for, said: "Well, he received the third degree because he had two other degrees; and he received the second because he had one; and the first because he didn't have any."

Thomas Jefferson had little use for the medical profession. In particular President Jefferson abhorred graduates from Philadelphia medical schools. "This nation," said Old Tom, "is overrun with young lads from the Philadelphia school, who, with their mercury and lancet in hand are vying with the sword of Bonaparte which shall shed the most human blood."

Jefferson's wry humor stabbed again at physicians when he said: "Whenever you find three physicians standing together, look skyward for the vultures hovering about."

★

John Quincy Adams kept a diary, and his first entry after assuming the presidency described the throng at the inaugural: "The crowd was excessive, the heat depressive and the entertainment bad." He later told a friend that he was unimpressed and would have rather been home in bed than at the inaugural.

★

William Howard Taft's wife was an extremely pushy woman. A story is told that on Inauguration Day, President Taft pointed a finger at his wife and said: "Now look here, I'm in the White House now and I'm not going to be pushed around any more."

★

When President Teddy Roosevelt was shot in the chest by a gunman, a whole army of doctors rushed over to take care of him.

The President would have none of the attention. "Get them out of here," he demanded. "I don't want to fall into their hands and have the same experience that McKinley and Garfield had."

★

"When you're out, you're out" is a truism that many politicians find out coldly and brutally. Herbert Hoover always related a little story to prove the point. After leaving the White House, he checked into a Canadian resort for a needed rest.

When he placed his name on the hotel register, the clerk looked at it and seemed impressed.

"Are you any relation to G-man Hoover?" he asked.

"No," said Herbert Hoover.

The clerk sized up the distinguished guest and came on again: "I suppose you're part of the Hoover family that manufactures vacuum cleaners?"

Again Hoover said: "No."

"Oh well," said the hotel clerk, "that's all right. But we *do* get a kick out of entertaining relatives of real celebrities."

★

The young son of a friend of President Jackson eyed a job in the War Department which was filled by a very efficient Whig. When he applied to Secretary of War Cass for the position and was refused, the young man took his case to Jackson.

The President called in Cass and asked him why he didn't give the job to the young man. Cass explained that the duties were of a peculiar nature, and the person now filling the position had special training and aptitude for the work and should not be removed. Jackson flared.

"By the eternal, Cass," he shouted, "do you mean to tell me there is an office in your department filled by a Whig which cannot be filled by a Democrat? Then abolish the job."

The young man was appointed.

★

Theodore Roosevelt was one of the most impatient men ever to sit in the President's chair, but he was often frustrated by the pace of congressional decision-making. Roosevelt wanted the Panama Canal built in a hurry, so he went to work on the project without the final approval of Congress. He explained his actions in this way: "I took the Canal Zone and let Congress debate. While the debate goes on, the canal does too."

★

President Andrew Johnson, despite his drinking habits, could cut up his enemies with verbal shots. He gave it to Horace Greeley, the publisher, by calling him "a man possessed of all heart and no head." Then he pinned Greeley again by calling him a "sublime old man."

Johnson saved his best slug for General U. S. Grant and referred to him as a "dullard, whose brain could have been compressed within the periphery of a nutshell."

★

President William Howard Taft had lots of funny lines and used them effectively. One of his best concerned meeting his wife-to-be Helen at a wintertime sliding party shortly after he graduated from Yale.

Taft asked Helen to accompany him down the slope on his sled. She accepted. "And," said Taft, "she and I have been sliding downhill ever since."

★

When a Southern politician announced that he was running for President as a favorite son, a dedicated enemy announced: "That is the most unfinished sentence I have ever heard."

★

Self-assured Jimmy Carter ran for President as a born-again Christian. In the course of his campaign, the former Georgia governor made quite a production of selecting a running mate on the Democratic ticket.

As the selection process proceeded, one wag commented: "I can't see why Jimmy Carter is bothering to select a vice-presidential candidate. Way down deep he probably feels he doesn't need one. Hell, man, if Jimmy dies in office, he will simply Rise Again!"

★

Woodrow Wilson once observed: "People never remain the same after they come to Washington. They either grow or swell, usually the latter."

★

Many years ago a certain President had a low popularity level in the State of Kansas. One of the state's two senators visited the

President and said he wanted a friend appointed postmaster of Topeka.

The President's private secretary took the senator aside and said: "You may want to talk with the President about this appointment, but I think I should tell you he wants to appoint a very personal friend."

Thereupon the senator exploded: "Well, for God's sake, if he has *one* friend in Kansas, let him appoint him."

★

During the impeachment trial of President Andrew Johnson, bitterness and hatred flowed through the national capital, and this was reflected in many Senate speeches.

One Johnson hater offered this penalty for the President: "He should be imprisoned during his natural life, and then hung until he is dead."

★

President Lyndon B. Johnson had a tremendous fondness for his wife Lady Bird. When someone asked him about his affection for Mrs. Johnson, he said: "Only two things are necessary to keep one's wife happy. First is to let her think she's having her own way. Second is to let her have it."

★

When Jimmy Carter came off the peanut farm to grab the Democratic nomination for President, it took Big Labor by surprise. The Meany crowd had bet on anybody but Carter, and now they had to make a decision whether or not they would support the former Georgia governor.

A high-ranking AFL-CIO executive solved the Carter quandary by announcing: "We wanted a Democrat in the presidency, no matter what. As soon as Carter won the nomination we began finding virtues in him that even his mother didn't know he had."

★

After the Mexican War and the annexation of Texas, Southern California, New Mexico, Arizona, and other lands, President

Zachary Taylor commissioned General William T. Sherman, then a captain, to look over the new possessions and see what they were worth, for they had never been surveyed.

Captain Sherman was gone two years and during that time he penetrated every corner of the new territory. When he returned to Washington he called on the President.

"Well, Sherman," said President Taylor, "what do you think of our new possessions? Will they pay for the blood and treasure spent in the war?"

"Do you want my honest opinion?" replied Sherman.

"Yes, tell us privately just what you think."

"Well, Mr. President," said Sherman, "it cost us one hundred million dollars and ten thousand men to carry on the war with Mexico."

"I know," said President Taylor, "but we got Arizona, New Mexico, Southern California, Texas and . . ."

"Oh, sure we did," interrupted Sherman, "but I've been out there and looked them over—all that country—and between me and you I feel that we'll have to go to war again. Yes, we've got to have another war."

"For what?" asked the puzzled Taylor.

"Why, to make them damned Mexicans take the damned place back again!"

★

President Thomas Jefferson's humor was a bit acerbic, as is evident in his comment about newspapers. He said: "The most truthful part of a newspaper is the advertisements."

★

The humorist Will Rogers visited President Warren G. Harding in the White House. After they had passed the time of day, Rogers said: "I'd like to tell you some of my latest jokes, Mr. President."

"Oh, you won't have to do that, Will," said President Harding. "I appointed them."

President James A. Garfield likened office-seekers to alligators: "They open their mouths for a horse but are perfectly willing to settle for a fly."

The President enlarged the story by pointing out an instance where an individual requested one of the highest positions in the Government. He was told he could not have it. He came back for a lesser appointment and was still refused. He dropped down another notch and still another, until he finally accepted a position as deputy doorkeeper of the Senate coal cellar.

★

During the inauguration of President Kennedy, a massive crowd jammed into the area in front of the Capitol. A senator was caught in the crush and was unable to break through to his place on the platform. While the tugging and hauling were going on, a man with a big Western hat turned to the senator and said: "Would you mind holding my hat for a minute?"

"What?" the senator snarled. "Me hold your hat? I want you to know, mister, that I am a United States senator!"

"What of it?" said the Westerner. "Despite that I'll trust you."

★

At the birth of President Cleveland's second child, no scales could be found to weigh the baby. Finally the scales that the President always used to weigh the fish he caught on his trips were brought up from the White House cellar. The child was found to weigh twenty-five pounds.

★

Harry S Truman was a pepper pot and was never one to shy away from a battle. After his successful presidential campaign where the slogan "Give 'em hell, Harry" caught the imagination of the voters, Truman denied he gave anyone hell.

"All I did," he explained, "was to tell the truth. They thought it was hell."

During the height of the secession crisis, Prince de Joinville asked Lincoln what policy he was going to follow, now that the very existence of the American republic seemed in peril.

"I have no policy," said Lincoln. "I pass my life in preventing the storm from blowing down the tent, and I drive in the pegs as fast as they are pulled out."

★

President Lincoln was discussing a certain book on Greek history with a visiting diplomat. Old Abe commented that it was a very tedious account of the Greeks. "I don't agree," said the diplomat. "The author of that book is one of the most profound scholars of the age. Indeed, it may be doubted whether any man of our generation has plunged more deeply into the sacred fount of learning."

"Or come up drier," said Lincoln.

★

Shortly after John F. Kennedy had taken over the presidency, Ted Sorensen, JFK's brilliant speech-writer, lunched with Richard Nixon, the defeated candidate. "I certainly wish I had said some of those things Jack said in his inaugural speech," said Nixon.

Sorenson felt rather proud. "What part," he asked, "the part about not asking what your country can do for you?"

"Heavens no," said Nixon, "the part that starts, 'I do solemnly swear . . .'"

★

Senator Charles Sumner of Massachusetts was a pompous man. He lorded it over everyone within reach. President U. S. Grant said of the giant senator: "The reason Sumner doesn't believe in the Bible is because he didn't write it himself."

★

President Taft was a huge man, and when he walked the floors literally bent under his weight. Inevitably, he was the subject of many humorous stories, not the least of which was one about his visit to the home of an old friend. It was a small house and not well built. As Taft walked about, it seemed the house shook in every rafter.

When Taft went to sleep that night, the bed gave way, dumping the President on the floor. His friend hurried to the door.

"What's the matter, Bill?" he cried anxiously.

"Oh, I'm all right, I guess," Taft good-naturedly called out to his friend, "but say, Joe, if you don't find me here in the morning, look in the cellar."

★

President Harry S Truman had a little sign on his desk at the White House, and it pretty well conveyed his feelings about the presidency. It read: "Always do right. This will gratify some people and astonish the rest."

★

Lyndon B. Johnson, whose humor was of the backroom variety most of the time, often introduced his wife Lady Bird as "my own secretary of war."

★

During the Truman administration, a leading industrialist completed a tour of service with the federal government. Returning home, he was given a testimonial dinner by his Truman-hating silk-stocking Republican friends.

When the guests were seated at the head table, a powerful Republican turned to the guest of honor and asked: "Ernie, tell us. What do you think of Harry Truman?"

The industrialist shook his head. "No," he said, "I can't possibly tell you. If I told you what I thought of that little guy, it would positively shock you."

The conversation shifted to other subjects. When the ladies had retired to the lounge room, the powerful Republican started his inquiry again. "Look, Ernie," he said, "the ladies have left the room. We aren't easily shocked. Tell us. What is your opinion of that runt?"

Still Ernie was adamant. After the last guest had gone home, just before midnight, the hard-nosed Republican grabbed the guest and sidled him off into a corner, whispering: "Look, Ernie, we're alone now; my wife is out of earshot. What do you think of Harry Truman?"

"All right," said Ernie, looking over his shoulder, "I like the little son-of-a-bitch."

★

President Theodore Roosevelt loved theatrics. One of his sons put it this way: "Dad always had to be the center of attraction. When he went to a wedding, he wanted to be the bridegroom; and when he went to a funeral, he wanted to be the corpse."

★

A sharp photographer managed to talk President Calvin Coolidge into posing in a cowboy outfit in the Black Hills of South Dakota. The photo, which showed Silent Cal in chaps, a wool shirt, bandana, and oversized Stetson which dropped over his ears, did the President no good.

Will Rogers was at that time burlesquing his way as a candidate for President and having the time of his life. A fellow comic named Raymond Hitchcock, who was campaigning for Rogers, came up with this witty piece of advice: "Vote for Rogers for President—and at least we'll have a President who won't look funny in a cowboy suit."

★

One night at a reception for President Grover Cleveland, one of the guests, Frank H. Brooks, shook hands with the guest of honor. "Mr. Cleveland," remarked Mr. Brooks, "I am very glad to thank you personally for the only political honor I've ever received."

"What was that?"

"You appointed me consul to Trieste."

"Ah, indeed. How did you like Trieste?"

"I didn't go there. You afterwards changed the appointment to consul general to St. Petersburg."

"Well, then, how did you like St. Petersburg?"

"I didn't go there, either. Family reasons finally compelled me to decline the appointment."

"Shake hands again," exclaimed President Cleveland. "I have never before, to my knowledge, had the distinguished honor of shaking hands with a Democrat who refused two offices."

★

A visitor at the White House said to Franklin Delano Roosevelt: "I see that Republican Wendell Willkie has his eye on the presidential chair?"

"Yes," said FDR, smiling, "but look what *I've* got on it."

★

One of the worst pests Lincoln had to face was a bald-headed man who cornered the President time and again seeking a government job.

When the man finally worked himself into the President's office, Lincoln listened to him for a few minutes and then walked over to a cabinet, took a bottle from it, and, proffering it to the man, said:

"Did you ever try this stuff?"

"No," the man replied after looking at the label, "what is it for?"

"It is said that this will grow hair on a pumpkin," replied Lincoln. "Take it and try it for several months. If hair doesn't grow immediately, keep on trying. Rub it in well each day for about ten months then come back and let me know how it works."

"Will it work, Mr. President?" asked an aide after the bald-headed man had left.

"Only to keep him out of here," said the President wearily.

★

A visitor who collected cigar bands was permitted to see President Coolidge. Noting that it was a great chance to obtain a Coolidge cigar band, he rather emotionally asked Cal for one.

The President went to the drawer, opened it, took out a cigar, removed the band, and handed it to the collector. Later someone said to Coolidge that he thought it would have been nice if he had given him the cigar as well.

Coolidge replied: "Well, he only wanted the band, didn't he?"

★

Every President has his troubles, and Millard Fillmore was no exception. When he had the first bathtub installed in the White House in 1851, a national scandal virtually ensued. Red-blooded Americans who generally took a bath once a year, if at all, complained that the chief executive was a sissy. The deadly cartoonists and reporters of the period had a great time with the issue.

Fillmore was not renominated for the presidency. There were other factors, of course, but some historians contend that part of the opposition came from those who believed that Fillmore's desire to take a bath every Saturday night in a bathtub was too ladylike. "After all," one editor wrote, "the Presidency is a man's job."

The President never did get it across that the bathtub was for his wife.

★

President Eisenhower's favorite ex-President joke had to do with golf. When a reporter asked him if he noticed anything different since leaving the White House, Ike smiled and said: "Yes, a lot more golfers are beating me."

★

A White House porter named Jim O'Neil had become involved in a violation so flagrant that President Jackson felt he should be fired.

"Do you believe the story about me?" O'Neil asked the President.

"Certainly," Jackson replied. "I have heard it from two different senators.

"Faith, man," said O'Neil (and the response saved his job), "if I believed all that the twenty senators said about you, it's little I'd think you fit to be President."

Jackson dismissed O'Neil with a shake of the head and told him to go back to work and not get into any more trouble.

★

Coolidge stories are endless, and a favorite with the Washington press was one in which the President walked into the office of his secretary and greeted a newsman with this inquiry:

"What's the news?"

"I have just come from the Shipping Board where they sold the United States Lines for several million dollars," the correspondent replied.

"That so?" asked the President. "Who gets the money?"

★

Lincoln was visited one day by a federal officer who tendered his resignation. "All right, Addison," said the President, "I accept your resignation, but nothing can compensate me for the loss of you, for when you retire I will be the ugliest man left in the employ of the government."

★

President Andrew Jackson had many qualities, some good and some bad. However, gallantry was one of his strong suits, as was demonstrated on a visit to Philadelphia. A hale, buxom young widow greeted Jackson with a shake of both hands, at the same time exclaiming: "My dear General, I am delighted to see you—I have walked six miles this morning to enjoy this rare felicity."

The President brought himself to his full height and with an air of dignified gallantry replied: "Madam, I regret that I had not known your wishes earlier. I certainly would have walked halfway to meet you."

★

Speaking at a Washington luncheon, President John Kennedy poked fun at a certain Washington lawyer who had made it a point of knowing everybody. The lawyer was reputed to have received five million dollars as his lobbyist fee following passage of an important piece of legislation.

Said Kennedy: "This man is a modest, self-effacing, unselfish, and dedicated individual. All he asks in exchange for his selfless assistance to officeholders is to have the name of his law firm printed on every dollar bill."

★

When President Wilson asked for the passage of daylight-saving legislation, Senator Frank B. Brandegee of Connecticut cried: "Great heavens! Having regulated the earth, is he now taking charge of the solar system?"

★

A delegation from Kansas, calling upon Theodore Roosevelt at Oyster Bay, was met by the President with coat and collar off. "Ah, gentlemen," he said, mopping his brow, "I'm delighted to see you, but I'm very busy putting in the hay now. Come down to the barn and we'll talk things over while I work."

When they reached the barn, there was no hay waiting to be thrown into the mow. "James!" shouted the President to his hired man in the loft. "Where's that hay?"

"I'm sorry, sir," admitted James, "but I just ain't had time to throw it back since you forked it up for yesterday's delegation."

★

President Kennedy attended the National Football Foundation dinner in 1961, and during his remarks he said: "Politics is an astonishing profession. It has enabled me to go from being an obscure member of the junior varsity at Harvard to being an honorary member of the Football Hall of Fame."

★

President Lyndon B. Johnson was a "to-the-core" Democratic politician. He knew all the angles and loved to give advice to party members starting out on the campaign trail. "Don't waste your time," he said, "telling Democrats about the qualities of our party. That is like telling people already in the pews what a sin it is not to come to church."

One of the cutting little jokes out of Washington involved the man who went to a psychiatrist and said to him: "Doctor, I'm in rough shape. I'm in politics, but I can't make a decision, I can't give a speech, I'm losing my friends, I'm not sure of what I'm doing. As a matter of fact, everything is wrong."

"Then, why don't you get out of politics?" the psychiatrist asked.

"I can't," the politician said. "You see, I'm the President."

★

When former President Taft was visiting Hampton Institute, in Virginia, he was overheard talking to a charming woman who was also to be a speaker at the final convocation. Handing the woman her wrap, Mr. Taft said: "Perhaps you had better carry it yourself. If we should be separated and I were found with a wrap I might be accused of having stolen it."

"Why, Mr. Taft," she said laughingly, "are you accustomed to such accusations?"

"My dear lady," replied Taft, "I am accustomed to anything. You see I have been President of the United States."

★

When Rupert Hughes wrote his controversial book, *George Washington*, revealing George as a man who could handle a goblet as well as a girl, the Washington press piled into the White House for a comment from Silent Calvin Coolidge.

"Our editors think, Mr. President," said the spokeman for the press, "that you should resent these aspersions on George Washington's memory. Will you say something for publication?"

President Coolidge thought a moment and then walked to the window, where he parted the curtains. "I see," said Cal, "that his monument is still standing."

★

President Grant felt that Postmaster General Jewell should be removed from the Cabinet, but he knew that a direct approach would bring resistance. One day, while talking over some matters with Jewell, Grant casually remarked: "Jewell, how do you think your resignation would look written out?"

Thinking it all in fun, Jewell took a piece of paper and scribbled out his "resignation." He handed it to Grant, laughing. "How does that look, Mr. President?"

Grant took a puff of his cigar, looked at the paper a moment, then replied: "That looks fine. I will accept it."

The President was serious and Jewell was out of the Cabinet.

★

At the height of his presidential service, Woodrow Wilson was stricken with a serious illness. Reports had him raving mad and suffering periods of delusion. The rumors were widespread around Washington that mental illness had set in, and many politicians probed away trying to find out if this was a fact. Among the inquisitive politicians was Senator Albert B. Fall, who had bitterly opposed Wilson over the years. He visited Wilson's sickroom to find out for himself what the truth was on the President's illness.

Fall said to Wilson: "I've been praying for you, sir."

"Which way, Senator?" said Wilson sharply.

When Senator Fall had left, the President said to his wife: "Imagine him praying for me. Is he trying to get me in wrong with the Almighty?"

★

An elaborate menu had been prepared for President Coolidge on the occasion of his first trip down the Potomac on the yacht *Mayflower*. Cal scanned the card carefully, frowned, and said:

"I took Latin and Greek, but I can't understand this. What I want is roast beef and baked potatoes, and put them down there so I'll know what I'm eating."

★

Coolidge once told a friend: "Many people don't understand why I'm President—least of all my father."

★

One of the games Presidents play is to make sure that everything that goes wrong is blamed on the previous administration.

"Elect me and I'll straighten out everything" suddenly gives way after the election to: "Look at the mess the previous administration left." Every President tries to get across the point that, had he been elected instead of George Washington, everything would have been rosy for the past two hundred years.

At a Washington dinner, President Kennedy admitted that the job was no sinecure when he said: "I used to wonder when I was in the House of Representatives how President Truman got into so much trouble. Now I'm beginning to get the idea."

Kennedy showed up at a meeting of the National Security Council one day, opened a folder filled with briefs of United States problems. He said: "Now let's see, did we inherit these problems or are they our own?"

Just before the meeting broke up, President Kennedy brought some humorous relief to the meeting by announcing: "I had plenty of problems when I came in, but just wait until the fellow that follows me sees what he will inherit."

★

Lyndon B. Johnson's favorite back-home-in-Texas story concerned the schoolteacher who was hired for one of the outlying district schools. The examining board asked him: "Do you believe the world is round or flat?"

"Doesn't matter," said the confident teacher, "I can teach it either way."

★

During Woodrow Wilson's service as President, there was a certain senator who had a habit of speaking out of the side of his mouth in real tough-guy fashion. Once while listening to the senator explain some legislation, Wilson whispered to another senator seated nearby: "That man is the only person I have ever known who can whisper in his own ear."

★

Lyndon B. Johnson always brought down the house at fund-raising dinners for the Democrats by stating: "I think it is essential the United States of America remain a two-party country. I'm a fellow who likes small parties—and the Republican party can't be too small to suit me."

★

President Eisenhower was a man who had faced countless dangers over a lifetime of military service. However, when called upon to address groups of women, he became extremely nervous. To an aide, he once whispered: "I'd rather face a cannon than these women."

In any event, one day he was called upon to address an organization of women meeting in Washington for a three-day convention. The President gave them the full treatment: military training, missiles, comparative strength of America vs. that of her enemies, weapons, the nation's firepower, etc. In fact, it was one of his best speeches to a women's group. When he had finished he asked: "And now, are there any questions?"

A neat little lady in a green dress arose and asked: "Will you tell us why Mamie always wears bangs?"

★

On one occasion, a man of tremendous importance in the business world rushed in on President Coolidge. With much trumpeting and tumult he presented the President with a new plan.

"What do you think of it, Mr. President?" he inquired.

"Won't 'mount t' anything," was the instant response.

"Well, I guess I'll be going."

"Wal," said Coolidge with his Yankee twang, "any time you've got anything you think we ought t' hear, come in."

★

President James Garfield once served as president of Hiram College in Ohio. The father of one of his students visited Garfield and asked if he could push his boy through school in order that he could obtain an early degree. He said he needed him in his business and didn't want the boy to waste too much time on education.

Said Garfield as he refused the request: "When God wanted to make an oak he took a hundred years, but He made a squash in two months."

★

President Wilson had a favorite story concerning a visit he made to the monument of Mark Twain in Hannibal, Missouri.

His pilgrimage was quiet and unannounced. Unknown to the natives, he asked one of them if he remembered Tom Saywer.

"Never heard of him," the Missourian replied.

"Do you recollect Huckleberry Finn?" asked the President.

"Finn? Finn?" pondered the native. "I remember a family of Finns up the road a piece, but I don't know if there was a Huckleberry among them."

The President tried again. "Do you recall Pudd'nhead Wilson?" he smiled.

"Sure do," said the native knowingly. "Voted for him twice."

★

One of President Truman's best stories concerned his own boyhood and the fact that he had such weak eyes he couldn't play baseball. "Since I could not see the ball," said Truman, "they gave me a very special job."

"What was that, Mr. President?" somebody asked. "Cheerleader?"

"No," said Harry, "umpire."

★

On one of President Franklin Roosevelt's campaign tours, he invited the mayor of a small city to ride in the open car with him. They were late for a scheduled meeting, and Roosevelt ordered the driver to speed up. As the machine whirled through the center of the town, the people on the sideline were but a blur. Finally the mayor said, "Mr. President, do you think you should be riding so fast?"

Roosevelt laughed and said: "Oh, it's all right—they know who I am."

"That may be so," responded the mayor, "but do you mind slowing up a bit so they can see who's with you?"

Colonel Edmund W. Starling, who guarded five Presidents as head of the White House secret service detail, had a great fondness for President Calvin Coolidge. He had a fund of little stories about Coolidge which he enjoyed telling to his friends.

One of Starling's favorites concerned a visit made by President Coolidge to Key West, Florida, upon his return from a conference in Cuba. Coolidge was tired and was looking for a little relaxation. Riding with the mayor of the city, Coolidge asked him if there were any picture shows in town.

"Why, yes, Mr. President," said the mayor. "We have five good picture shows in town. Two of them, I am told, are very good."

The President looked at the mayor very solemnly and said: "Do you get any free passes?"

Before the bewildered mayor could reply, Coolidge continued: "They used to give me free passes when I was mayor of Northampton."

★

Because of his huge size, President Taft was the butt of many stories. Not a particularly sensitive person, Taft told lots of stories on himself also. He often brought the house down with the tale of a train trip he took through the Midwest in the days when trains seldom stopped at the smaller towns.

Taft had made plans to stop at a little place in Kansas to visit some friends. He was informed that the train never made special stops "except for large parties."

"Oh, a large party is getting off at that station," Taft told the railroad conductor.

When the conductor asked the name of the party, Taft jovially said: "It's me."

★

President Warren G. Harding was known as the "Great Handshaker." Talking with Henry Ford one day, Harding said: "I think I have shaken hands with at east twenty-five per cent of the American people."

"Yes," said Ford, looking at one of his Model T tin lizzies

parked at the curb, "and I suppose I have shaken the bones of about half the population of the United States."

★

Someone asked Woodrow Wilson how long he would prepare for a two-minute speech. He said: "Two weeks."

"How long for an hour speech?"

"One week."

"How long for a two-hour speech?"

"I am ready now," said Wilson.

★

No man ever approached the presidency with more fear than Abraham Lincoln. Untried in national affairs, he truly believed that the American people had made a mistake in electing him.

Lincoln confided in a friend that if he could select his cabinet from the legal fraternity that had traveled the circuit with him in the early days, he believed he could avoid war or settle it without battle, even after the fact of secession.

"But, Mr. Lincoln," said the friend, "those old lawyers from the circuit are all Democrats."

"That I know," said Lincoln wearily, "but I would rather have Democrats I know than Republicans I don't know."

★

Westchester County, New York, is a Republican stronghold in which President Franklin Delano Roosevelt had few friends. He liked to tell the story of the commuter from Westchester, who always walked into the railroad station, handed the newsboy a quarter, picked up the morning paper, glanced quickly over the front page, then handed the paper back to the newsboy and raced for the train.

Curiosity being what it is, the newsboy finally asked the customer why he only glanced at the front page of the paper.

"Checking the obituary notices," said the commuter.

"Yes, but they are over on Page 22, and you never look inside the paper," the boy objected.

"Look, boy," came the bitter reply, "if the son-of-a-bitch I'm interested in dies, it will be on Page 1."

★

Harry Truman put it this way: "The President of the United States hears a hundred voices telling him that he is the greatest man in the world. He must listen carefully to hear the one voice that tells him he is not."

★

Former President Gerald R. Ford told a California Republican dinner crowd that he was America's first instant Vice-President, based on a resignation, and also America's first instant President, also based on a resignation. "The situation became so confusing," said Ford, "that the United States Marine Corps Band didn't know whether to play "Hail to the Chief" or "You've Come a Long Way Baby.""

★

Military reservists were being drawn up on Pennsylvania Avenue one day to be reviewed by President Lincoln and Secretary of State Seward. As he watched the young soldiers move in formation, Old Abe commented to Seward: "Mr. Secretary, I suppose there are a hundred men in those ranks who could hold your job or mine."

★

As a candidate for President, Jimmy Carter appealed to every imaginable segment including those who believe in UFO's. Carter let it be known through the media that years earlier he had sighted a "glowing light" in the sky and figured it out to be a UFO.

Others insisted, however, that the "glowing light" might just have been his well-lit brother Billy, "a little higher than usual."

★

Pianist Roger Williams played for President Harry S Truman's inaugural. When the performer had finished, Truman took over the piano to play a few numbers. At the conclusion, Williams said to HST: "Mr. President, you would have made a great pianist."

"Yes, I know," quipped Truman. "A helluva lot of people wish I'd stuck with it."

★

A reporter asked former President Eisenhower about mistakes he had made during his administration. "Two of them," said Ike with a grunt, "are now sitting on the Supreme Court."

★

Senator Everett Dirksen had a surefire way of getting under President Johnson's skin. Whenever the President called the senator, he said: "Hello, Everett. This is Lyndon."

Dirksen answered: "Lyndon who?"

★

Speaker Sam Rayburn of Texas had been in the House for forty-eight years. A reporter once asked him how many Presidents he had served under.

Looking the newsman straight in the eye, Sam replied: "Son, I never served *under* no President. I served *with* eight."

★

Personal hatred for President Jackson was high while he was the resident of the White House. One senator who had lost a bout with the fiery Jackson remarked bitterly: "I don't wish Jackson any harm, but I shouldn't care if the Almighty took a fancy to him."

★

Secretary of State Henry Kissinger was charged with having a fat ego, something Henry never denied. "In fact," said a by-stander, "Henry admitted that he was the only Secretary of State under whom two Presidents had served."

The presidency of the United States is the hottest seat in government, and during a period of presidential crisis Richard Nixon asked former President Lyndon Johnson for some advice.

"All I can tell you, Mr. President," said Johnson, "is that the President is like a jackass standing alone in the middle of a field in a driving hailstorm. There's nothing he can do but stand there and take it."

15

His Most
Superfluous Highness

During the Federal Constitutional Convention of 1787, the functions and proper form of address to be given the President of the United States were discussed at length.

The titles of English kings, "Sire," "Dread Sir," "Defender of the Faith," "Most Exalted Majesty," etc., were noted and pondered. Washington himself was in favor of "High Mightiness," used by the Statholder of Holland. When it was suggested that the President's title should be "His Excellency," Benjamin Franklin, always ready with a quip, observed: "In that case, I suppose the Vice-President ought to be called 'His Most Superfluous Highness.'"

Old Ben's suggestion, though never adopted, nevertheless set the tone for the ongoing political attitude toward the vice-presidency of the United States. With minor exceptions, any man who became Vice-President suffered instant anonymity. Most Chief Executives considered Vice-Presidents as little more than stowaways on the ship of state—or, in private conversations, something worse.

Through the decades the vice-presidency has been well described as "a collection of duties in which the incumbent can serve actively and honorably so long as he doesn't become too much of a nuisance to the President."

John Adams, the nation's first Vice-President, was far from happy with the job. President Washington grabbed all the headlines, and Adams felt that he was being shunted aside. Old John complained bitterly, saying: "My country has in its wisdom contrived for me the most insignificant office that ever the invention of man contrived or his imagination conceived."

Friction has often developed between the nation's two highest officeholders, much of it due to jealousy on the part of one or the other. As one President put it: "Can you imagine that cluck only a heartbeat away from running this country?"

Down through the years, Vice-Presidents have been given little to do but preside over the Senate, which almost always kept them at arm's length. The other duty was to collect their pay. One lonely Vice-President confided to a senator one day that he hoped the President would remember the name if they ever accidentally met someplace. Another V-P groaned: "This G—— d—— job is not an office; it is a dilemma."

Many capable men in both parties have been sidetracked into the vice-presidency, never to be heard from again. Others refused to be trapped, calling the vice-presidency America's answer to the catacombs of ancient Rome. They preferred to take their chances as governors, senators, congressmen, or whatever. "I'm too young to be buried alive," said an Eastern governor who had been approached to accept the Democratic nomination for Vice-President.

Thomas R. Marshall, Vice-President under Woodrow Wilson, and one of the most humorous of all Veeps, got the message early in his service in Washington. He had left the spacious offices of the governor of Indiana and then found the Vice-President's chamber in the Capitol so small it was necessary to keep the door open to obtain enough air to breathe.

What irked Marshall more than anything were the Senate guides. Taking groups on a tour of the Capitol, the guides pointed out the Vice-President's office as sort of a curiosity.

One day Marshall exploded. When a group of tourists gawked at his tiny office, Tom went to the doorway and cried: "If you look on me as a wild animal, be kind and throw some peanuts at me; but if you are really desirous of seeing me, come in and shake hands."

Blunt-spoken Harry Truman became Vice-President under Franklin Delano Roosevelt. In no time at all Truman became immobilized. Events whirled in every direction and nobody bothered to tell Harry what was going on. Frustrated and angry, Truman exploded with this remark: "The vice-presidency is about as useful as a cow's fifth teat."

Richard Nixon, as President Eisenhower's Vice-President, tried to find his own place in the sun, despite the tradition that Vice-Presidents should remain out of sight and anonymous. Reportedly close to Ike, Nixon still was not the man at the President's side during many of the great decisions made by the administration. In fact, pressed by newsmen for a comment on Nixon's contribution to the affairs of state, Eisenhower replied that if given a little time he might think of something. Ike later tried to explain it was an offhand remark and not intended the way he said it. However, it was the same type of observation other Presidents made about their second man.

When Jack Kennedy ran for President in 1960, he took on Senate Majority Leader Lyndon Johnson as his running mate. The two were as suited to each other as a pit dog and an alley cat. It was an uneasy accommodation, and when Camelot made it to the White House, Johnson was hit by a thousand elbows as the Kennedy clan moved him to the back of the bus.

For all his enormous knowledge of government, Johnson was not the man on the inside during the Kennedy years. A few photographs with the President, for Texas consumption, gave LBJ a little limelight. For the most part Johnson was consigned to the barbecue, roast beef, and rubber chicken circuits. It was galling and humiliating for the once-powerful Lyndon Baines Johnson. When LBJ's sputtering and backroom complaining reached the ears of the President's staff, it was brushed off. "There's only one 'big' man around here," was the comment, "and that ain't a cowboy from Texas."

Fate made Lyndon Johnson President of the United States. At the 1964 Democratic Convention, after accepting his own nomination, LBJ toyed with the nomination of Hubert H. Humphrey for Vice-President.

Johnson kept HHH on the string until the last minute, and then before a nationwide television audience boyishly announced his choice. It was not a serious moment as Johnson called upon the delegates to nominate Humphrey. Convention analysts delared that Johnson had come under the spell of the same power drug as his predecessors. For all his kidding and needling, he nevertheless was telling one and all that Old Lyndon was boss.

During the Johnson years, Hubert Humphrey picked up the barbecue and Rotary Club circuit where Johnson had left off. When he was working the hinterland as Vice-President, Humphrey developed a monologue which greatly impressed the Democratic faithful. Though extremely humorous, the monologue nevertheless conveyed to the audience in a subtle manner that Humphrey had no illusions about the job of Vice-President.

"I thrive on activity," said Humphrey. "The President knows this and is giving me extra duties. In fact, before the President tosses out the ball to start the American League season, he always lets me rub up the ball."

There was irony in that remark, but no more than in another in the same speech, in which Humphrey declared: "My wife Muriel says I don't have enough to do and that I should get a part-time job in the neighborhood drugstore."

Among Vice-Presidents, Spiro Agnew was probably the most unusual in history. Spiro started out a candidate for Vice-President as unknown nationally as the coach of Slippery Rock College. When Nixon picked him as his running mate, Agnew was only six years removed from the presidency of his home-town Parent-Teacher Association. The puzzled electorate chorused: "Spiro *who?*"

When advised that nobody knew him, Agnew came up with the understatement of the year. "I realize," he observed, "that my name is not exactly a household word."

From that moment on, Spiro Agnew went on the attack. He developed a flair for Agnewisms which received good press. On the banquet and fund-raising circuit, Agnew became a sensation. No Vice-President of either party had ever been able to draw the faithful to the banquet tables like Spiro the Hero. His ability to put together mind-boggling statements and jawbreaking phrases made him a great crowd pleaser and splendid copy for the press. Agnew dug words out of the dictionary that had been dead for a hundred years, and used them to spear Democrats and Republicans alike, not to mention the press, peace groups, and whatnot.

In the short space of a few years since he came out of the mists at the Republican Convention in Miami in 1968, Spiro Agnew did more for vice-presidential visibility than any other man in history. He demummified the job, stood as his own man, throwing his own shadow. Agnew looked like the first Vice-President who would be talked of in equal terms with the President. Sadly, he blew the whole thing out the window with alleged indiscretions and was compelled to resign.

"It figured," cracked a newsman. "Here was a guy who came into the vice-presidency a nobody. He attempted to become somebody and damn near made it. Just when he was going good, they made him a nobody again."

The 1972 presidential election continued—at least among the Democrats—the age-old vice-presidential syndrome. *Who* would accept the nomination? Democratic hopeful George McGovern beat the bushes, trying to snare anybody with a name. The pickings were so slim that George even put a couple of mayors on his list, and not many presidential candidates had ever done that before. Finally, after winding up with a basketful of refusals, McGovern came up with Senator Thomas Eagleton of Missouri.

One of the world's great unknowns, Eagleton suddenly found himself getting more publicity than McGovern, all of it adverse. Personal problems finally drove Eagleton off the ticket, and McGovern cast around for a replacement.

Well-known Democrats scampered out of town, leaving no forwarding addresses. Others warned: "Tell George not to call me. I'll call him," then took the phone off the hook. One of McGovern's aides was asked if George had found a running mate as yet? "Running mate is right," sighed the downhearted aide. "All our Democratic mates are running—away."

But no matter what the job is in politics, there is always a warm body available. After McGovern had agonized for some time and his lists were getting lean, he came up with Sargent Shriver, one of Ted Kennedy's in-laws.

An old political bridesmaid, Shriver had been waiting for years for lightning to strike. He was always under the wrong tree until a desperate George McGovern tapped him to be his running mate.

When Shriver accepted the assignment to run with McGovern, a veteran Washington writer commented: "Running for vice-president will be a good thing for Sarge. It'll keep him busy for a few weeks. He wasn't doing anything anyway but playing tennis."

Thus another vice-presidential aspirant was kissed off even before he got started.

Following his confirmation as Vice-President, Gerald Ford's unassuming manner gained for him a high rating in national polls. This outraged a partisan Democrat and former congressional colleague of Ford's, who growled: "What the hell, we voted to confirm Ford in the expectation that he would restore the vice-presidency to its traditional role of political anonymity. Now that son-of-a-gun is more appealing to the public than the rest of us and I charge that to be a breach of faith on his part."

The resignation of Richard Nixon opened the way for Vice-President Gerald Ford to move to the White House, leaving the vice-presidency vacant. There was no wild rush of candidates to fill the post. Some of Ford's best political friends went hunting or fishing. "He'll never find me here," laughed a senator, as he broiled a couple of trout in a hideaway camp in Maine. The word around Washington was "Not available. Not even just to talk."

Ford finally selected former Governor Nelson Rockefeller of New York. There were others, of course, but Rockefeller seemed to be the one most eager to accept. He had passed up the offer to run for Vice-President at least a couple of times before, snorting such remarks as: "Who the hell wants to be the invisible man?" and "I have no inclination to be standby equipment."

Now the situation was different. Rockefeller had lost his political base when he resigned from the Governorship of New York. The presidency was out of reach for the sixty-six-year-old multimillionaire. There wasn't much around in politics for hyperactive Rockefeller, so he swallowed his pride and accepted Ford's bid to come aboard as Vice-President of the United States.

Following a grueling investigation by House and Senate committees, Rockefeller was confirmed, but not before some wag commented: "Christ, you'd think they were going to appoint him as one of the twelve Apostles. Didn't those birds understand his only task will be to stay reasonably healthy?"

"Well," said another cynic, "I wouldn't be too certain of that. If the country gets too far into financial trouble, Vice-President Rockefeller might write a check and take care of the national debt."

★

Vice-President Lyndon Johnson had a storehouse of Confederate jokes he loved to tell around the White House. One of his favorites had a hard-bitten Texan leaving his home town in 1861 to fight against the Union soldiers.

"We can lick those damyankees with broomsticks," he boasted. Two years later the doughty warrior came home minus a leg. His colleagues asked him what had happened, reminding him that when he went away he bragged of being able to lick the North with broomsticks.

"We could," said the Texan, "but the trouble was the damyankees wouldn't fight with broomsticks."

★

Vice-President John Nance Garner hated social events, but because of his position he was forced to attend many of them. One night because of his wife's indisposition he was compelled to go alone to a social function where the cream of Washington society was present.

When he arrived back in his apartment, his wife asked him how the affair went off, to which Garner answered: "Just fine."

"Who was there?" Mrs. Garner asked.

"Just about everybody," said the Vice-President.

"What were the women wearing?" quizzed Mrs. Garner.

Garner groaned: "Nothing above the table. And I didn't look underneath."

Warren G. Harding was one President who failed to grasp the full impact of the job. Like all Chief Executives, however, he had few words of praise for the vice-presidency. When someone asked him what the Vice-President did, Harding replied: "Oh, he handles the odd jobs around here and gets a good night's sleep to boot, which is a hell of a lot more than I can get."

★

"If a man would rather be right than President," observed a Washington writer, "then, my God, what would he rather be than Vice-President?"

★

Vice-President Alben W. Barkley once defined a "bureaucrat" as a Democrat who holds an office that some Republican wants.

★

The vice-presidency was a bore to Lyndon Johnson. He indicated his distaste for the job with a story about a chauffeur who had served Johnson during his days as Majority Leader and who now had been transferred to the Vice-President's limousine.

"One day," said Johnson, "I noticed he was becoming very grumpy. This was strange, for my chauffeur was ordinarily a very cheerful fellow. I asked him what his trouble was and this is the way he put it: 'Well, I don't mean to be personal or anything like that, but my wife thinks I ought to get a job driving somebody important.'"

★

In his youth Vice-President Charles G. Dawes was a poor speaker. As one of the lawyers in an important case, he was opposed by a seasoned attorney whose eloquence always attracted a large crowd. It was a hot July day, and the courtroom was literally steaming as the veteran lawyer worked up to his oratorical peak. Except for the judge, the listeners were transfixed.

Red-faced and perspiring, the magistrate mopped his brow, loosened his collar, and at last removed his coat and turned to the speaker: "Mr. Attorney," he interrupted, "I wonder if you would let Dawes speak for a while. I want to thin out the crowd."

★

Vice-President Alben Barkley was presiding over the Senate when a heated argument broke out between Scott Lucas of Illinois and Kenneth McKellar of Tennessee. The cross fire continued for a considerable period of time. Finally, Lucas sat down and listened to McKellar drone on. It was hot and late, and, drained by the oratory, Lucas finally yawned. Immediately McKellar protested vehemently, insinuating that Lucas was mocking him.

Barkley looked out at the two debaters, then turned to the parliamentarian and said: "The yawn of the senator from Illinois will be stricken from the record."

★

One unnamed President got himself in hot water during a discussion over the duties of his vice-president, for whom he had little use. When asked what assistance he gave the President, the deadly answer was: "Oh, him. I've got him in charge of replying to all the anonymous letters we receive here at the White House."

★

Thomas R. Marshall, Vice-President under Woodrow Wilson, probably made the most lasting statement of all Vice-Presidents when he coined the phrase: "What this country needs is a good five-cent cigar." A first-class wit, Marshall also said: "I come from Indiana, the home of more first-rate second-class men than any other state in the Union."

★

The unkindest cut of all so far as Vice-Presidents are concerned was the story which made the Washington rounds when Calvin Coolidge was second man in the national capital.

As the story was told, a fire broke out in a midtown hotel where Vice-President Coolidge was staying. The guests were routed from their rooms by the fire. When the blaze had subsided, many of the guests started back for their rooms, Coolidge among them. They were halted by the night manager, who shouted:

"Hey, you, get back there!"

"Sir," said Coolidge, pushing up to the manager, "you are speaking to the Vice-President."

"Oh, that's different. Go ahead."

As Coolidge left the desk, the manager yelled after him: "Wait a minute. What are you Vice-President of?"

Said Coolidge tightly: "The United States."

"Get back here," snapped the clerk. "I thought you were vice-president of the hotel."

★

When debate flared up in the Senate regarding a home for the Vice-President, South Dakota's Senator George McGovern offered this advice: "As for the argument that the country cannot afford to build a home for the Vice-President, I can only say it doesn't make sense. If we can afford an aquarium for the fish in the national capital, we can surely afford a home for the Vice-President."

★

Among United States senators, the office of Vice-President has little appeal. A number of years ago, during discussion of candidates for the second spot on the national ticket, a certain senator asked a colleague if he should take the nomination for Vice-President. "It's all right," was the response, "if your mother never finds out about it."

★

Charles G. Dawes, Vice-President under Coolidge, made an excellent comment on the duties of the Veep: "All I do is preside over the Senate, listen to the boring debate with no privilege of being able to answer back, and look at the newspapers every morning to check on the state of the President's health."

★

Many Vice-Presidents have been more interested in the President's health than they were in the health of the country. One newsman put it this way: "When the Vice-President greets the President, he learns to shake hands and feel his pulse at the same time."

★

Just after he had been elected Vice-President in 1920, Calvin Coolidge was invited to dinner by somebody he did not know. He asked his secretary to find out who the man was. She reported that the fellow was not listed in the Social Register.

"You can't tell much from that," said Coolidge, "I've only been in it myself for half an hour."

★

Some of Lyndon Johnson's aides were worried that Hubert Humphrey would try to upstage the President when the two got together as the 1964 Democratic ticket. When Humphrey heard the charge, he quipped: "That's like Rembrandt worrying about a college art student."

★

Vice-President Lyndon B. Johnson was talking with Speaker Sam Rayburn one day and commented on the brilliance of President Kennedy's Harvard advisers.

"You may be right, Lyndon," said Sam, "but I'd feel a whole lot better about them if just one of them had run for sheriff."

★

Thomas R. Marshall never took his duties as Vice-President with any degree of seriousness, knowing full well that history had long before his time relegated the job to the White House broom closet.

Marshall often told a story about a trip he made to Denver for a meeting. Walking about the town, he suddenly noticed that he was being followed by a policeman. Marshall stopped the officer and asked him why he was following him. The officer said he had been assigned to guard the Vice-President as he moved about town.

"Don't bother," said Marshall. "Nobody is crazy enough to shoot at a Vice-President. If you will go away and find somebody to shoot at me, I'll go down in history as the first Vice-President who ever attracted enough attention to have a crank take a shot at him."

★

Shortly after he became Vice-President, Calvin Coolidge was deluged with invitations to become honorary president of this club and that organization.

One day the president of a small Washington bank came to him, explained that his bank was small, new, but soundly managed—a worthy institution. Would Mr. Coolidge honor the bank with a deposit? Any amount, however small, would be appreciated.

"Why don't you make me an honorary depositor?" asked Coolidge.

16
Politicians at Large

John Randolph was one of the most irascible men ever to sit in the United States Senate. Almost to a man, his colleagues feared his fiery tongue.

Outside Congress it was no different, as was proved by an amusing incident that occurred one evening when Mr. Randolph stopped at an inn located near the fork of two roads.

The innkeeper was a fine old gentleman and, knowing who his distinguished guest was, he attempted to draw him into conversation but failed.

In the morning, Randolph, ready to continue his journey, called for his bill and paid it. The landlord, still anxious for some conversation, asked:

"Which way are you traveling, Mr. Randolph?"

"Sir?" said Randolph with a look of displeasure.

"I asked," said the landlord, "which way are you traveling?"

"Have I paid my bill?" said Randolph with a cold stare.

"Yes."

"Do I owe you anything more?"

"No."

"Well, I'm going just where I please; do you understand?"

"Yes," replied the shaken innkeeper.

Randolph stalked out the door and drove off. To the landlord's surprise, in a few minutes, one of Randolph's servants was back to inquire which of the forks in the road to take. Cupping his hands to his mouth, the landlord yelled at the top of his voice so Randolph could hear:

"You don't owe me a cent, mister; just take whichever damn road you please."

★

Governor Raymond C. Baldwin of Connecticut had a favorite story about party-line politics. It involved a Connecticut farmer who had butchered a hog. After dressing it down, the farmer hung the two halves in his barn.

During the night somebody broke into the barn and stole half of the hog. The next day the farmer was telling a neighbor of his misfortune:

"Some damn Democrat must have broken in and stolen half my hog," he complained angrily.

Said the neighbor: "How do you know it was a Democrat?"

"Very simple," replied the farmer. "If it had been a Republican who had broken in, he would have stolen the whole hog."

★

If a survey were taken among the wives of public officeholders, probably 80 per cent would wish their husbands out of the rat race and back with their families. Said one congressional wife: "Politics is for bachelors and grandfathers. It is not for fathers."

It takes a strong family structure to withstand the pressures of a political life. Observed another wife: "I always remind Harry who I am when he comes home. He's so darned preoccupied that he's liable to take me for just another voter."

Still another congressional wife said: "Congress, like war, is always harder on the women and children than it is on the men."

★

A group of former professors who had held positions in the Kennedy administration met in Washington for a reunion. They agreed that running government is different from writing and talking about it.

Once in government, the professors contended, there was no

time for thoughtful contemplation. The staffs were so large that their time was taken up just keeping track of things. To a man they stated there was no logical, coherent way to form policy.

Henry S. Rowan, a former Harvard professor who was a deputy assistant in the Defense Department, said it best when he told his fellow professors: "The Pentagon is like a log going downriver with twenty-five thousand ants on it, each thinking he is steering."

★

A testy Missouri congressman got his come-uppance on a Mississippi river steamboat one foggy night. Anxious to get downriver for an important speaking engagement, he was angered that the boat had stopped. Searching out the captain, the irate congressman demanded to know why the boat was not moving. "Too much fog. Can't see the river," replied the captain.

"But you can see the stars overhead," insisted the politician.

"Yes," replied the urbane captain, "but until the boiler busts, we ain't going that way."

The congressman wisely went to bed.

★

The involvement of clergymen in politics has become so commonplace that it has affected many parishioners.

Two stalwart churchgoers met one day and the first asked: "Well, Sam, what's going on in politics and world affairs these days?"

"Damned if I know," was the response. "I haven't been to church for the last two Sundays."

★

One of Senator Tom Connally's best stories concerned the posse that had just captured a horse thief and was preparing to string him up. One member of the posse spoke up: "May I say a prayer for this man?"

The deputy in charge of the posse protested: "Are you trying to sneak this yaller varmint into heaven when he ain't fit to live in Texas?"

In the summer of 1916, Woodrow Wilson asked Henry Ford to help finance his election campaign, since Ford was a strong advocate of peace. Ford refused outright but suggested that he would send a letter to every purchaser of a Ford car in America, advocating Wilson's election.

The President agreed to the deal, and Ford, true to his word, set up an office in New York City and sent a letter supporting Wilson to every Ford owner.

Sometime later when the subject came up concerning Ford's efforts in the campaign, Wilson remarked: "Old Henry Ford's patriotism and peace efforts were measured along with the sales of his cars."

★

Governor Ben Butler of Massachusetts was one of the stormy petrels of his time. His favorite story concerned a dinner conversation on the merits of Philadelphia and Boston. A guest from Philadelphia commented that Boston was a compact and substantial city, but was not as well laid out as Philadelphia.

"No," said Butler, "Boston is not as well laid out as Philadelphia, but she will be when she is as dead as Philadelphia."

★

A member of the Massachusetts House had been appointed to a special committee set up to investigate the growing menace of pornography. He became so wrapped up in the subject that he accepted invitations to speak around the state.

Appearing one afternoon before a ladies' club, he proceeded to castigate X-rated movies, telling his audience: "Why, our committee saw a movie last night, which included rape, homosexuality, lesbianism, and in fact almost every kind of perversion you could think of. It was a disgrace to the human eye."

Then he concluded: "And now, ladies, are there any questions?"

Simultaneously three ladies cried out: "Where's it playing?"

★

Many congressmen dislike the city of Washington, and it has always been that way. A number of years ago, a veteran representative was standing on the train platform when a starter came over and asked: "Mister, do you want to go to Washington?"

"Hell, no," was the congressman's instant reply. "Dammit, I have to."

★

America is not the only country that brings down its politicians with ridicule and satire. Behind the Iron Curtain political humor is rampant but more secretive than in the United States. One story is told about a comrade who arrived at the voting place and asked for a ballot. He was handed a sealed envelope to drop in the ballot box.

Taking the envelope, he started to open it when a man at the desk jumped up and screamed: "Stop, don't open that."

"What's the matter?" asked the voter. "I just want to see who I am voting for."

"You must be out of your mind," said the official. "Don't you know that this is a secret ballot?"

★

Shortly after Mike DiSalle had been badly beaten for governor of Ohio, he was chosen to teach a course in "practical politics" at the University of Massachusetts. When the news arrived of Mike's appointment, a wag remarked: "That's about like hiring Tommy Manville (many times married) to teach home economics."

★

Upon his return from Russia a few years ago, Bob Hope described the hotel situation in Moscow. "Yes, they have television in every room there," he declared. "Only, of course, it watches you."

★

Congress never had a better storyteller than Alben Barkley. One of his best concerned a widow who showed up at the town cemetery with a package of grass seed and a watering pot. The caretaker watched as the lady stopped by the grave of her late husband. She planted the seed and was watering it from the pot when the caretaker moved in and asked her:

"What are you doing there, ma'am?"

"I'm planting some grass seed on my husband's grave," she replied.

"What's the use of watering it?" said the caretaker. "It will get enough water when it rains."

"That may be," said the widow, "but when my husband died last winter, he made me promise that I would not marry again until the grass grew on his grave—and frankly, mister, I had a good offer last night."

★

Former Senator Sam Ervin of North Carolina claimed that more common sense comes out of the hills of his state than from any college campus in America. One of Sam's favorite stories concerned a crusty old backwoodsman who told his country preacher: "You aim to try and tell me that the Lord loves me when he ain't even ever knowed me?"

The pastor thought a moment and said: "Lish, let me put it this way. It's a whole heap easier for the Lord to love you *without* knowin' you than it would be *if* he knowed you."

★

A Sunday-school teacher was telling of Jesus' triumphal entry into Jerusalem on a donkey, when a youngster in the front row piped up and said: "I didn't know Jesus was a Democrat."

★

The mayor of a flourishing town near London was convicted of extensive frauds. The next mayor was also involved in fraudulent activities that landed him in jail. Despite their convictions, portraits of the two former mayors were placed in the town council chambers in accordance with a long-standing rule.

When the third mayor left office after two terms of exemplary service, he was asked why he had not presented his portrait to the council. He was informed: "There's a vacant space between the two former mayors."

"I don't care to have my picture there at present," said the outgoing mayor. "If they'll remove the other portraits I'll put mine up. At present it is too suggestive of the Crucifixion."

★

The late Governor Harold Hoffman of New Jersey was a top-flight storyteller, and most of his yarns were on himself. Hoffman always got a laugh from a story having to do with a period when the New Jersey voters were down on him for a few bad gubernatorial decisions.

It seems Hoffman went to a well-known Newark restaurant with a friend. After sitting forty-five minutes in the crowded little bar area, waiting to be called to the dining room, Hoffman became uneasy and said to his friend: "I dislike doing things like this, Jack, but perhaps it would help if you told them who I am."

Hoffman's friend shrugged his shoulders and said: "I dislike telling you this, Governor, but I did—fifteen minutes ago."

★

Shortly after the Revolution, during the period of the first Congress, an American visited London. The Earl of Dartmouth asked him how many members the first Congress included. The reply was "Fifty-two." The Earl pondered a moment and then said: "Why that is the number of cards in a pack." Then he added: "How many *knaves* are there?"

"Not one," returned the American. "For, you see, *knaves* are *court* cards."

★

The people of the North and South of Ireland pass up no opportunity to tell jokes about each other. One of the best North-South-of-Ireland stories concerns an official of Northern Ireland, who visited Dublin on government business. Once there, he went to a tailoring shop and bought some cloth for a suit.

The tailor told him that he had enough goods there to make a suit and two pairs of trousers. He took the goods up north, but his own tailor measured the material and said: "You've been given a short measure. There isn't enough goods here for a suit."

On the next trip to Dublin, the Prime Minister took the goods and rushed to the tailor. "My tailor up north said there isn't enough goods here for a suit. Why did you tell me you could make a suit and two pair of pants out of it?"

"Sure, because down here you're not as big as you are up there," was the quick response.

★

Governor Tom Marshall of Indiana was a top-flight chief executive and a first-class wit. Not only did his repertoire of stories involve Indiana politics, but he had many good yarns about neighboring Kentucky and the mountaineers of that state.

One of Marshall's favorites concerned a family reunion in a Kentucky hill town which terminated in a free-for-all. The offenders were lugged off to court where the justice of the peace questioned one old lady as to the particulars of the fight. Her description was typical of the mountaineers' attitude toward strife and bloodshed.

"I tell ye, Jedge," she said. "Jim Howard got himself into an argument with Henry Gates. Henry smashed Jim over the head with a stick of cordwood and busted his head open. Then Jim's brother cut Henry up with a butcher knife and Dick Collins shot him through the leg. Pete Lilly went at Dick with an ax, and from that point on, Jedge, we just naturally got to fightin'."

★

When Frank Lausche was governor of Ohio, he had a favorite story about himself and a walk he took in front of the State House one day. Lausche noticed a mother with a camera and a little boy. He stopped to talk to them and then suggested: "Would you like to take a picture of me with your son?"

The mother replied: "I am sorry, sir, I have only one shot left and I want to take a picture of the squirrels."

★

At a gathering in Washington, Adlai Stevenson introduced

Rose Kennedy, mother of the President, Attorney General, and Senator, as "the head of the most successful employment agency in America."

★

Looks are always deceiving, as was proven when Senator Daniel Webster was compelled to proceed at night by stage from Baltimore to Washington. He had no traveling companion and the driver had a sort of criminal look about him, which produced alarm in the senator. Despite that, Webster felt he had better keep going, for he had to be in Washington for a meeting the next morning.

As Webster told the story, it went like this: "I endeavored to tranquilize myself and had partly succeeded when we reached the dark woods between Bladensburg and Washington—a proper scene for murder or outrage—and here, I confess my courage deserted me.

"Just then the driver turned to me, and with a gruff voice, inquired my name. I gave it to him. 'Where are you going?' he asked. The reply was 'To Washington. I am a Senator.'

"Upon this, the driver seized me fervently by the hand and exclaimed, 'How glad I am! At first glance I took you for some sort of a desperado!'"

★

In the course of a political campaign, a pretty young Republican worker fell in love with an equally energetic Democratic worker. They were married, and when the next election came around, a call went out to the home of the young couple to assist in the campaign.

"We can't get involved in politics this year," said the new bride. "We are spending our time trying to launch a third party."

★

Early Texas governors were not noted for their education. It was said of one chief executive that he thought "grammar" was his father's mother. On one occasion he went hunting and forgot his gun. He phoned his secretary and asked him to send the gun.

The secretary said: "The phone connection is poor; I can't catch that word; please spell it." The governor replied:

"G as in Jesus; U as in onion; N as in pneumonia—GUN you damn fool!"

★

After a trip to Washington some years ago, Lewis Douglas, former ambassador to Great Britain, was asked how a member of the Democratic administration was handling a particularly vexing problem.

"You don't have to worry a bit," said Douglas. "He's got the situation right in the hollow of his head."

★

Politicians are a vain lot, as was demonstrated by a well-known female psychologist while speaking before a group of congressmen. During the course of her remarks, she commented: "It's a shame that politicians attach so little importance to the way they dress. Why, right this minute as I look out at this group, I notice that the smartest politician in this room has his tie on crooked."

As if on cue, every politician in the room immediately put his hand to his tie.

★

Two senators, one a Democrat and the other a Republican, had fought bitterly for nearly twenty years. Finally, a peacemaker stepped in. "Look, boys," he said, "why don't you cut out this constant fighting? Let's go across the street and have a few drinks and make peace."

When each had a highball in hand, the third party said: "Now, make a toast to each other." One raised his glass and purred: "Here's wishing for you what you're wishing for me."

"I'll be an SOB," yelled the other, "you're starting in all over again."

"Is there such a thing," asked the musically inclined young tourist of Senator Vandenberg "as 'The Washington Waltz'?"

"There sure is," said Vandenberg, smiling.

"How does it go?" the young lady asked.

"Well, the one I know," said Vandenberg, "goes like this: one step forward, two steps to the rear, and then the sidestep. Every politician in Washington is good at this particular waltz."

★

Senator George G. Vest of Missouri was a robust man until his early seventies, when he started to decline physically. Concerned friends asked him what his trouble was. Said Vest: "Well, I am in the same position as an old friend of mine back home. He saw forty doctors and each one told him he had a different malady. Finally he took the case into his own hands and discovered that all that ailed him was Anno Domini. And I think I have the same affliction."

★

Speaker Tom Reed's favorite story concerned an old potato farmer in Maine for whom the Speaker obtained a postmastership. The small-town post office handled only about thirty letters a year. A few months after the appointment, Reed started to get complaints that no mail was coming out of the town.

When he went back to Maine, he dropped over to the post office where his friend was warming his feet against the stove. "What has been happening to the mail here?" asked Reed.

"Well, Tom," said the postmaster, "the danged bag ain't full yet."

★

Speeding out of Washington one evening, a congressman was halted by a highway patrol trooper. Before the officer had time to pull out his ticket book, the congressman said: "Now look here, Corporal, I admit I was going a bit fast, but I'd like to point out to you that I am a congressman . . ."

He got no further as the trooper stopped him with: "Ignorance is no excuse."

Politicians must be very careful of what they say around children, as the following story illustrates. A governor of a Western state once visited the home of an influential state senator who had a ten-year-old son. During the entire dinner, the boy gazed intently at the governor.

Finally the youngster asked: "Are you really and truly a governor?"

"Yes," replied the great man laughingly, "I really and truly am."

"I've always wanted to see a governor," continued the child, "for I've heard Daddy speak of 'em."

"Well," rejoined the governor, "now that you have seen one, are you satisfied?"

"Yes, sir," answered the youngster, without the slightest impertinence, but with an air of conviction, "yes, sir. Daddy can't be right, though. You don't look like a jackass to me."

★

When Tom Marshall was governor of Indiana he often told a story about a man who left the Presbyterian Church to become a Christian Scientist.

One of his friends met him and asked what he thought of his new church. His answer was typical of Indiana backcountry thrift. "It's just as good as my old church," said the Hoosier, "and a damn sight cheaper."

★

Senator Ben (Pitchfork) Tillman of South Carolina is credited with having said: "Texas has more trees and less timber; more rivers and less water; more resources and less cash; more itinerant preachers and less religion; more cows and less milk, and you can see farther and see less than any damn country in the world."

★

A sadder but wiser congressman had a disastrous experience with a gold mine speculation. One day a number of colleagues were discussing the subject of speculation, when one of them said

Some years ago, Representative Olin Teague of Texas visited Greece. At an embassy party he was introduced to the popular Greek drink *ouzo*. After the first glass, he noticed the furniture moving around. "This is a powerful drink," he said to the ambassador.

"Not particularly," the ambassador replied. "This happens to be an earthquake."

★

Political reputations can often be difficult to shake, as was pointed up at a Washington hotel dining room many years ago. A well-known but crafty senator was enjoying his meal when he noticed that the waiter was constantly hovering over him. Eventually, the exasperated senator asked: "What are you doing standing over me while I'm eating my meal?"

"Excuse me, sir," said the waiter, fumbling for his napkin, "but you see, sir, I'm responsible for the silver."

★

Senator Charles Sumner of Massachusetts was haughty, self-possessed, and difficult to please, an attitude which made him the butt of many Capitol Hill jokes. One of the more popular anecdotes about him had Sumner passing away and arriving at St. Peter's gate, where he was asked the usual questions.

"What is your name and where did you live?"

"I am Senator Charles Sumner and I come from Massachusetts."

"You may come in," said St. Peter, "but I know you won't like it here."

★

The very popular governor of Massachusetts Jim Curley had a storehouse of tales about his supporters in the back wards of Boston. One of them concerned an Irish longshoreman who boasted that he could lick any man in Boston and in the whole state of Massachusetts as well. Finally, he added New England to his list.

Curley met the man one day and noticed that he was bruised,

to this member: "Old chap, as an expert, give us a definition c the term 'bonanza.'"

"A bonanza," replied the burned congressman with emphasi "is a hole in the ground owned by a champion liar."

★

Another of Senator Sam Erwin's favorite stories comes straigh out of the mountain region of North Carolina. It was the custor in this area to hold religious meetings at which the oldest membei of the congregation were called upon to stand up and publicl testify to their religious experiences.

On one such occasion an ancient mountaineer named Ephrair Swink, whose body was all bent and distorted with arthritis, wa present. All the older members except Ephraim stood up and gav testimony to their religious experiences. Uncle Ephraim kept hi seat. Thereupon the moderator said: "Brother Ephraim, suppos you tell us what the Lord has done for you."

Old Uncle Ephraim rose with a groan as he tried to straighte: his bent and twisted body. Then he said: "Brother, the Lord ha mighty near ruint me."

★

While traveling through Arizona Governor Glasscock of Wes Virginia noticed the dry, dusty appearance of the country "Doesn't it ever rain around here?" he asked one of the natives.

"Rain?" the native spat. "Rain? Why, say, pardner, there's bull frogs in this here town over five years old that hain't learned tc swim yet."

★

Jack Kennedy was always being kidded about his father's money and was even accused of using his wealth to buy votes. At a Grid-iron dinner in Washington, the witty JFK defused the accusation by declaring: "I have received the following telegram from my generous father: 'Dear Jack, Don't buy a single vote more than is necessary. I'll be damned if I'm going to pay for a landslide.'"

battered, and barely able to walk. "What happened?" said the governor.

"I tried to cover too much territory," was the response.

★

Like all politicians, Mayor Fiorello La Guardia was often hurt by the ingratitude of the average citizen. At City Hall he sometimes dispensed with his battery of assistants and answered the phones himself. La Guardia figured that this kept him closer to the people. One day he took a call from an irate woman in the Bronx. "The plumbing in my house is on the bum," she shrieked, "and the bathroom is all clogged up. But the landlord and the cops won't do anything about it."

"Think nothing of it," responded La Guardia. "I will have it fixed immediately. Call me later and let me know if it is okay."

In no time, the entire emergency crew of the New York City Department of Buildings was at the lady's home and the plumbing was repaired pronto, at no cost to the citizen.

Later on that day, the woman called the mayor to thank him. La Guardia accepted the call. "Now, you can do me a favor, madam," said the Little Flower. "Next time I run you can vote for me!"

There was a pause at the other end of the line, then a burst of angry language hit La Guardia's ear as the woman shouted: "Vote for you? Are you nuts? Don't you know I'm a lifelong Democrat?"

★

Christophe, King of Haiti, offered this comment on New England enterprise and ingenuity: "Hang up a bag of coffee in hell," said His Majesty, "and a Yankee would go down and bring it back without being singed."

★

"Religion has changed," Senator Everett Dirksen once told a group of divinity students. "The ancient church tried to save its young from being thrown to the lions; now we are glad if we can save them from going to the dogs."

When he was advised that President Richard Nixon had installed secret tape recorders in the Oval Office to record conversations, unbeknownst to visitors, Senator Bob Dole of Kansas commented: "Thank goodness I only nodded."

★

Illinois Congressman Ebon C. Ingersoll loved self-deprecating humor, and one of his best stories concerned a speech he was to deliver in St. Louis for which he had been offered a fat fee.

As Ingersoll told it, he arrived at the hall and noticed a man standing near the entrance. He had a forlorn look on his face and was also carrying a scraggly puppy in his arms.

Ingersoll inquired of the man if all was well: "Why, no, sir," said the man, "I want so much to hear you speak, but I have no money and I am trying to sell my puppy to raise enough money to buy a ticket."

"Oh," said Ingersoll expansively, "be my guest." With that, he led the man inside, found a safe place for the puppy and a front seat for the man.

"Well," said Ingersoll later, "when I had finished my oration and condemnation of the government, I sought out the man and asked him how he had liked my speech."

" 'I'm glad I didn't sell my dog,' was the man's response as he patted his puppy and headed for the exit."

★

One of Senator Chauncey Depew's "chestnuts" with which he regaled many an audience was his famous dog story.

"My father let me go to the circus," said Depew, "after I had just finished a five-acre field of corn. While in town, I saw for the first time in my life a spotted coach dog. I bought it and took it home. When my father saw the spotted dog, he said it would frighten the cattle.

"I assured my father it was a blooded dog and would be no trouble. The next day I took the dog into the woods to try him on a coon, but it started to rain. The next thing I knew the dog's spots had disappeared.

"With a long face, I took the dog back to the dealer, complaining that the rain had washed the spots off the dog and, instead of a fancy coach dog, all I had was a white mongrel.

"'Great guns, boy!' exclaimed the dog dealer. 'There was an umbrella went with that dog. Didn't you get the umbrella?' "

★

Every governor is sooner or later approached by lovers of the arts who complain that the chief executive is not giving enough attention to their interests.

When some intellectuals told a Kentucky governor that he was neglecting music, the governor responded: "Gentlemen, you are misinformed. I've never authorized a single campaign expense that did not include a brass band or a group of country singers."

★

Many years ago, a United States senator was stranded by a flood. He finally waded through the water and mud until he arrived at the town hotel. As he registered, he remarked to the clerk: "Boy, this flood is just like the deluge."

"What was that, stranger?" said the clerk.

"I said, my good man," answered the senator, "that this was just like the deluge. You know, Noah, the Ark, Mount Ararat."

"Sorry, no," said the clerk, shrugging, "the water has been so high that we ain't had no papers delivered here for more 'n three days."

★

Senator Chauncey Depew was a world traveler. Among his favorite stories was one about a friend who, on his way to Europe, was experiencing violent seasickness.

Calling his wife to his bedside, the man said in a weak voice: "Mary, my will is in the care of the Commercial Trust Company. Everything is left to you, dear. My various stocks you will find in my safe deposit box."

Then he said fervently: "And Mary, I just want one thing from you. Bury me on the other side. I can't stand this trip again, dead or alive."

Governor Herman Talmadge was being interviewed on a Florida television broadcast, in the course of which he was asked: "Is it true, Governor, that thousands of Georgians have migrated to the better life in Florida, and how do you feel about the exodus?"

"I agree," replied Talmadge, "that lots of people have left Georgia for Florida and I feel that it raises the level of intelligence in both states."

★

Former Speaker of the House Carl Albert got plenty of mileage from a story about a young fellow who approached a farmer's house and told the farmer: "I was at the wheel of that hay truck down the road when the load of hay overturned a while ago—and . . ."

"Come right in, boy," said the farmer. "You've come to the right place for help. But cool off first. Have a glass of cider."

"No," said the boy, "Paw wouldn't like it."

"Come on. Have a glass of cider!" the farmer insisted, and although the boy protested that "Paw wouldn't like it," he nevertheless drank the cider.

"Now, how about some supper?" insisted the hospitable farmer.

"No," said the boy, shaking his head, "Paw wouldn't like that either."

"Listen, son," the farmer again insisted, "you've *got* to have supper," and the boy did. When they had finished the farmer pushed his plate back and said; "We'll go down now and reload the hay. By the way, where is your paw?"

The youngster shrugged his shoulders and said: "Under the hay."

★

"The trouble with this country," said a chronic complainer, "is that for the last year or so, it has been running on automatic pilot."

★

Vice-President Alben Barkley loved to tell stories about the Kentucky mountaineers. One of his best concerned the new preacher who came into a hill town for his first sermon. It was an eloquent sermon and his prayers seemed to cover the whole category of human wants.

After the services one of the deacons asked a crusty old mountaineer what he thought of the new minister. "Don't you think he offers a good prayer, Jasper?" the deacon asked.

"He mos' suttenly does," said Jasper. "Why, that man axed fo' things off the good Lawd the other preacher never knowed he had."

★

Senator Zebulon B. Vance told a story about a preacher who aspired to public office. A powerful and emotional man, he exhorted the crowd to help him win the election. "Then," said Zeb, "like all preachers, he asked for a collection. He handed his hat down and asked that it be passed around. When the hat had gone through the crowd it arrived back at the platform without a single penny in it. The preacher looked into the black emptiness of the hat and then raised his hands in pious fervor.

" 'Anyway, dear Lord,' he cried, 'let us be thankful that this hat got back safely through this crowd.' "

★

One of the best observations on the Republican vs. the Democratic approach to government was made by a Boston newsman of long experience at the State House. "As I see it," he said, "the G.O.P. is long on principles and short on political savvy. The Republicans love government and hate politics, while the Democrats love politics and find that government is a nuisance to them."

★

An admirer suggested to Mayor Fiorello La Guardia that the city of New York should erect a statue to the Little Flower for his work among the people. La Guardia nixed the suggestion and told the story of the statue of Christopher Columbus in Columbus Circle.

"That statue comes to life once a year on Columbus' birthday," said La Guardia. "One day, a reporter waited around until Old

Chris came to, on his annual reincarnation. The reporter asked Columbus a question: 'After all these years of being a statue, Mr. Columbus, what is the first thing you say when you come to life each year?'

" 'Why don't somebody kill the damn pigeons,' answered Columbus.

"Do you get it, son?" said La Guardia. "No statues for me."

★

When former President Harry Truman returned to civilian life after World War I, he went into the haberdashery business with a friend. After a few years, the business went under.

Shortly after the doors had closed, Truman met a neighbor who asked: "What happened?"

"Nothing happened," explained Truman. "We just lost our shirts."

★

Many British newspapers did not appreciate Irish politicians, particularly when they became members of Parliament. The press considered every Irishman an obstructionist. When an eccentric Belfast member passed away, a British newspaper concluded his obituary in this way: "A great Irishman has passed away. Heaven grant that many as great, and who wisely love their country, may follow him."

★

The mayor of a Midwestern city was having a difficult time with the electorate. To ease the burden, the mayor went fishing on a nearby lake. While attempting to pull in a big fish he lost his balance and fell overboard. He would have drowned had not three young men noted his plight, plunged into the lake, and rescued him.

When he had recovered from the ordeal, the mayor identified himself and told the boys that they could have anything they wanted for saving his life.

At first the boys refused, but when the mayor insisted, one of the youngsters said: "All right, if you insist, I'll take a bicycle."

The mayor then turned to the second lad and asked him what he would like to have: "Well, if that's what you want to do, I'll take a pair of skis."

"And now you," the mayor said, pointing to the third boy, "name it and it's yours."

The boy shifted his feet and said: "If it's all the same to you, Mr. Mayor, I'd like a military funeral."

"A military funeral . . . ? Why?" asked the puzzled mayor.

"Because," the boy replied with a shrug of his shoulders, "when my father finds out whose life I helped save, he'll kill me."

★

"Sure I'm in favor of the two-party system," bellowed a big Chicago labor leader, "so long as the Democrats hold all the offices."

★

Many years ago a state senator from a western Massachusetts farm district was appointed chairman of the Joint Legislative Committee on Agriculture. The senator, a well-known and articulate farmer, received many invitations to address farm and garden clubs throughout the state.

During one such speaking engagement before a ladies' garden group the senator-farmer advised that one of the best fertilizers was old cow manure.

When the question-and-answer period came up, an elderly lady rose and said that she had enjoyed the senator's speech and was going to heed his suggestion on old cow manure.

"But," she pleaded, "where am I going to find an old cow?"

★

During a visit to a Kentucky town Alben Barkley met a querulous citizen who whined about hard times for about fifteen minutes.

"Why, man," said Barkley, "you ought to be able to make a lot of money shipping green corn to the Northern markets."

"Yes, I orter," was the sullen reply.

"You have the land, I suppose, and can get the seed?"

"Oh, sure."

"Then why don't you start the project?"

"'T'aint no use, mister," sadly replied the native. "That damned woman of mine is too lazy to do the plowin' and the plantin'."

17

The Political
Merry-Go-Round

A man violently opposed to Franklin Delano Roosevelt and the
New Dealers was a great admirer of Abraham Lincoln. It so happened that he had never owned a radio. When he saw the announcement that a prominent senator would deliver a radio address on February 12, he decided to purchase a radio immediately.

On Lincoln's Birthday, the man settled back and listened to
the splendid tribute to the Great Emancipator. He was seriously
annoyed, however, to hear the speaker say in closing: "Fellow citizens, we refer to Honest Abe as the Great Emancipator, but I ask
you, have we ever had a greater emancipator than the present incumbent?"

There was nothing the man could do about it, and he had to
accept the situation. On February 22, he listened to another
splendid oration by another speaker. The same thing happened at
the close of the speech:

"Fellow citizens," cried the orator, "we think of George Washington as the Father of his Country, but I ask you, has this country ever had such a father as Franklin Delano Roosevelt?"

That was too much for the anti-New Dealer. Angrily he packed the radio and took it to the store where he had purchased it. "I want my money back!" he demanded.

"What's the matter with it?" inquired the clerk. "Doesn't it work?"

"It works all right," admitted the man, "but I don't like what I hear on it." Then he went on to explain the Lincoln Day and Washington's Birthday orations.

"Oh, don't let that bother you," said the clerk. "You'll hear a lot of other things on the radio. Why don't you keep it? Anyway, those were political talks and more than that the anniversaries are all over now—"

"Like hell they are," shouted the anti-New Dealer. "That's the trouble—Easter's coming."

★

Benjamin Franklin's advice on campaign fund-raising is as sound today as when he gave the following guidance to a fund-raising committee: "First," said Franklin, "call upon all those you know will give something; next apply to those you are uncertain whether they will give or not; and finally those who you are sure will give nothing, for in some of these you may be mistaken."

★

When Assistant Secretary of Defense Carter L. Burgess resigned to become President of Trans World Airlines, he was awarded an exceptional civilian service medal by the Army.

Secretary of the Army Brucker was the speaker for the occasion. He laid it on with a long and glowing tribute about Burgess' work as Secretary of Defense. When it was over, Burgess said: "I am sorry my mother is not here. She not only would have enjoyed this ceremony, but she would have believed every word of it."

★

Henry Kissinger, Nixon's top diplomat and a Harvard man, found himself in hot water with conservatives over his engineering of the President's trips to China and Russia. Kissinger had this to say: "It has been my first real exposure to right-wing extremists.

They sound very much like left-wing extremists, only their vocabulary is not as good."

*

FDR was the butt of many Republican jokes, particularly when it came to his taxation policy. One of the best concerned two ardent members of the G.O.P. who were having their child christened before the war. In the church the father was holding the baby in front of the baptismal font. When the clergyman asked the Christian name of the child, the father gave the name of Roosevelt.

His wife, an anti-Rooseveltian, looked aghast. When the ceremony was over she asked: "Why in the name of God did you call him after that man? You know how I dislike the sound of that name."

"Well," replied the husband, "I just couldn't resist it. As I held our child in my arms, he started smiling at me. And in a little while he was soaking me."

*

Anti-Republicanism was once rampant in South Boston, Massachusetts, home of the Boston Irish politician. A young man went to confession bent upon unloading a feeling of guilt about his involvement with a young girl. "It was like this, Father," he commenced. "I went to this Republican picnic . . ." Here the priest interrupted with: "Yes, and now go on with the rest of your sins."

*

Jimmy Walker, New York's fast-moving and controversial mayor, once said: "My philosophy on mudslinging in politics is this: Don't be in a hurry to sling it back. Wait until it cakes."

*

"Curiosity," once said Senator George Vest of Missouri, "is one of man's greatest motivators." Vest then went on to explain, in his humorous style, how curiosity affected a situation in a neighborhood church in his native state.

"The services were proceeding well," said Vest, "when a young lady in the balcony leaned too far over the railing and fell. Her dress caught on the chandelier and there she was suspended in mid-air. The minister saw the undignified predicament and immediately thundered at the audience:

" 'Any man in this congregation who turns around and looks up will be struck stone blind.'

"One of the parishioners, whose curiosity was getting the better of him, but who feared the clergyman's warning, finally turned to his seat companion and whispered:

" 'I'm going to risk one eye.' "

★

After a few years in the political trenches, veteran officeholders adopt the following little verse:

> Among life's dying embers,
>   These are my regrets,
> When I'm right, no one remembers,
>   When I'm wrong, no one forgets.

★

Harry Truman's favorite story concerned the period after he left the White House. It seems he went calling on a friend on Park Avenue in New York and rang the wrong doorbell. The man who answered accepted his apology, then did a double-take and exclaimed:

"Say, did anybody ever tell you you're the spittin' image of that old SOB Harry Truman?"

★

During the 1960 election campaign, an elderly lady asked a friend at a tea party in New York: "What do you think of Henry Cabot Lodge?"

"I prefer Grossinger's," was the immediate response.

★

"The people in America should have very little to worry about," commented a Chicago editorial writer several years ago. "The

Democrats have promised to take care of them from the cradle to the grave and Khrushchev has promised to bury them."

★

When Senator Edmund Muskie became chairman of the Democratic Senatorial Committee, he stated that he had plans to promote the senatorial "workhorses." Said Muskie: "There has been too much recognition given to the Senatorial 'showhorses.'"

★

It was the late Martin Lomasney, celebrated "Mahatma" of Boston politics, who gave this advice: "A man is a fool to put anything down in writing, if he knows how to talk. And he shouldn't talk if he is able to nod and shake his head."

★

An old Boston Irish politician was on his deathbed. The priest came to administer the last rites. "Michael," the priest said, "you have not long to live, but before you go, I want you to renounce the devil."

"I'm sorry I can't do that," the old politician said in a weak voice. "At this point, I'm in no position to offend anyone."

★

When Dean Acheson was having his troubles as Secretary of State, he jumped into a taxicab in front of his office one day. The cabdriver slowed down and subjected Dean to a long look, absolutely devoid of expression. Finally the driver said: "Ain't you dat guy Dean Acheson?"

"Yes," replied the embattled secretary, "do you want me to get out?"

★

Frank Daley, an old-time Democratic publicist and product of Massachusetts State House politics, had this comment on Boston politics: "Anyone born in Boston," said Frank, "doesn't study politics. He acquires it by osmosis."

Daley also had a newspaperman's conception of what a politician should be. Said Frank: "A politician has no control over how, when, or where he is born, but at least he can arrange things to die at a respectable time and give the newspapers a chance to properly prepare his obituary."

★

A woman was ushered into a mayor's office seeking welfare aid for herself and several small children.

"What is your husband's occupation?" the mayor asked.

"My husband has been dead for fourteen years," was the reply.

"Whose children are these?"

"They're mine."

"I thought you said your husband has been dead for fourteen years?" queried the puzzled mayor.

"He is, but I ain't," was the prompt response.

★

One of the best political stories out of Democratic South Boston concerned the ward chairman who suffered an accident and was taken to the hospital. "Which ward do you wish to be taken to?" said the doctor. "A pay ward or a—"

The old partisan looked up at the doctor and through his pain gave this order: "Any ward at all, doc, so long as it's safely Democratic."

★

Senator Chauncey Depew was asked what kind of exercise he took. The senator answered: "I get my exercise acting as pallbearer for some of my friends who exercise."

★

The Massachusetts Senate has a program which involves the employment of young college students as pages for the senators. One such youngster went to the president and tendered his resignation.

"How long have you been here?" the president asked.

"Five months," replied the boy.

"And you don't like politics and the legislative business?"

"No, sir, it's no good," was the boy's comment, "and to tell you straight, Mr. President, I'm sorry I learned it."

★

Newspaper readers who believe that editors are not above coloring political news will find food for thought in the following announcement, which appeared in a Southern newspaper that had just changed editors: "We therefore announce that hereafter our policy, politically, will be independent. On all other questions, we will endeavor to print the truth."

★

"Why is it," asked a reporter, "that politicians very seldom ever tell the truth?"

"Well," said the candid old politician, "there just ain't that much truth around."

★

"The trouble with this country," commented a sideline observer, "is that it has forgotten, in its concern with the Left and the Right, that there is an Above and a Below."

★

It was Premier Malenkov's birthday and the Russians decided to make it a legal holiday. An aide went around trying to sell tickets at ten rubles apiece for a celebration in honor of the Premier.

"It'll be a great affair for him," the aide stated. "We're also giving prizes and you people may win one."

"I'd rather knock his teeth down his throat," answered one worker.

"That's the first prize," came the gleeful retort.

★

The father of U. S. Supreme Court Justice William J. Brennan once observed: "You've got to remember, there's a difference between Democrats and Republicans. Democrats would steal a hot stove. Republicans put their gloves on first."

★

When Arthur C. Townley was promoting his National Non-Partisan League many years ago, he gave the following instructions to his membership solicitors: "Find out the damn fool's hobby and talk it. If he likes religion, talk Jesus Christ; if he is against the government, damn the Democrats; if he is afraid of whiskey, preach prohibition; if he wants to talk hogs, talk hogs— talk anything he'll listen to, but talk, talk, talk until you get his G—d— John Hancock to a check for six dollars."

★

Visiting a cemetery one day, a group of people stopped at a stone that, among other things, read: "Here lies a politician and an honest man." A wag in the group commented: "Can you imagine that, two people in one grave?"

★

When Senator Paul Fannin of Arizona accepted a service club bid to help out in a charity drive by selling newspapers, he took a stand in front of a big resort hotel in Phoenix. He was doing well until two young boys saw him. One was overheard to say: "How's that for fickle fate: one day he's a big shot in Washington, next day he's selling papers in Phoenix!"

★

Much to everyone's surprise, a crooked lawyer won a seat on his local city council. "It baffles me," said a voter, "how a crook like you could get elected."

"I'll admit," said the lawyer, "that everyone knows me to be on the shady side. But they also know my opponent was a crook too. It just happened that he knew more people than I did, and they voted for me to keep him out of office."

★

Former President Harry Truman arrived home one afternoon to find his wife Bess burning some letters he had written her. "Bess, you can't do that," Truman remonstrated. "Think of history." Mrs. Truman answered sweetly: "That's what I am thinking of, Harry dear."

★

The teacher was doing her best to explain the political system to her fifth-grade class. She asked: "Who can give me a good, clear definition of a politician?"

A youngster in the middle of the room volunteered: "I can, if you will tell me which party he belongs to."

★

General George Marshall was guest of honor at a huge Washington dinner attended by Mamie Eisenhower. Former Ambassador Joseph C. Grew was the toastmaster. In his remarks Grew said that Marshall wanted nothing more than to retire to Leesburg with Mrs. Eisenhower. While the guests roared, Grew squirmed unhappily at the faux pas and murmered: "My apologies to the general."

Mamie smiled at him and asked: "Which general?"

★

A professor said to a political science class: "Many of you are Republicans because your fathers were Republicans, and many of you are Democrats because your fathers were Republicans."

★

When the chairman of a program asked Wendell Phillips, the abolitionist, what his terms were for a speech, Phillips replied: "If I lecture on antislavery, nothing. If, on any other subject, one hundred dollars."

★

At a large party, Mrs. Henry Clay, chaperoning a young lady, passed through a room where gentlemen were playing cards, Mr. Clay among them. "Is this a common practice?" inquired the young lady.

"Yes," said Mrs. Clay; "they always play cards together."

"Doesn't it disturb you to have Mr. Clay gamble?"

"No, dear," said the old lady composedly, "he 'most always wins."

*

Senator Dwight Morrow of New Jersey was very absent-minded. One day, he was reading some papers on a train when the conductor asked for his ticket. Frantically, Morrow searched for it.

"Never mind, Mr. Morrow," the conductor said. "When you find it, mail it to the company. I am certain you have it."

"I know I have it," exploded Morrow. "I've got to find it, for I want to know where the hell I am going."

*

Woodrow Wilson summed up a certain breed of politicians: "Only two things move political bosses—fire and fodder. Fodder in front of their noses, fire underneath them."

*

Oliver Wendell Holmes, often quoted for his "Oh, to be eighty again" when passing a beautiful damsel, enjoyed spoofing the "nine old men" of the Supreme Court. He told of two jurists, ages eighty-five and ninety, who went to the funeral of a colleague, age ninety-two. After the services, one judge turned to the other and said, "Don't you think we're wasting our time going back home?"

*

"America certainly is a strange place," said a foreign visitor. "You can berate, malign, and abuse the mayor, governor, and the President, but don't try it on a traffic cop."

*

Mark Twain and Senator Chauncey Depew were traveling on the same ship, and each was invited to make a speech. Twain spoke for twenty minutes and made a great hit. Then it was Senator Depew's turn. He rose and said:

"Mr. Toastmaster, ladies and gentlemen: Before this dinner Mark Twain and myself made an agreement to trade speeches. He has just delivered my speech, and I thank you for the pleasant manner in which you received it. I regret to say that I have lost the notes of his speech and cannot remember anything he was to say."

Depew then sat down to the accompaniment of laughter. The next day Twain met an Englishman who had been at the dinner. "Mr. Clemens," he said, "I consider you were much imposed upon last night. I have always heard that Mr. Depew is a clever man, but really, that speech you made last night struck me as the most infernal rot."

★

When a fund-raiser contacted an elderly Republican woman and asked her to buy a hundred-dollar ticket to a G.O.P. dinner, the lady hesitated a moment, and then said: "Heavens, I could never eat a hundred dollars' worth of food."

★

In 1931 Babe Ruth held out for eighty thousand dollars a year to play ball for the New York Yankees. A critic scolded him for asking for so much money during such hard times. "Why, that's more money," the critic told Ruth, "than President Hoover gets."

"So what?" answered the Babe. "I had a better season last year than he did!"

★

When a tax-conscious congressman visited Paris, he was asked by a Frenchman what he thought of the Eiffel Tower. "To me," said the congressman, "it looks like the Empire State Building after taxes."

★

Treasury Secretary Andrew Mellon was once asked the difference between direct and indirect taxation. "The former," he explained, "is somewhat like daylight robbery, while the latter is like going through a man's pockets while he's asleep."

★

"Instead of hundreds of federal bureaus," said a Midwestern banker, "the United States needs only five: one to raise the wages of everybody who works, one to increase the pensions of people who do not work, one to increase the price of everything we sell, one to reduce the prices of everything we buy, and one to raise the money to pay for it all."

★

Senator Charlie Hogan, who served for almost thirty-five years in the Massachusetts legislature, was also a fine lawyer. Whether or not they could pay, Hogan represented his constituents before the courts of his district and had many amusing experiences doing so. One of them involved a derelict who appeared in district court charged with habitual drunkenness. The judge started to lecture the drunk. "Just look at you," he said, "broken down, busted, down-at-the heels. Alcohol has ruined your life."

The defendant looked up at the judge and said: "Thank you, Judge. Everybody else says it's my fault."

★

An American and a Dutchman were talking. "What does your flag look like?" asked the American.

"It has three stripes," replied the Dutchman, "Red, white, and blue. We say they have a connection with our taxes—we get red when we talk about them, white when we get our tax bills, and we pay them until we are blue in the face."

"That's just about what it is here," replied the American, "only we see stars, too."

★

A Russian peasant appeared at a government bureau to take an examination for a position as garbage disposal deputy. He was asked two questions by the examiner:

"What is your attitude toward religion?" asked the examiner.

"Religion," said the peasant, "is a capitalistic fantasy. Religion is an opiate offered to the proletariat to deaden their sensitivity to imperial subjection."

"And what about churches and synagogues?" continued the examiner.

"They are symbols of decadent democracy and reaction," was

the earnest response. "And furthermore they should be burned to the ground and the ashes spread on the ocean."

The examiner smiled and said: "That's all. You will be notified."

Outside, the peasant met a friend, who asked him how he had made out. "With God's help," answered the peasant, smiling, "I think I will pass."

★

It was a raucous Democratic ward committee meeting in a rough section of Buffalo, New York, and the chairman was striving desperately to control the audience.

Finally, a beefy-faced ward worker shouted: "What we would like to know is what did you do with the campaign contributions?"

Just at that moment a chair fell out of the gallery and hit the inquirer on the head, knocking him out cold. He was carried from the hall in a state of unconsciousness.

Amid deep silence from the audience, the ward boss then said calmly: "And now, are there any more questions?"

★

When Ronald Reagan was elected governor of California, he received a letter from Governor Pat Brown which stated:

"There is a message in *War and Peace* that every new governor with a big majority should have tacked on his office wall. In it young Count Rostov, after weeks as the toast of elegant farewell parties, gallops off on his first cavalry charge and then finds real bullets snapping at his ears.

" 'Why, they're shooting at me,' he says, 'me, whom everybody loves.' "

★

A hard-bitten but deaf Vermont Republican of great age hated the Democrats. In the course of events he was invited to visit his nephew in Georgia. The old man had been warned that Georgia was as Democratic as Vermont was Republican.

Sunday morning the nephew took the venerable Republican to

church. At the conclusion of the services, the aged Vermonter asked: "Who was that young preacher, son?"

Shouting into his uncle's ear, the nephew said: "He's the son of a bishop."

"I know, I know," the uncle shouted right back, "ain't all these Democrats—but what's his name?"

★

A cocktail party story around Washington describes a typical modern American: "A typical American," so the story goes, "is one who drives home from an Italian movie in his German car. When he arrives there he takes off his Hong Kong jacket, sits on his Danish furniture, kicks off his Spanish shoes, drinks Brazilian coffee, fortified by Irish whiskey, out of an English bone china cup. Then with his Japanese ball-point pen writes to his congressman protesting that imports are ruining his business."

★

Two bitter partisans, one a Democrat, the other a Republican, were arguing the merits of their respective parties. "As I see it," screeched the Democrat, "the Republican Party is on the road to hell."

"Better," returned the Republican, "than the Democratic Party, which don't know where the hell it is going."

★

Small Massachusetts towns hold annual town meetings during which all citizens have a right to question their public officials. On one occasion, the chairman of the board of health in a tiny upstate town announced that the community had a particularly good year from a health standpoint. "In fact," he said, "the death rate has been only 11.7."

When he had completed his report, a citizen rose and said: "I don't understand what you mean by 11.7. Would you please explain it to us?"

Whereupon the old chairman of the health board replied: "Well, I'm not sure myself just what it means, but I think it means that we had eleven deaths and seven at the point of death."

★

Senator Everett Dirksen was a fine storyteller and many of his yarns were drawn from the days of the old frontier. One of Dirksen's favorites concerned a circuit court judge who had a fondness for corn liquor.

"One day," said Dirksen, "the judge had imbibed too freely and went out to the stable to throw a saddle on his horse. A young lawyer watching the operation noticed that the judge had the pommel where the cantle should be. Tapping the judge on the shoulder, he said: 'Your Honor, do you mind if I tell you that you have that saddle on backwards?'

"The judge stepped back, and with a great show of dignity, he said haughtily: 'How the hell do you know in what direction I am going?' "

★

Elbert Hubbard, author and publisher, once said that a conservative was a man who was too cowardly to fight and too fat to run. Someone else described a conservative as an individual who wanted no change in the things forced on the world yesterday by the radicals. Another observation of a conservative was that he was a man who would not look at the new moon out of respect for the old one.

Many liberals contend that a conservative is a man who won't agree that anything will work. They illustrate their point with a story of Robert Fulton's first steamboat and a cranky conservative who was standing in the crowd along the shore as Fulton worked feverishly to prepare his invention for its historic journey along the Hudson River.

As the firewood was being piled into the boilers and smoke started to bellow from the stack, the old conservative shouted above the crowd: "It'll never start. It'll never start. . . ."

When the steamboat pulled away from the shore to the cheers of hundreds, the old conservative, not a bit convinced about the whole thing, yelled at the top of his voice: "It'll never stop! It'll never stop . . . !"

*

No First Lady in history ever traveled the miles registered by Eleanor Roosevelt. During her years in the White House, Eleanor found her way to the remotest parts of the earth, chasing various causes. Naturally, stories developed on her travels and one of them went this way:

Deep in the wilds of a rugged Rocky Mountain forest a rock was found with this inscription: "We were the first people to travel through these woods. (Signed) Lewis and Clark."

Underneath there was another legend, which read: "That's what you think. (Signed) Eleanor Roosevelt."

*

Ambassador Elliot Richardson is not known for his wit and humor. However, during his campaign for lieutenant governor of Massachusetts, he told a stock story from one end of the state to the other, and it always brought a good laugh.

As Richardson told it, a scoutmaster was giving a lecture to some young scouts on the hazards of camping. "And, boys," warned the scoutmaster, "you must be careful of snakes. If one of these snakes happens to bite you on the hand, just take out your knife and crisscross the place where the snake bit you and suck out the poison. Are there any questions?"

A freckle-faced boy in the rear of the room raised his hand and asked: "Mr. Scoutmaster, you say if a snake bites you on the hand, you cut it with a knife and suck out the poison? What do you do if a snake bites you on the rear end?"

"Well, I'll tell you, son," replied the scoutmaster with a straight face, "that's when you find out who your friends are."

*

A North Carolina school committeeman informed his neighbor that the school board had decided not to renew the contract of the man who taught science in the high school. The neighbor expressed surprise at this action of the board, stating that he understood that this particular teacher had attended many colleges and earned many degrees.

The school committeeman replied: "That's the trouble with him. He has been educated way past his intelligence."

★

Historically, state legislators have a bad image among the electorate. Many citizens condemn them as being little short of pirates. A story has been told of a legislative junket which took place in an Eastern state. A planeload of legislators headed out of the state airport, bound for a certain destination at taxpayers' expense.

No sooner was the plane airborne than the pilot radioed the tower that it was being hijacked to Cuba by three desperadoes.

Ten minutes later the pilot again radioed the tower. This time he reported that all was well again aboard the plane. This was his message: "These desperadoes made a big mistake in hijacking this plane, especially with all these legislators aboard. The legislators have relieved them of their wallets, watches, rings and other valuables, and with increased enthusiasm and satisfaction, have ordered me to continue on to the assigned destination."

★

John Kenneth Galbraith, noted professor of economics at Harvard University, made this observation of political reporting and its effect on politicians: "The volume of political comment substantially exceeds the available truth, so columnists run out of truth and then must resort to imagination. Washington politicians, after talking things over with each other, relay misinformation to Washington journalists, who, after intramural discussion, print it where it is thoughtfully read by the same politicians, who generally believe it. It is the only successful closed system for the recycling of garbage that has ever been devised."

★

The incoming mayor of a Midwestern city had promised extensive budget cutting. When someone asked the fire chief if he expected the ax to fall on his appropriations, the chief commented sadly: "This guy is for real. He means business, and if he carries out his threatened cuts for the fire department, I am afraid that if the alarm goes off, we might have to go down to Hertz and rent a truck."

★

When Joseph Ely left office as Massachusetts governor some forty years ago, he made a few pertinent political observations. Said Governor Ely: "Politicians are seldom in the right frame of mind for effective work because they are continually guarding their popularity. Roosevelt started getting elected in 1936 before he was even inaugurated in 1932."

Ely then went on to state: "Politics is full of intrigue, distorted values and excitement. Political life is an abnormal existence that goes on day and night. Politicians give false emphasis to the importance of their work. They read all the political news and suppose that everyone else does also."

★

Little stories creep up around all public servants. Governor Michael Dukakis of Massachusetts is no exception. A no-nonsense chief executive, Dukakis demands loyalty and agreement on his positions. A State House story had him remarking: "Whenever an important decision comes up, we put it to a vote of my cabinet. My ten cabinet members have ten votes and I have eleven."

★

There was unconscionable graft during the heyday of the Tammany Hall regimes in New York City. One of the stories that surfaced at the time concerned a stranger who approached a Tammany Hall ward heeler and offered a bribe for a certain political favor.

With apparent indignation, the ward heeler responded: "I want you to know I never take money from perfect strangers." Then reaching for the money and depositing it in his pocket, he added with a wink: "But who's perfect these days?"

The mayor of a stormy Eastern city had declared that he was not running for re-election. A poll had given him the message that he would not be re-elected. The mayor, however, continued to battle everybody in sight right up to the end of his term.

On his final day in office, city hall workers, as was the age-old custom, gave a party for the outgoing mayor and presented him with a gift package.

As the presentation was being made, a disgruntled worker in the back of the room, commented: "He'd better drop it in a bucket of water before he opens it."

★

Senator Howard Baker of Tennessee, commenting on the growing lack of interest in American history, told of a plane trip he made to the West Coast to speak at a Lincoln club dinner honoring the former President. On the flight to San Francisco, Baker became the center of some attention because of his role in the Watergate hearings. Finally, a young lady asked him where he was going. "Oh," said Baker, "I'm on my way to San Francisco to speak at a Lincoln club dinner."

"San Francisco?" said the girl. "Gee, my father lives in San Francisco and he owns a Lincoln. Maybe he'll be at the dinner."

★

Fisher Ames, a congressman from Massachusetts in the late eighteenth century, gave the following description of America when it was a new democracy:

"Monarchy," said Ames, "is like a full-rigged ship, trim and beautiful, with all hands at their stations and the captain at the helm. It executes its maneuvers sharply and operates with the greatest of efficiency. But if it hits a rock, the frail hull is crushed and the vessel sinks.

"Democracy, on the other hand, is like a raft—hard to navigate, impossible to keep on course and distressingly slow. But if it runs onto a rock it simply careens off and takes a new course."

Ames added that with the virtue of always staying afloat, America has disadvantages too. "Damn it," he said, "your feet are wet all the time."

18

Short and Sweet
Political Quips

Politicians are like criminals. They are judged by the number of times they are losers.

*

Lots of politicians think they are big guns, when in fact they are small bores.

*

Any politician who takes credit for the sunshine must understand that he must accept blame for the rain.

*

In a political campaign, virtue and righteousness prevail if they have a fat campaign chest and a damn good organization.

*

Politics is modified war.   —Elihu Root

Politics has got so expensive that it takes a lot of money just to get beat with. —Will Rogers

★

A politician who tries to please everybody often look like a small puppy trying to follow four boys at the same time.

★

Politics is the science of who gets what, when and why. —Sidney Hillman

★

Influence in politics is far more rewarding than power.

★

A statesman is a politician who has been dead for at least fifteen years. —Harry S Truman

★

Every rising politician comes to learn that the road to political success is smoothest everywhere but in his own home town.

★

Most politicians say what they think without thinking.

★

A big city politician is one who has the gift of grab.

★

Politics is the business of obtaining money from the rich and votes from the poor on the pretense of protecting one from the other.

★

Politicians always belong to the opposite party.

Politics is a game of give-and-take, with more takers than givers.

★

Politicians are the soul of honor. When they break a promise, they are willing to make two new ones to replace it.

★

A politician is a person who loves the government for all it is worth.

★

Like pilots, politicians gain reputations in storms.

★

A political platform must be built ingeniously so that a candidate can keep standing on it while the opposition is dismantling it plank by plank.

★

The trouble with some politicians is that they have more solutions than the country has problems.

★

Politics is the art of looking for trouble, finding it everywhere, diagnosing it wrong, and then applying unsuitable remedies.

★

A politician is a person who would travel two hundred miles to deliver a speech he wouldn't walk across the street to hear.

★

Today's political promises are tomorrow's taxes.

★

If a politician tries to buy votes with private money, he's a crook; but if he tries to buy votes with the people's money, he's a great liberal.

A politician: One that would circumvent God. —Shakespeare

★

In politics what begins in fear usually ends in folly.

★

Good politicians and bad politicians are less than they seem.

★

Politicians deal mostly with people who want something or who are trying to avoid something.   —Walter Lippmann

★

Sometimes a politician will come right out and run for office on a campaign of planned extravagance.

★

A politician needs seasoning just as much as soup does.

★

Physicians bury their mistakes, while mistakes bury politicians.

★

The trouble with political jokes is that very often they get elected.

★

A politician is very often a man who has risen from obscurity to be something worse.

★

The average politician talks at the rate of 125 words a minute, whether or not he has anything to say.

There's nothing wrong with this country that a good smart politician can't exaggerate.

★

A politician, like a helmsman, exposed to all winds, temperature, and moisture, soon gets to be weatherproof.

★

Politics is the business of loud promises and poor performances.

★

The toughest part of politics is to satisfy the voter without giving him what he wants.

★

It is the smart politician who can keep the note of envy out of his voice while accusing his opponent of fooling the public.

★

Kissing babies is a politician's way of offering lip service to the voters.   —Edmund J. Kiefer

★

Most politicians get the votes of the people who don't know them and lose the votes of the people who do know them.

★

It is little wonder politicians get hard-boiled. They are always in hot water.

★

Many politicians have wide-open mouths and narrow minds.

★

In politics many a nobody becomes a somebody and then becomes known by everybody. Then everybody tells him they knew him when he was nobody and they knew he would someday be somebody.

★

Practical politics consists in ignoring the facts. —Henry Adams

★

No wonder the world is so sick. All our politicians are diagnosing the trouble without asking any questions.

★

A demagogue is a person who cashes in on the ignorance of the people.

★

Political difference is wholesome. It's political indifference that hurts.

★

In today's free-love market and open society, the fact that a politican is running around with another woman might give him just enough mystique to assure his election.

★

Public opinion is the handiwork of a few.

★

As long as the public believes that anyone should hold public office, it will cost them money.

★

Political historians state that no new campaign promise has been invented in the past four thousand years. This does not bother modern-day candidates. They keep trying to invent new ones.

In politics you have to learn to do what you can, and understand that it's never enough.

★

You cannot be made great by a political election.

★

When they stop writing about you in politics, you're dead.
— Senator Claude A. Swanson

★

Political campaign: A matter of mud, threat, and tears.

★

If the statements of opposing political candidates are true, none of them are fit to hold public office. — Francis Roman

★

Politics is the diplomatic name for the law of the jungle.
— Ely Culbertson

★

Political pie—Apple sauce and plums.

★

Political parties are conspiracies against the rest of the nation.
— Lord Halifax

★

Politics is the art of putting people under obligation to you.
— Colonel Jacob L. Arvey

★

Politics is the science of appealing successfully to the emotions and imagination of the voters.

Politics is the only profession to which a man can devote forty years and then be insulted if somebody says he's good at it.

★

A "Lame Duck" is a politician whose goose has been cooked.

★

Politics has always been a rough game, but there are certain rules, and the first is to utter no falsehood that cannot be refuted easily.   —Charles Michelson.

★

Politics makes strange postmasters.

★

When a politician swears on the Bible that a thing is so, and immediately goes ahead and proves it, I know he is lying.
        —Samuel Bonom

★

When a politician says the country is going to rack and ruin, he means it is going to ruin unless he gets to the feed rack.

★

A political banquet has been described as a feast of overcooked roast beef, undercooked mashed potatoes, and half-baked speeches.

★

In public speaking, a full stomach and an empty head go together.   —Bertrand Lyon

★

A Washington cocktail party is a social gathering where people stand around with a drink in one hand and a knife in the other.

Congress has been described as a national inquisitorial body, created for the purpose of acquiring valuable information and then doing nothing about it.

★

Congress has an advantage over other comedians: They make a joke and it becomes a law.   —Will Rogers

★

Many congressmen who act like *oaks* in their district are in reality *willows* in Washington.

★

Congress is a perpetual re-election society.

★

Congress has been described as an area of wide-open spaces, completely surrounded by teeth.

★

There are some congressmen, who, if their constituents were cannibals, would promise them missionaries for dinner.

★

Almost all congressmen are interested in the youth vote. You can tell it by the dye in their hair.

★

If Congress found itself on a jet plane about to crash, it would take time out to appoint a landing committee.

★

If ever there was an American criminal class, it's probably Congress.   —Mark Twain

★

Congress is a body of men completely surrounded by red tape.

Great speeches are not born in a day.

★

When a speech is too long, the end makes one forget the middle, and the middle, the beginning.

★

Let your speech be better than silence, or be silent.
—Dionysius the Elder

★

The minute you ain't yourself in front of an audience, you're in trouble. —Will Rogers

★

Give me the right word and the right accent and I will move the world. —Joseph Conrad

★

The object of oratory is not the truth, but persuasion.
—François de La Rochefoucauld

★

If oratory is a lost art, leave it that way.

★

It is a way of calling a man a fool when no heed is given to what he says. —Pythagoras

★

An orator is merely a fellow who is willing to lay down your life for his country.

★

Great talkers are little doers. —Benjamin Franklin

It is the heart that makes men eloquent.

★

The worth of a political speech is when the crowd goes away saying, not, "what a wonderful speech," but rather, "I will do something."

★

When a man is giving a speech, never shout "Louder!" The man who talks so you can't hear is not saying anything important.

★

What can be more pathetic than an empty speaker, pouring forth himself before a full house?   —John H. Holmers

★

One minute of keeping your mouth shut is worth an hour's explanation.

★

Lungs and language are requisites in the United States Senate.

★

Politicians should remember the capacity of the mind to absorb is limited to what the seat can endure.

★

After-dinner speaking is the art of saying nothing at length.

★

Silence is not always golden. Sometimes it is just plain yellow.

★

An orator is an individual who gasses the audience instead of electrifying them.

In Spain a man throws the bull and is called a matador. In America he is called a Senator.

★

It is easier to look wise than to talk wisdom. Say less than the other fellow and listen more than you talk; for when a man's listening he isn't telling on himself and he's flattering the fellow who is. —George Horace Lorimer

★

I never was hurt by anything I didn't say.   —Calvin Coolidge

★

A lobbyist is anyone who opposes legislation I want. A patriot is anyone who supports me. —Charles Smith

★

A lobbyist is a man whose job is merely to know how and know who.

★

The more a fellow knows in a Democracy the less liberty he's got.

★

We live under a constitution, but the Constitution is what the judges say it is. —Chief Justice Charles Evans Hughes

★

A conservative is someone who buckles himself in going through a car wash.

★

A conservative is a person who does not think anything should be done for the first time.

A liberal is a person who will give you a solution even though you don't have a problem.

★

A liberal is a man who leaves the room when the fight starts.

★

A liberal is a person with both feet firmly planted in the air.

★

When aliens cuss the United States, that's communism. When a Senator does it, that's leadership in politics.

★

Nobody need worry anymore about Washington going to the left. Indeed, nobody need worry that Washington is going anywhere.   —Heywood Broun

★

The Aztec emperors took a public oath each year to keep the sun on its course. That may have been the beginning of the election promise.

★

The United States is a pretty good union, even if the dues are a little high.   —Alan Frazer

★

When you tell a small child that Washington never told a lie, make it clear to him that you are referring to the man and not the city.

★

Whether or not they will admit it, nevertheless the public begs to be fooled.

Four hostile newspapers are more to be feared than a thousand bayonets.   —Napoleon I

★

The President of the United States serves a four-year sentence with time off for good behavior.

★

There was a time when only Heaven protected the poor working girl. Now it takes a union, a wage and hour law, unemployment compensation, health insurance, a pension and women's liberation.

★

If I had been a good pianist, I never would have been President of the United States.   —Harry S Truman

★

There is seldom a collision between the office seeking the man and the man the office.

★

If your opponent calls you a liar, call him a thief.
                                        —Big Bill Thompson

★

Americans are stubborn people. About the only thing that will change their opinion of a candidate is to have him elected.

★

Never handle a hot poker on the front porch   —Frank Kent

★

A man can fail many times, but he isn't a failure until he begins to blame somebody else.

How is it possible for those who are men of honor in their persons, thus to become notorious liars in their party?   —Addison

★

A third party is as unpopular in politics as it is in love.

★

Many people consider the things government does for them to be social progress—but they consider the things government does for others as Socialism.   —Chief Justice Earl Warren

★

Patriotism very often is scoundrelism in disguise.

★

Washington has been described as one huge fog bank, completely surrounded by legislative fog horns.

★

"My country right or wrong," is like saying, "My mother, drunk or sober."   —Gilbert Keith Chesterton

★

There's no way America can have a revolution after the year 2000. If the rate of increase continues as it has for the past 30 years, in 30 years, all of us will be working for the government.

★

A government bureau is where the taxpayer's shirt is kept.

★

Taxes are like golf. You drive like hell for the green and then wind up in the hole.

★

What this country needs is a relief program for the taxpayer.

If Patrick Henry thought taxation without representation was bad, he should see it *with* representation.

★

Taxes are not like old soldiers—they don't fade away.

★

The best form of taxation is that which will be paid by somebody else.

★

Taxation is the science of plucking the goose to obtain the greatest amount of feathers with the least amount of squawking.

★

Taxes: the greatest sneak thief in government.

★

If the Democratic candidates and the Republican candidates were as unqualified as their opponents claim, the country would be in terrible shape no matter who got elected.

★

A legislator is a person who works hard at his job of separating the wheat from the chaff, and then puts the chaff into law.

★

Laws are not passed, they are purchased.

★

A majority is a large number of people who have become tired of trying to think for themselves and have decided to accept someone else's opinion.

★

An expert is a man who decides quickly and is sometimes right.
—Elbert Hubbard

It is more pleasing to a man's vanity to be hated than to be despised.

★

Controversy equalizes fools and wise men in the same way, and the fools know it.

★

Nothing is more fallacious as facts, except figures.

★

A statesman is a man who finds out which way the crowd is going and then jumps out in front and yells like hell.

★

A statesman is a former politician who has mastered the art of holding his tongue.

★

Diplomacy is easy on the brain but hell on the feet.
—Charles G. Dawes

★

A diplomat is a man who knows how far to go before he goes too far.

★

Economy is a great revenue. —Cicero

★

Liberty is being free from the things we don't like in order to be slaves to the things we do like.

★

When a man has gone to his everlasting rest, you don't know if he has died or taken a job with the government.

Get mad enough and you do things you ought not to try.
—Governor George Romney

★

Those who seek to please everybody, please nobody.   —Aesop

★

It's better to be roasted than ignored.   —Frank Kent

★

There's got to be a president who understands something besides government.

★

You can't use tact with a congressman. You must take a stick and hit him on the snout.
—from *The Education of Henry Adams*

★

Like the weather, Congress often seems to be a subject of conversation about which very little can be done.

★

What people want is not necessarily the kind of government they ought to have.   —Sherman Adams

★

Politics has more interpreters and prophets than any other calling.

T